Microsoft

6 Microsoft® Office Business Applications for Office SharePoint® Server 2007

*Rob Barker, Joanna Bichsel,
Adam Buenz, Steve Fox,
John Holliday, Bhushan Nene,
and Karthik Ravindran*

PUBLISHED BY
Microsoft Press
A Division of Microsoft Corporation
One Microsoft Way
Redmond, Washington 98052-6399

Library of Congress Control Number: 2007939308

Printed and bound in the United States of America.

1 2 3 4 5 6 7 8 9   QWT   3 2 1 0 9 8

Distributed in Canada by H.B. Fenn and Company Ltd.

A CIP catalogue record for this book is available from the British Library.

Microsoft Press books are available through booksellers and distributors worldwide. For further information about international editions, contact your local Microsoft Corporation office or contact Microsoft Press International directly at fax (425) 936-7329. Visit our Web site at www.microsoft.com/mspress. Send comments to mspinput@microsoft.com.

Microsoft, Microsoft Press, Active Directory, ActiveX, BizTalk, Excel, Expression, Expression Blend, Fluent, FrontPage, InfoPath, IntelliSense, Internet Explorer, Microsoft Dynamics, MSDN, Outlook, PerformancePoint, PivotChart, PivotTable, PowerPoint, ProClarity, SharePoint, Silverlight, SQL Server, Visio, Visual Basic, Visual C#, Visual Studio, Windows, Windows Server, and Windows Vista are either registered trademarks or trademarks of Microsoft Corporation in the United States and/or other countries. Other product and company names mentioned herein may be the trademarks of their respective owners.

The example companies, organizations, products, domain names, e-mail addresses, logos, people, places, and events depicted herein are fictitious. No association with any real company, organization, product, domain name, e-mail address, logo, person, place, or event is intended or should be inferred.

This book expresses the author's views and opinions. The information contained in this book is provided without any express, statutory, or implied warranties. Neither the authors, Microsoft Corporation, nor its resellers, or distributors will be held liable for any damages caused or alleged to be caused either directly or indirectly by this book.

Acquisitions Editor: Ben Ryan
Developmental Editors: Devon Musgrave and John Pierce
Project Editors: Michelle Goodman and Kathleen Atkins
Editorial Production: ICC Macmillan Inc.

Body Part No. X14-25663

Contents at a Glance

Table of Contents

What do you think of this book? We want to hear from you!

Microsoft is interested in hearing your feedback so we can continually improve our books and learning resources for you. To participate in a brief online survey, please visit:

www.microsoft.com/learning/booksurvey/

What do you think of this book? We want to hear from you!

Microsoft is interested in hearing your feedback so we can continually improve our books and learning resources for you. To participate in a brief online survey, please visit:

www.microsoft.com/learning/booksurvey/

Introduction

The work that Office Business Applications perform is at the heart of the requirements for information gathering and document processing that companies and organizations of all sizes face today in a business environment and economy characterized by mobility; a worldwide network of customers, partners, and suppliers; new compliance and regulatory requirements; and a need for broad visibility into business processes and the information that supports and governs them. Factors such as these drive the need for organizations to integrate business applications, documents, and workflows and transform the content of documents into business information they can act on.

6 Microsoft Office Business Applications for Office SharePoint Server 2007 offers examples of approaches that software developers and solution architects can take to extend the 2007 Microsoft Office system and provide business information to users. In this book, you'll also find descriptions of Microsoft Office Business Application patterns that provide professional developers with guidance for developing their own custom 2007 Office system business solutions.

The 2007 Office system has numerous capabilities that address current business conditions, including the Open XML file formats, a highly programmable user interface, and an ability to more easily link to back-end and line-of-business data systems. The support of XML, for example, provides a means to define information workflows and document management capabilities. An organization's IT staff can integrate systems such as SAP, Siebel, or Microsoft Dynamics with 2007 Office system applications so that workers can perform operations such as invoicing or ordering when working in an Office application rather than in the back-end system itself.

6 Microsoft Office Business Applications for Office SharePoint Server 2007 focuses also on how to develop Office Business Applications on Microsoft Windows SharePoint Services and Microsoft Office SharePoint Server 2007, platforms that developers can use to create collaboration applications as well as applications and features that support business intelligence, workflow, data calculation, team workspaces, document life-cycle management, content management, knowledge discovery, and project management.

Information workers use an array of tools and devices to perform their jobs and collaborate with others: e-mail, desktop applications, mobile devices, Web browsers, Web conferencing, portals, and specialized line-of-business applications. Individual workers, project teams, and departments all need the capabilities provided by collaborative workspaces and the ability to archive and access information as projects are completed and new ones begin. Windows SharePoint Services, an integrated part of the Microsoft Windows Server operating system, provides services that enable teams and developers to build such workspaces. Windows SharePoint Services 3.0 can be tightly integrated with the 2007 Office system, further enabling information workers to make use of workspaces for organizing meetings, managing projects, authoring documents, and other activities that they frequently manage from traditional Office applications. Windows SharePoint Services 3.0 can also be integrated with line-of-business applications, providing access to data that workers need to update and analyze.

Office SharePoint Server 2007 builds on the Windows SharePoint Services framework and provides services such as search in portal sites, team sites, and content management sites; user profiles and audience targeting; and single sign-on to facilitate integration with enterprise data systems. Office SharePoint Server 2007 also introduces the Business Data Catalog, which enables integration between enterprise portal and line-of-business applications; new document management capabilities; Web content management, which provides tools for site branding, creating multilingual sites, and building content deployment solutions; Microsoft Office SharePoint Server 2007 Excel Services, a technology for viewing, calculating, and extracting values from a workbook through a Web browser or through a Web service; and Microsoft Office Forms Server 2007, which lets information workers use a Web browser to interact with form templates designed with Microsoft Office InfoPath 2007.

Six of the seven chapters in this book provide examples of the functionality and capabilities that can be included in a solution developed with Windows SharePoint Services, Office Share-Point Server 2007, and the 2007 Office system. These examples often show sample code, some of which was developed and tested on beta versions of Microsoft Visual Studio 2008. You'll see a Web Part that displays data from Active Directory, as well as examples of how to implement Excel Services to perform calculations and how to manage business processes with workflows. The examples are meant to show off features and concepts and to help generate ideas for solutions that can be developed or deployed in your own organization.

Who This Book Is For

6 Microsoft Office Business Applications for Office SharePoint Server 2007 will appeal to a variety of technically minded readers. Solution architects, for example, will find diagrams and discussions in the application chapters describing the components of the solution and their relationships. Developers will find a steady supply of sample code and development tips that demonstrate coding and implementation details. Technical decision makers will find summaries and related information about the business purpose and value of Office Business Applications and learn in more detail how Office Business Applications can be used to manage and automate business processes.

The examples provided are also applicable to organizations of various sizes. Small and medium-size businesses in markets and industries that rely on the extensive and regular use of documents and information technology—consultants and law firms, for example—will recognize advantages in examples such as the budgeting, sales forecasting, and statement of work solutions presented in Chapters 2, 3, and 5, respectively. Larger organizations will see the advantages of developing these capabilities within relevant workgroups, as well as the examples about site provisioning, security, sales force automation, and business intelligence in Chapters 4, 6, and 7, all of which are applicable to work at the enterprise scale.

About This Book

Each chapter in this book was written by a different individual, all of whom bring experience and expertise to the arena of Office Business Applications. Several of the authors work in the Office product group at Microsoft as technical program managers and developer evangelists. Several others are working software developers and consultants who are members of the Windows SharePoint Services MVP (Microsoft Most Valuable Professional) community.

Here is a quick summary of the contents of *6 Microsoft Office Business Applications for Office SharePoint Server 2007.*

- **Chapter 1, "Getting Started with Office Business Applications" (Rob Barker, Microsoft Corporation)**   An overview of OBA platform capabilities, OBA services, and the main architectural components of an OBA. This chapter also provides detailed descriptions and diagrams of a number of OBA application patterns that can be combined and adapted when developing custom applications.

- **Chapter 2, "Managing and Automating the Budget Approval Process" (Steve Fox, Microsoft Corporation)**   A combination of out-of-the-box workflows, Excel Services, Web Parts, and custom user interface elements that form an application used to approve and monitor budgets. This example demonstrates how to combine SharePoint technologies with Visual Studio Tools for Office customizations within the 2007 Office system environment. A workflow developed in Windows SharePoint Services ties the approval process together.

- **Chapter 3, "Managing Sales Forecasting with an Office Business Application" (Joanna Bichsel, Microsoft Corporation)**   The sales forecasting solution combines the features of a workflow, a custom Ribbon and task pane, Open XML, the Business Data Catalog, and Excel Services. In the solution, a salesperson creates a forecast in Office Excel 2007 using a custom task pane to pull up data from the Business Data Catalog by using a custom Ribbon. When the salesperson considers the forecast complete, she initiates a workflow that saves the spreadsheet to a SharePoint document library, generates a report, and sends an e-mail message to her manager for approval. In this chapter you'll also see an example of how to work with the *ServerDocument* class, which enables the manipulation of custom XML cached data.

- **Chapter 4, "Provisioning and Securing a Virtual Learning Workspace" (Adam Buenz, Microsoft Windows SharePoint Services MVP)**   The OBA presented in this chapter consists of several moving pieces that form a framework for building, securing, and extending virtual learning workspaces (VLWs) that are appropriate for universities and academic institutions that deploy the Microsoft Office SharePoint Server 2007 or Windows SharePoint Services 3.0 platform. Several key elements make up the VLW application: automated site provisioning, automated site security provisioning and enforcement, and the enhancement of user interaction. Automated site provisioning is demonstrated through the use of reusable workflow activities that also introduce high-level programmatic tasks related to the Windows SharePoint Services security model.

- **Chapter 5, "Creating a Statement of Work with Open XML Formats" (John Holliday, Microsoft Windows SharePoint Service MVP)**   The OBA solution described in this chapter shows how you can use Office Open XML to generate a statement of work document in a variety of formats. It explores the details of an XML schema (XSD) for a statement of work and then describes a C# application programming interface (API) that generates the statement of work document based on the schema. To show one way that users can make use of the schema and collect the information needed for the final statement of work, the chapter presents a Microsoft Office InfoPath 2007 form template that can serve as a vehicle for entering data and then generating the statement of work in the format you need. At the end of the chapter you'll see how to call the API from a custom feature in Windows SharePoint Services.

- **Chapter 6, "Sales Force Automation" (Bhushan Nene, Microsoft Corporation)**   The OBA for sales force automation manages important elements of the opportunity-to-order business process by using an Office Outlook 2007 add-in, an Office Word 2007 add-in, and Office SharePoint Server 2007 to access and integrate information from an enterprise CRM system. The solution provides salespeople with a consistent user experience and enables them to review and gather data more easily and collaborate with customers and coworkers. You'll see an example of how to view a CRM system's product catalog in a custom task pane in Office Word 2007 and how to track and associate sales opportunities in Office Outlook 2007.

- **Chapter 7, "Business Intelligence: A Manufacturing Plant Floor Analytics OBA" (Karthik Ravindran, Microsoft Corporation)**   Overview of the architecture of a business intelligence solution designed to manage plant floor operations. The chapter includes a description of Microsoft's business intelligence solutions and includes an example of how to implement a Microsoft Silverlight component. The chapter presents an Office Business Application that illustrates the range of Microsoft business intelligence products and capabilities, including Microsoft Office SharePoint Server 2007, Microsoft SQL Server (including SQL Server Analysis Services and SQL Server Reporting Services), Microsoft PerformancePoint Monitoring Server, and Microsoft Office Excel 2007.

Additional Resources

A wealth of information is available about developing Office Business Applications and the 2007 Microsoft Office system. Here are some of the resources suggested by contributors to this book.

Resources on Microsoft.com

- Business Data Catalog Information Center: *http://msdn2.microsoft.com/en-us/office/ bb251754.aspx*

- Business Data Catalog Software Developer's Kit: *http://msdn2.microsoft.com/en-us/library/ms563661.aspx*

- Content Types Software Developer Kit: *http://msdn2.microsoft.com/en-us/library/ms479905.aspx*

- Excel Services Information Center Portal on MSDN: *http://msdn2.microsoft.com/en-us/office/bb203828.aspx*

- How Do I? Screencasts: *http://msdn.microsoft.com/office/learn/screencasts/*

- Introduction to Content Types: *http://office.microsoft.com/en-us/sharepointserver/HA101495511033.aspx?pid=CH101779691033*

- Microsoft Office SharePoint Server 2007 Software Developers Kit: *http://msdn2.microsoft.com/en-us/library/ms550992.aspx*

- MSDN OBA Developer Portal: *http://msdn.microsoft.com/oba*

- MSDN Office Developer How-To Center: *http://msdn2.microsoft.com/en-us/office/bb266408.aspx*

- OBA Central: *www.obacentral.com*

- Office 2007 Software Developers Kit: *http://msdn2.microsoft.com/en-us/library/ms376609.aspx*

- Office Developer Center: *http://msdn2.microsoft.com/en-us/office/default.aspx*

- Office Developer Webcasts: *http://www.microsoft.com/events/series/officedeveloperlive.mspx*

- Ribbon User Interface: *http://msdn.microsoft.com/office/tool/ribbon/default.aspx*

- Visual Studio Tools for Office Developer Center: *http://msdn2.microsoft.com/en-us/office/aa905533.aspx*

- XML File Formats: *http://msdn.microsoft.com/office/tool/xml/2007/default.aspx*

Blogs

- Building Office Business Applications:
  - *http://blogs.msdn.com/oba*
  - *http://blogs.msdn.com/Joanna_Bichsel/*
  - *http://blogs.msdn.com/rbarker/*
  - *http://blogs.msdn.com/javeds/*

- Brian Randell's blog: *http://sqljunkies.com/WebLog/brianr/* for information about SQL Server, Microsoft Office, and Visual Studio Tools for Office (VSTO)

- Eric Carter's blog: *http://blogs.msdn.com/eric_carter/* for information about Microsoft Office and VSTO

- Microsoft Office fluent interface: *http://blogs.msdn.com/jensenh/*

- Office Developers: *http://blogs.msdn.com/erikaehrli/*

- Open XML File Formats:
  - *http://blogs.msdn.com/brian_jones/*
  - *http://blogs.msdn.com/dmahugh/*
  - *http://blogs.infosupport.com/wouterv/*

- Paul Stubbs' blog: *http://blogs.msdn.com/pstubbs/* for information about Microsoft Office, VSTO, and OBAs

- Scott Guthrie's blog: *http://weblogs.asp.net/scottgu/* for information on a variety of topics

- SharePoint Products and Technologies:
  - *http://blogs.msdn.com/sharepoint/*
  - *http://blogs.msdn.com/mikefitz/*
  - *http://www.u2u.info/Blogs/Patrick/default.aspx*

- Visual Studio extensions for SharePoint and SharePoint Designer: *http://blogs.msdn.com/alexma/*

- Visual Studio Tools for Office: *http://blogs.msdn.com/vsto2/*

Companion Content

You can download a Virtual PC image that contains a full working model of the business intelligence solution for manufacturing described in Chapter 7 from the book's Web site, *http://msdn2.microsoft.com/en-us/architecture/bb643797.aspx*. In Chapter 7, you will find steps for walking through this demonstration to see how the business intelligence technologies are implemented.

System Requirements

To work with the VPC image of the manufacturing plant floor analytics OBA, your system must meet the following minimum requirements:

- A supported Microsoft Windows operating system (Windows XP, Windows Vista, or Windows Server 2003)

- Microsoft Virtual PC 2007

- Minimum memory requirement for the VPC image: 1 gigabyte (GB)

- Hard disk space for the VPC image: 16 GB

- Processor (recommended): 1 gigahertz (GHz) or greater

Setting Up and Logging On to the VPC

In Microsoft Virtual PC 2007, create a virtual machine named PF Analytics OBA from the virtual hard disk (VHD) you can download from the book's Web site. To log on to the VPC image, follow these steps:

1. Use the VPC 2007 console to start the PF Analytics OBA virtual machine.

2. Log on to the virtual machine using the following user credentials:

   User name: **administrator**

   Password: **pass@word1**

3. Wait for the warm-up scripts to fully complete prior to proceeding to the next task.

Support for This Book

Every effort has been made to ensure the accuracy of this book. Microsoft Press provides support for books and companion content at the following Web site:

http://www.microsoft.com/learning/support/books/

If you have comments, questions, or ideas regarding the book, or questions that are not answered by visiting the site just mentioned, please send them to Microsoft Press via e-mail to

mspinput@microsoft.com

Or via postal mail to
Microsoft Press
Attn: 6 Microsoft Office Business Applications for Office SharePoint Server 2007 Editor
One Microsoft Way
Redmond, WA 98052-6399

Please note that Microsoft software product support is not offered through the above addresses.

Acknowledgments

A number of people were involved in the publication of this book. Thanks go first and foremost to the book's contributors, who gave their time and expertise to this project: Rob Barker, Joanna Bichsel, Adam Buenz, Steve Fox, John Holliday, Bhushan Nene, and Karthik Ravindran. Rob Barker, Mike Fitzgerald, and Ben Ryan deserve credit for envisioning and initiating the project. For their work reviewing and contributing to Chapter 1, we thank Bhushan Nene and Chris Keyser. For help with envisioning the sales force automation OBA described in Chapter 6, a special thanks to Mauricio Ordonez. His insight into the 2007 Microsoft Office system was critical in formulating a compelling scenario.

Thanks also are due to Kathleen Atkins, Michelle Goodman, Leo Kelly, Becka McKay, and John Pierce for their roles in developing, editing, and producing this book.

Chapter 1
Getting Started with Office Business Applications

—Rob Barker, Microsoft Corporation

Over the past two decades, companies and organizations have spent billions of dollars buying, installing, deploying, and maintaining line-of-business (LOB) systems to manage customer data, inventory, billings, product life cycles, and many other types of business information and processes. Modern businesses would not be competitive and thus would be unable to survive without these applications. LOB systems, however, are often accessible only to a few elite power users who require expensive training in these applications' proprietary—and sometimes arcane—user interfaces. Making information from LOB systems available to people who need it requires the information to be extracted from the systems, whose processes are designed to ensure its integrity and control.

Over the same time, the personal computer and the software developed for it have catalyzed a revolution in how people work, ushering in the information economy. These technologies have profoundly affected the way people work and the way that companies are organized. Many people today would find it impossible to envision a work environment that lacked e-mail, spreadsheets, word-processing documents, and a Web browser. These tools have become a given in the work environments for hundreds of millions of people and have had a tremendous impact on personal productivity. But while these tools help people gain insights, make decisions, take actions, and collaborate, their use has been largely constrained to local or personal information.

The activities that most affect a business's performance tend to be different from the transactional and transformational jobs that lend themselves to mechanization and automation—jobs on an assembly line and jobs in data entry, for example. An established and growing class of employees works by exchanging information and making judgments about a variety of data gleaned from diverse interactions. People in this class are called *information workers*. They include salespeople, marketing managers, product designers, lawyers, engineers, and so on. They are usually among the highest-paid employees in an organization because they make the most significant contributions to a business. The significance of their contributions, however, often depends on how easily and consistently they can access information they need. This dependence on access to information and its integration brings to light a new type of software application, called an Office Business Application.

What Is an Office Business Application?

Office Business Applications (OBAs) are a breed of application that combines the productivity tools in the 2007 Microsoft Office system with information and processes defined in LOB systems. OBAs represent the best of both worlds, and they are being included in innovative solutions developed by some of the world's largest software companies—including Microsoft with Dynamics Snap; Duet, a partnership of Microsoft and SAP; independent software vendors (ISVs) such as Open Text, Epicor, Business Objects, and KnowledgeLake—and used by multinational corporations, including Chevron Corporation, Del Monte Corporation, The London Stock Exchange, and Elite Model Management.

But you need better reasons to build an OBA than simply to put a pretty face on an established set of functionality. Although OBAs provide value in a number of situations, four common cases follow:

- **Make aspects of application functionality available to a broader audience.** The interfaces for LOB systems are often complex and require significant training to use effectively. These systems might also be ignored by the majority of users because the value derived from using the application does not equal the effort required to learn it. By providing a capability that is better integrated with tools that most information workers use every day, the barrier to adoption can be drastically lowered. Examples of this include:

  - ❑ Integrating functionality into the Microsoft Office Outlook 2007 calendar that links an appointment with a customer to an LOB billing system

  - ❑ Integration with Office Outlook 2007 that associates a scheduled meeting with a sales opportunity recorded in a customer relationship management (CRM) application

  - ❑ Employees reporting vacation time to an LOB human resources system through time reserved in the Office Outlook 2007 calendar

  - ❑ Feedback on an interview with a prospective employee entered in Office Outlook 2007 that is automatically inserted in a human resources system

  - ❑ Hosting a centralized budgeting spreadsheet using Microsoft Office SharePoint Server 2007 and Excel Services (in Microsoft Office SharePoint Server 2007)

  - ❑ Exposing customer data from a CRM system in a SharePoint site using the Business Data Catalog (BDC)

- **Gain control and insight into the interactions around processes managed by LOB systems.** Today, many activities that affect business performance are interactions between information workers. These interactions are typically captured in documents and e-mail exchanges. The decisions that result from these interactions ultimately require an update of information within an LOB system, but the path that leads to the decision and the documentation supporting the decision often remains ad hoc, unmanaged, and opaque. By integrating and tracking the flow of these interactions more formally, businesses gain more realistic insights, extend elements of best practices into hitherto ad-hoc interactions, and ensure a level of tighter control and improved auditing, which helps meet corporate compliance requirements. Examples include proposal generation, statements of work, and deal negotiation solutions.

- **Provide information in context, inside the tools information workers use.**   Examples include offline access to sales opportunities, accounts, and customer data through Outlook for sales representatives; access to account information, purchase orders, and incident information in Microsoft Office Word 2007 for assembling information in documents; and options for acting on a particular piece of information embedded in an Office Word 2007 document or in an e-mail message through recognition of the embedded content.

- **Create a collaborative context around an LOB activity.**   LOB applications can often be enhanced by sharing information between a collaboration site such as a Microsoft Office SharePoint Server 2007 team site and an LOB construct. One example would be creating a team site around an incident or sales opportunity or creating a dashboard related to a store's performance.

To help you understand what technologies and capabilities make up the foundation of OBAs, the next several sections will describe the platform's capabilities and supporting services.

Platform Capabilities

Figure 1-1 shows the platform capabilities and supporting technologies that form the framework for OBAs. I'll review the platform capabilities in this section and then describe the supporting technologies in the section that follows.

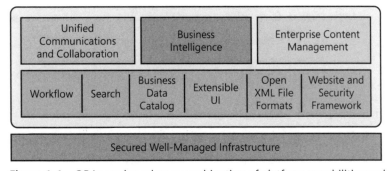

Figure 1-1   OBAs are based on a combination of platform capabilities and supporting technologies.

Enterprise Content Management (ECM)

Organizations can manage diverse content by having a consistent design and process for Web, document, and records management, enabling a classification of content types with metadata, policies, and workflows. Enterprise content management provides for searches across multiple repositories and LOB systems. Functionality from Microsoft Content Management Server 2002 (MCMS) has been incorporated into Office SharePoint Server 2007, and with this functionality, users can take advantage of Web content management features directly from the Office system platform. This integrated Web content management system controls consistency by enabling content types that define certain documents or collections of information, master pages that can define the look and feel of an entire site, and page layouts and logos that provide for consistent branding and images for Web pages.

The single content management and collaborative system provided by Office SharePoint Server 2007 eliminates the need for the separate solutions offered by Microsoft SharePoint Portal Server 2003 and MCMS. Users can create Web sites that are dynamic, customized for team or individual need, and centered on the content the site manages.

Business Intelligence (BI)

SharePoint Server 2007 builds on traditional portal and dashboard solutions to provide users with business intelligence portals that can be used for data manipulation and analysis. Users can create some dashboards from multiple data sources without using code. Key performance indicators (KPIs) can be defined from a variety of sources, including Excel Services, SharePoint lists, and SQL Server Analysis Services cubes. When information such as this is hosted in SharePoint Server 2007, it is available for other SharePoint Server 2007 services, such as search and workflows.

The business intelligence functionality allows you to do the following:

- Consolidate ETL, OLAP, data mining, and reporting capabilities
- Synthesize high volumes of LOB data into your data warehouse with XML, Web services, and RSS sources
- Incorporate newer data sources with traditional LOB data
- Use Office Excel 2007 with SQL Server Analysis Services to make sense of large amounts of data
- Tap into LOB data within spreadsheets and reports using the BDC

Unified Communication and Collaboration

In the new world of work, the focus is on the work, not where the work occurs. Individuals come together to solve problems, develop plans, and embrace opportunities, but coming together no longer requires or even implies that individuals are sitting in the same room or even in the same country. The physical and logical barriers that once defined a team or workgroup are dissolving. The 2007 Microsoft Office system supports communication and collaboration through a number of contextual capabilities. Teams can collaborate by using workspaces, for example, which can be large and relatively centralized, supporting entire divisions of business units, or fit the needs of ad-hoc workgroups that need a way to work together quickly.

OBA Services

Six services support the capabilities and OBA framework within the 2007 Microsoft Office system:

- **Workflow**   The integration of the Windows Workflow Foundation (WWF) into Share-Point Server 2007 allows developers to create simple workflows and attach them to SharePoint Server 2007 document libraries. Microsoft Office SharePoint Designer 2007 can be used to create custom workflows without coding. For power users and developers, the Workflow object model is available in Microsoft Visual Studio 2005.

- **Search**   SharePoint Server 2007 Enterprise Search is a shared service that provides extensive and extensible content gathering, indexing, and querying and supports full-text and keyword searches. By coupling BDC data with Microsoft Office Forms Server 2007 and search, organizations can build searchable server-side applications that allow users to interact with previously segregated data within the context of the organization's portal. Search is central to the 2007 Office system platform's efforts and provides multiple ways to integrate with and extend search, including:

  - ❑ Controlling the presentation of search results using XSLT transforms and custom Web Parts

  - ❑ Presenting LOB data in the search index by using the BDC

  - ❑ Including custom content in the search index using protocol handlers and IFilters

  - ❑ Consuming the search index from remote clients via Web services

- **Business Data Catalog**   The BDC allows enterprise data to be exposed to Web Parts, Office Forms Server, and search. Developers can use this capability to build applications that allow users to interact with LOB data in easy-to-use interfaces designed on the basis of substantial usability studies.

- **The Microsoft Office Fluent interface**   A major improvement in the 2007 Office system for developers is the work performed on the extensibility model to enable more platform power. Developers now have the ability to customize the Ribbon to expose both core features of the 2007 Office system as well as their individual applications. In addition, the 2007 Office system offers more managed code support as well as improved security and management through a common application trust model.

- **Open XML file format**   The adoption of the Open XML file format in the 2007 Office system facilitates server-side document creation and manipulation without the need to instantiate the client applications on the server. Server advances, such as document property promotion, workflow, and search, are among the many capabilities that are available to OBAs now that the underlying documents are consumable by server-side processes.

■ **Website and Security Framework**   The Website and Security Framework is a common site framework for all types of sites: intranet, extranet, and public facing. This framework integrates with ASP.NET 2.0, allowing support for ASP.NET master pages and native ASP.NET Web Parts.

A common role-based security model that integrates with Active Directory directory services, the Website and Security Framework also exposes a greatly improved site template model. This model allows solution creators to combine required features into site templates that users can provision themselves and then configure and customize.

Attributes of an Office Business Application

OBAs also have certain attributes that are enabled by the platform capabilities and the supporting technologies. When you build an OBA, the following attributes make your solution more robust and allow you to focus on solving the particular business problem being addressed by your application:

■ **Ease of use**   Information workers today often have no choice but to request LOB application experts to export useful business data from an LOB system into tools such as Excel. This process provides the data in a disconnected fashion. OBAs bridge this gap by presenting business data in the user interface with which information workers are familiar. Information workers can now analyze the data using tools they already know how to use, thereby facilitating more informed decision making and actions.

■ **Role-based**   OBAs formalize people-centric processes and connect them back to system-centric processes. They let workers perform a particular task from start to finish without having to shift context, pull data from various data sources manually, or perform analyses in disparate applications. OBAs are also built with a common identity and security system.

■ **Collaborative**   A great deal of the activity required to accomplish a business task happens outside enterprise systems. The OBA platform allows developers to capture all aspects of a business process within a 2007 Office system application. The ability to share and connect with others is built into the platform and supports both formal and informal processes (such as workflows), allowing for more complex applications.

■ **Configurable**   OBAs are serviceable by their end users, adaptive, and highly customizable by both IT developers and end users. Because the collaboration and business rules are not hard-coded into the presentation tier, end users have considerable control over configuring applications for their own needs. Power users can arrange their portals the way they like and set business rules for certain tasks using familiar tools. As business needs change, IT developers can rebuild and redeploy the business tier components, thus maintaining their business applications relatively easily and with less code.

- **Contextual**   OBAs focus on business interactions, analytics, and actions. They allow users to make decisions and act within the context of the business problems at hand. OBAs do not reinvent the wheel for functions such as data access, data interactions, workflows, analysis, and reporting, but they do make use of these capabilities from the underlying platform. Thus business applications can build on the foundational capabilities of the Office system to provide business capabilities of their own.

How OBAs Extend the Development Paradigm

Having the common services described in previous sections in a single platform is a breakthrough for developers. With fewer platforms and tools to learn and with a common deployment model, developing OBAs in conjunction with .NET applications and Web services provides for faster development at a lower cost. As a developer, you can add to your knowledge of building multitier applications and extend it to the OBA platform.

In Figure 1-2, the four major areas show how information is presented and consumed by end users, how information is processed, how collaboration occurs, and how information is stored. Information is made available through an Office SharePoint Server 2007 portal that has sites composed of pages and pages composed of Web Parts. A Web Part is the most basic building block of the portal. Solution providers can develop Web Parts and incorporate Web Parts that are provided out of the box, one of which provides Office Excel 2007 spreadsheets and charts and another the capability to view lists and tables.

Web Parts are aggregated within pages. This aggregation can be assembled by users from the collection of Web Parts made available to them, or dashboard templates can be created from these pages. For example, developers can create standard dashboards for business functions involved in sales, inventory, or any other business area.

Developers can also create and package template sites along functional lines. An entire site can be deployed as part of an OBA solution. Users can also work with personalized My Sites in which they can create pages from scratch using the Web Parts made available to them or simply pull in links to standard dashboards that are appropriate for their role.

Information is processed and can be worked on by the users of a site through a number of services within the 2007 Office system. For example, documents live in document libraries, and forms live in form libraries. Document libraries for spreadsheets can be registered with Excel Services, and the worksheets they contain can then be distributed through thin-browser views of charts and tables. You can also present business data in lists and tables in Office SharePoint Server 2007 through the BDC. You could create a report to show this information, either through a combination of Excel Web Parts and spreadsheets presented through Excel Services or through reports designed and published through Microsoft Office Business Scorecard Manager or OLAP cubes maintained in SQL Server Analysis Services.

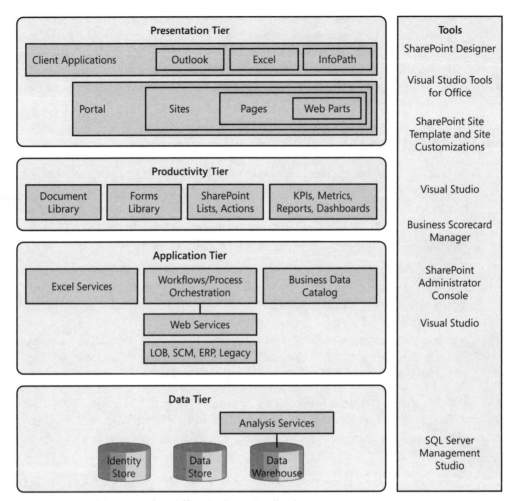

Figure 1-2 Architecture of an Office Business Application.

You can use Visual Studio 2005 or Microsoft Office SharePoint Designer 2007 to create workflows and then associate these workflows with document and form libraries. You can specify to Office SharePoint Server 2007 which workflows to invoke on a document when it is modified or created. These workflows might be related to a business process (document approval, for example) or to document life-cycle management (for example, record expiration dates).

Finally, you can access the information that lives in back-end systems through the BDC or by workflows. This information can be presented through a Web service interface or through direct data connectivity. The BDC makes information available in lists and tables within Office SharePoint Server 2007 and allows the association of actions that can be taken on that data. These actions become available through a drop-down menu on the table, invoking specified URLs and passing in context. These URLs can correspond to a Web service or link to a 2007 Office system document that is prepopulated by the context that is passed in from the BDC.

Major Components of an Office Business Application

As with any application platform, certain layers should be included in every OBA. These layers are separated into three tiers for this discussion: the client tier, the middle tier (which includes both the application and productivity subtiers), and the data tier.

Client Tier Considerations

Most solutions need to provide a way for users to interact with the application. When you are developing solutions based on the 2007 Office system, several user interface (UI) elements are available to you. The 2007 Office system client UI has been redesigned with an eye toward a more effective user experience, and it has also been exposed to developers for building custom solutions. You can integrate these solutions into the Ribbon and the new application-level task pane within the client, using the UI framework that users are expecting and familiar with.

Forms Based (InfoPath)

InfoPath 2007, the forms designer of choice for Office SharePoint Server 2007, has several options for quickly creating forms, including the forms client, document information panels, and workflow forms.

- **Forms client**   You can design forms in the traditional Office InfoPath 2007 client or the new Visual Studio editor to control a form's functionality as well as its look and feel.

- **Document information panels**   A *document information panel* is a form that contains document metadata fields and is displayed in a client application. Users can use these panels to enter metadata about a file while working in a Microsoft Office system client application. You can create document information panels in Office SharePoint Server 2007 or in Office InfoPath 2007.

- **Workflow forms**   You can also use Office InfoPath 2007 forms with workflows in Office SharePoint Server 2007, enabling user interaction with the workflow form from the 2007 Office system client application instead of only through a browser.

Outlook Custom Form Regions

Form regions add custom functionality to standard Office Outlook 2007 forms. Form regions provide a range of options for presenting a UI:

- Customize the default page of any standard form.

- Add up to 30 extra pages to any standard form.

- Replace or enhance any standard form.

- Display custom UI in the reading pane in addition to the Document Inspector.

You can design the layout of a form region by using the Office Outlook 2007 Form Region Designer, shown in Figure 1-3. You can then import the form region into an application-level add-in project and use managed code to handle events in the form region. Before you test the form region, you define the region's properties and associate the form region with an Office Outlook 2007 message class.

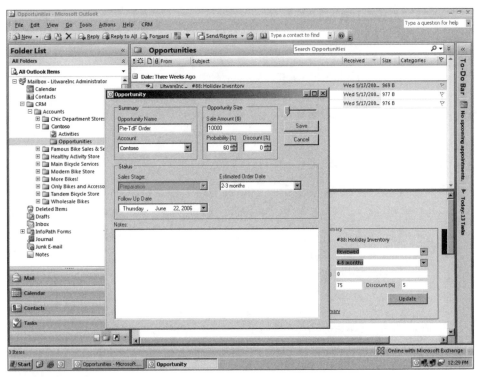

Figure 1-3 An example of an Office Outlook 2007 form.

Web Parts

A *Web Part* is a modular unit of information that consists of a title bar, a frame, and content. A *Web Part Page* is a type of Web page that contains one or more Web Parts and consolidates data, such as lists and charts, and Web content, such as text and images, into a portal built around a common task. By connecting Web Parts, you can present data from two Web Parts in alternate views, perform related calculations between two Web Parts, and filter a Web Part by using values from another Web Part—all on one Web Part Page. Web Parts are the basic building blocks of any Office SharePoint Server 2007 solution and are also an important part of any Office Business Application. The Web Parts that can be used in an OBA belong to one of two groups:

- **Built-in Web Parts** Web Parts such as BDC Web Parts, Excel Services Web Parts, and business-intelligence Web Parts.

- **Custom Web Parts**   Web Parts developed by you or by third parties. You can use custom Web Parts to extend the built-in capabilities and functionality of Office SharePoint Server 2007 and to provide customized behaviors. Custom Web Parts are based on ASP.NET and can be developed using Microsoft Visual Studio 2005 and Microsoft Visual Studio extensions for Windows SharePoint Services version 3.

Ribbon Extensibility

Most of the features accessed by using menus and toolbars in previous versions of Microsoft Office can now be accessed by using the Ribbon, the new user interface element that brings a unified customization model to many 2007 Office system applications. This control provides a way to organize related commands (in the form of controls) so that they are easier to find. Controls are organized into groups along a horizontal strip at the top edge of an application window. Related groups are organized on tabs that help users perform tasks. Developers can use the flexibility of adding or removing controls to provide a specific experience and specific functionality to users. This UI model also provides more consistency for developers by supplying the same Ribbon and task pane model across the applications.

Middle Tier Considerations

For practicality, you can combine the application tier and the productivity tier, as illustrated earlier in Figure 1-2, as the middle tier. The middle tier has the dual responsibility of handling information processing and collaboration.

The core of your application is the business functionality it provides. An application performs a business process that consists of one or more tasks. Business logic will usually evolve and grow, providing higher-level operations and logic that encapsulate logic that already exists. In many cases, you will need to compose functionality (a workflow, for example) to perform the required business logic.

Deciding Between Client Code and Server Code

Although your application architecture depends on specific solution requirements, it's pretty safe to say that the business logic should be abstracted from the client tier. A good general rule is that the client should consume the services exposed by the middle tier, which provides the gateway to the underlying data.

The Open XML standard used in the 2007 Office system enables server-side document manipulation scenarios and allows developers to include their own custom data on the client within a document that is generated programmatically from the server. Several of the 2007 Office system applications now save files by default in this open file format. Furthermore, updates have been released by Microsoft to allow client applications from previous versions of Office to read the new file formats. As mentioned earlier, storing the document as XML facilitates server-side document creation and manipulation without requiring the client applications to be instantiated on the server. Server advances, such as document property promotion, workflow, and search, are among the many capabilities available to OBAs now that the underlying documents are consumable by server-side processes. These documents can be generated by the middle tier on the fly, or they can be consumed by the middle tier after being presented on the client tier.

Business Data Catalog

One of the main methods for connecting to data is through the BDC, a business integration feature in Microsoft Office SharePoint Server 2007. The BDC is a shared service that can be used with Office SharePoint Server 2007 to present business data from back-end server applications without any coding. You can use the BDC to display data from SAP, Siebel, or another LOB application through Web services or databases.

The BDC, whose framework is shown in Figure 1-4, is a metadata repository that allows you to define business entities such as customers, invoices, and purchase orders. Once defined, these entities can be used throughout your Web sites and portals in ways such as the following:

- In search results
- In Web Parts and lists
- As a filtering mechanism in dashboards
- In document properties

These models for business entities will help maintain consistency in data and reduce errors and rekeying.

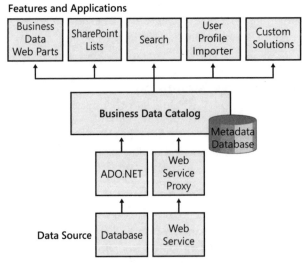

Figure 1-4   The Business Data Catalog.

The BDC is a key element of the infrastructure around which the other business data features of Office SharePoint Server 2007 are built.

The BDC provides access to the underlying data sources through a metadata model that is based on a consistent and simplified client object model. Typically, metadata authors with skills equivalent to those of a database developer describe the API of business applications by using the metadata model. Administrators register business applications in the BDC, after which the data in the business application is immediately available on a portal site through other Office SharePoint Server 2007 business data features and the SharePoint Server object model.

Data Connectivity

Business rules, data, and metadata are stored on the server in a typical application architecture. Exposing this content in an Office client workspace makes it more likely that information workers will enter and use relevant information in their work. This metadata can then be used within elements of the presentation tier. The metadata is eventually saved on the server and can then be used to categorize and search for the content. For example, you can look for all purchase orders with the *Customer* property equal to Contoso.

Data Connection Library

A *data connection library* is a new type of SharePoint Server document library in which organizations can publish connection files that provide a straightforward way for users to share, manage, and discover connections to external data repositories without requiring them to have knowledge of the technical details. Data connection files are easy to create and update, and solution designers can reuse them in 2007 Office system client applications.

Adapters

In addition to using data connection libraries, you can use the BizTalk Adapter Pack—a set of application adapters—to enable customers to bring LOB data into 2007 Office system client applications or any client that supports using Web services.

Excel Services

Excel Services, outlined in Figure 1-5, is part of Office SharePoint Server 2007. It extends the capabilities of Office Excel 2007 through the broad sharing of spreadsheets and improved manageability and security. Excel Services also provides a means for reusing spreadsheet models through a scalable, server-based calculation service and an interactive, Web-based user interface.

Excel Services has three core components: Excel Web Access, Excel Web Services, and Excel Calculation Services. Excel Services handles communication among the three components and load-balances the requests made to Excel Calculation Services.

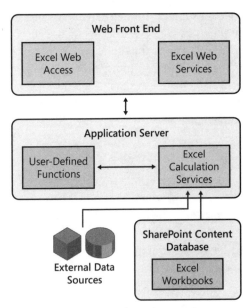

Figure 1-5 How Excel Services works.

The Excel Web Access, Excel Web Services, and Excel Calculation Services components can be divided into components that reside on the front-end Web server and those that live on a back-end application server. The Web front end includes Excel Web Services. The Excel Calculation Services component resides on the back-end application server, alongside any user-defined function assemblies that an administrator may have added.

Open XML

Open XML file formats allow developers to program Office documents outside the application that generated them. This standards-based format is the primary data transport between applications and users in an OBA. One key benefit of the new format is substantially smaller file sizes.

The Office XML formats are based on XML and ZIP technologies, thereby making them universally accessible. The specifications for the formats and schemas are published and made available under the same royalty-free license that exists today for the Microsoft Office 2003 Reference Schemas.

With Open XML at the center of the Office XML formats, exchanging data between Microsoft Office applications and enterprise business systems is greatly simplified. Without requiring access to the Office applications, solutions can alter information inside an Office document or create a document by using standard tools and technologies capable of manipulating XML and ZIP. A simple example is creating an Office Excel 2007 spreadsheet on the server without the need for Office Excel 2007.

Additional benefits of the Office XML formats include the following:

- **Easy to integrate business information with documents**   Office XML formats enable the rapid creation of documents from disparate data sources, thereby accelerating document assembly, data mining, and content reuse.

- **Robust**   The Office XML formats are designed to be more robust than the binary formats, and therefore help reduce the risk of lost information resulting from damaged or corrupted files.

- **Secure**   The openness of the Office XML formats translates to more secure and transparent files. You can share documents confidently because you can easily identify and remove personally identifiable information and sensitive business information such as user names, comments, and file paths.

- **Backward-compatible**   The 2007 Microsoft Office system is backward-compatible with Microsoft Office 2000, Microsoft Office XP, and Microsoft Office 2003. Users of these versions can adopt the new format with little effort and continue to gain benefits from using their existing files.

Workflow

A workflow can control almost any aspect of an item in Office SharePoint Server 2007. A simple workflow can require the approval of several users for a document such as a budget. A more complex workflow can require information to be gathered through forms, branching to perform different functions depending on the information gathered. Other complex workflow activities include creating a SharePoint task for a set of users, sending an e-mail message to the appropriate roles with the details of the task, and sending the data across the wire to a trading partner as an automatically generated acknowledgement.

Figure 1-6 shows a sample analysis for a workflow for a purchase order approval process.

PO Approval Process	Workflow
Review Current Budget Status	Collect Feedback
Verify Inventory	Verification
Get Manager's Approval If Over Approval Limit	Approval Review
Approve Purchase Order	Approval

Figure 1-6   A sample table analyzing workflows.

Microsoft provides two development tools for authoring workflows for Windows SharePoint Services: the Visual Studio 2005 Designer for Windows Workflow Foundation, and Office

SharePoint Designer 2007. In general, the major differences between the two tools are the following:

- Authoring workflows in the Visual Studio 2005 Designer for Windows Workflow Foundation is performed by a professional developer, who creates a workflow template that can be deployed across multiple sites and contains custom code and activities. The developer then passes the workflow template to a server administrator for actual deployment and association.

- Workflow authoring in Office SharePoint Designer 2007 is likely to be done by someone other than a professional developer, such as a Web designer or information worker who wants to create a workflow for a specific list or document library. In this case, the designer is limited to the workflow activities on the Safe Controls List, and the workflow cannot include custom code. The author of the workflow deploys the workflow template directly to the list or document library as part of the workflow authoring process.

Data Tier Considerations

Almost all applications and services need to store and access some kind of data. Your application or service might have one or more data sources, and these data sources might be of different types. The logic used to access data in a data source needs to provide methods for querying and updating data. The data your application logic needs to work on is related to *entities* that play a part in your business. The considerations discussed in the following sections will assist you in working with the data tier for an OBA.

Writing Data to LOB Systems

The XML file formats used in the 2007 help facilitate a way to write to an LOB system by using document assembly and disassembly and content tagging with custom schemas. Document assembly and disassembly give a developer the ability to quickly unpackage any Office document and retrieve the metadata holding the data that needs to be pushed to the LOB system. With the compression enhancements in the .NET Framework 2.0 and 3.0 to the *System.IO.Packaging* library, the design of custom compression libraries or the use of third-party utilities is no longer required to complete this step. Developers are now provided with a more reliable solution.

With content tagging, a document can store critical data needed for integration in a separate data file using a custom-defined schema based on the requirements of an LOB system. Processing the metadata by using the tagging approach leads to less overhead while the data is loaded and read and also removes the need to navigate through the formatting elements used to present the document.

Maintaining Mapping of Data Between Systems

Data in a document that is used to modify an LOB system must be up to date to ensure data integrity. A developer can use many different techniques to confirm the data's currency, depending on the type of document being processed. One of these techniques can often be applied to all documents that use the Office XML file formats. Office XML file formats allow a user to define the metadata needed by including a custom XML file in the compressed file. This data file holds the data required to render the document as well as to push the data back to the LOB system. The file can be defined with a custom schema for setting the guidelines of the metadata, but this is not required.

When the user loads the document for editing, a server-side process is needed to populate the compressed document file with the metadata and deliver it to the user after it is populated. The document the user sees is rendered with the metadata embedded, and as the user modifies the document, the 2007 Office system will keep the metadata file in sync. After all the changes are made, the user will save the document to a server-side application, such as Office SharePoint Server 2007, where this process will extract the metadata from the compressed file and render any changes back to the LOB data store or exposed service points. Inside Office SharePoint Server 2007, this process can be designed by using the new built-in workflow tools.

Developer Tools

Developers have several tools available to assist them in building Office Business Applications.

Visual Studio 2005 Tools for the 2007 Microsoft Office System Section Edition

Visual Studio 2005 Tools for the 2007 Microsoft Office System Second Edition (VSTO 2005 SE), a fully supported free add-on to Visual Studio 2005, gives developers the ability to build applications targeting the 2007 Office system. VSTO 2005 SE includes the following functionality:

- Application-level customizations and add-ins for the most popular Office applications, including for both the 2003 and 2007 versions of Office Word, Office Excel, Office Outlook, Office Visio, Microsoft Office PowerPoint, and the 2007 version of Office InfoPath. The safe loading, unloading, and management of managed add-ins is one of the most important features of VSTO 2005 SE.

- A programming model and run-time support for the Ribbon, custom task panes, and Office Outlook 2007 forms regions.

- Design-time support for Office InfoPath 2007 forms so that you can build your forms from the Visual Studio IDE.

- Support for Visual Studio 2005 Professional.

Office SharePoint Designer 2007

Office SharePoint Designer 2007 is specifically designed to help you create and customize Web sites and workflows built with Windows SharePoint Services and Office SharePoint Server 2007. It provides tools that IT professionals and solution developers need to develop SharePoint Server 2007–based applications and workflow solutions that address organizational agility and business process automation.

With Office SharePoint Designer 2007, you can design SharePoint workflows and applications without having to use traditional procedural coding languages or techniques. Instead, SharePoint Designer 2007 provides tools that you can use to do the following:

- Build conditional views and forms with validation
- Read, write, and present data from a variety of data sources, such as XML files, SQL databases such as Microsoft SQL Server 2005, and Web services
- Compile data from multiple sources to create flexible, customized views and reports
- Build Web Part Pages and connect Web Parts to create business applications

OBA Application Patterns

In the following sections, I'll describe OBA application patterns, which provide a breadth of approaches that you can use to extend and integrate LOB systems and the 2007 Office system. These application patterns in many cases are based on real-world implementations, and in other cases they are built on features and capabilities of the 2007 Office system that have a generalized solution rooted in input from customers and partners. Multiple patterns can be and typically are combined in a single OBA, and more sophisticated patterns emerge within scenarios involving specific applications and industries.

 Note   Customers and ISVs can often implement these application patterns in Office 2003, although for just about every case, the 2007 Office system and the latest release of Visual Studio Tools for Office make implementing the application patterns simpler and offer richer possibilities.

Office Applications as a Reach Channel

The objective of this pattern is to extend LOB application functionality to a broader user base by using Office applications as the channel. A complementary objective in many cases is to eliminate a duplication of effort. An example of extending LOB functionality to a broader set of end users is an employee self-service scenario such as updating employee personal information. An example of reducing the duplication of effort is a feature with which consultants can classify time for meetings entered in Outlook to track their time against billable projects. This pattern can be useful in situations in which system adoption is spotty because users see low value in the system and are annoyed by the duplication of effort; e-mail messages containing requests for updates are submitted to a few people who in turn reenter the information into an LOB system; or LOB functionality goes unused because training and maintenance efforts required to extend the LOB application's interface to a larger number of users are not sufficiently justified.

A developer can pursue the integration of 2007 Office system applications and an LOB system directly or through a mediated approach.

Direct Integration Pattern

In the direct integration pattern, access to LOB interfaces is projected directly into an Office client or is extended to an existing feature, such as in the Office Outlook 2007 calendar example mentioned previously. The back-end process remains unchanged and is minimally augmented by additional logic. Integration using custom Web Parts that access LOB systems and present functionality and services without a mediating feature also falls into this category. A good example is a solution that presents a Business Service Page (BSP) from an SAP system as a Web Part on a SharePoint site. (See Figure 1-7.)

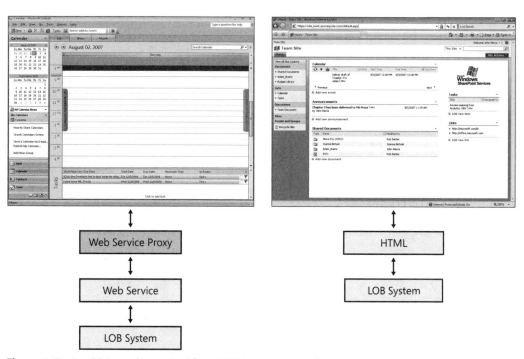

Figure 1-7   An OBA can interact with an LOB in a number of ways.

Mediated Integration Pattern

Although direct integration is a great approach for realizing value quickly and potentially making use of the frameworks that organizations have built around service-oriented architectures, this approach requires coding and doesn't facilitate the discovery and reuse, or construction and reuse, of a composite solution across systems.

A metadata-driven approach to systems, however, enables the achievement of loose coupling and reuse more easily, as well as augmentation and extension after development using more advanced frameworks. Microsoft pioneered this approach with the Information Bridge Framework (IBF). While Microsoft is no longer investing in IBF, in the 2007 Office system the BDC performs similar functions for managing entities and their related services across Web services and data sources (using ADO.NET) for Office SharePoint Server 2007 solutions.

The mediated integration pattern incorporates metadata stores such as the BDC to provide an additional level of abstraction over direct integration. (See Figure 1-8.) This approach allows read-only views to be presented in SharePoint without any development, and it also allows for the creation of compositions using SharePoint Web Parts. You can extend the BDC with custom code to support more sophisticated write-back operations to promote decoupling and reuse of the controls. In addition to mediating the Web service interfaces, the BDC framework provides common approaches to services, including security, with a single sign-on mechanism based on credentials mapping.

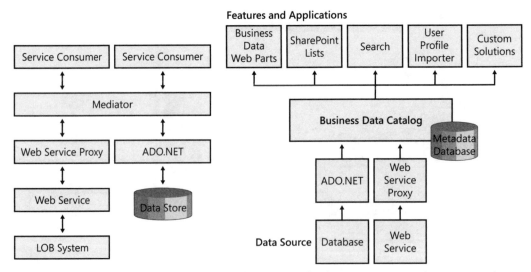

Figure 1-8   The mediated integration variant is a pattern that incorporates metadata stores such as the BDC.

Document Generation

Today a significant amount of information within an enterprise resides in documents. Structured LOB storage accounts for only one-third of the information in the enterprise. The rest is stored in documents on user desktops, often replicating (through manual means) information contained in LOB systems. The 2007 Office system and Open XML document formats provide ways to narrow this gap and create documents that contain LOB-related data that can be processed. This set of application patterns describes incremental approaches along this path. Documents generated from business data stored in an LOB system can be simple documents such as a marketing campaign letter or a table exported to Office Excel 2007, or they can be more complex: a proposal, a contract, or a budget spreadsheet.

The application-generated documents pattern is the most common pattern for integrating the 2007 Office system and LOB systems. In this pattern, outlined in Figure 1-9, the LOB system merges business data with a 2007 Office system document. This pattern commonly occurs in batch-oriented, server-side processing, although client-side generation is also feasible.

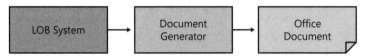

Figure 1-9   The application-generated documents pattern is the most common pattern for integrating the 2007 Office system documents (.docx, .xlsx, .pptx) and LOB systems.

Before the 2007 Office system was released, this pattern was a challenge to scale because an Office client was generally required to perform sophisticated document generation. In the 2007 Office system and Open XML file formats, document generation becomes simpler and far more scalable.

More Info   Open XML is an Ecma standard. More information and samples about Open XML can be found on the community site *http://openxmldeveloper.org.*

Intelligent Documents

Many LOB processes generate business documents that are used to exchange information with customers and partners, and information workers often create documents based on information in an LOB system. In many cases, 2007 Office system documents facilitate a more intuitive user experience and provide more useful functionality than a native LOB application for visualizing, analyzing, and manipulating LOB data. Some examples of such document-centric business processes are proposal generation, contract approval, budgeting, and forecasting. The data in these documents is dynamic and transactional—in other words, structured content persisted within the document can be used to update an LOB system, call an LOB service, or start a workflow in the LOB system. A snapshot of the LOB information moves with the document, turning the document into a container of information that can be acted on by client-side or server-side processing logic. As capabilities such as search become more intelligent, they will be able to parse embedded, structured information intelligently and provide information workers with a greater array of options. Document-centric processes are perfect candidates for building an OBA using intelligent document patterns.

Embedded LOB Information Pattern

In the embedded LOB information pattern, shown in Figure 1-10, LOB data is embedded in 2007 Office system documents created in applications such as Office Word 2007 or Office Excel 2007. A custom task pane (CTP) can provide a user interface to LOB data by using either the direct integration pattern or the mediated integration pattern described previously. With the Open XML file format, the ability to embed structured information and process the document is facilitated through the use of standard XML capabilities supported in all modern frameworks. An information worker can browse or search LOB data and merge (embed) it into a document. For example, a user can browse and search a product catalog from an LOB system using controls in a CTP and merge the product information into a sales quote document. The LOB data is embedded in the body of the document, or it can be embedded as an XML document part. In Office Word 2007 documents, you can present the data in an XML document part by binding it to content controls. This capability provides an abstraction between data and presentation and hence is a better approach than embedding data directly in the body of the document.

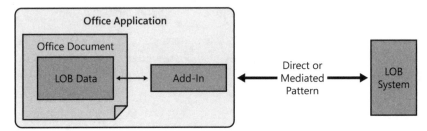

Figure 1-10   In the embedded LOB information pattern, LOB data is embedded in Office documents created in applications such as Office Word 2007, Office Excel 2007, and Office PowerPoint 2007.

Embedded LOB Template Pattern

When incorporating the layout of LOB data within a document would be beneficial, a more sophisticated approach is to create a document template, as shown in Figure 1-11. A template combines metadata from an LOB system with document markup (content controls, XML schema, bookmarks, and named ranges) bound to specific instances of LOB information at a later stage. The creation of such a template uses the aspects of the embedded LOB information pattern using a CTP, although in this case the add-in provides metadata information rather than instance information from the LOB system. The metadata is used to mark up the document schema to describe the embedding of LOB content within the document. This technique enables end users—without the involvement of developers—to create sophisticated document templates that can be processed automatically.

The markup, along with the Office Open XML file format, is subsequently merged with an instance of the LOB data to create a document. The merging can take place through an add-in within one of the Office client applications to provide an interactive user experience and enable offline capabilities, as shown in Figure 1-12.

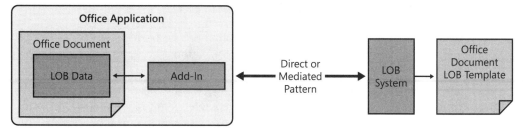

Figure 1-11 Creation of standard document templates that integrate with LOB data makes consuming and interacting with the data easier.

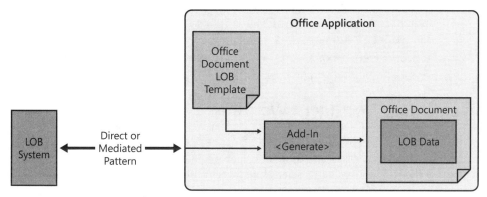

Figure 1-12 You can create documents interactively through a custom task pane that makes use of both document and LOB data.

The template is also ideal for server-side data merging and batch processing of multiple or complex documents, as shown in Figure 1-13.

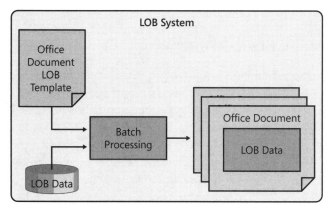

Figure 1-13 A document template is a recommended model for server-side data merging and batch processing because it allows for the separation of design and development.

LOB Information Recognizer Pattern

In this pattern, a fragment of document content is recognized as semantically meaningful information within the context of an LOB application. The recognition can be enabled through metadata and document markup (content controls, XML schema, bookmarks, named ranges, and so on) or by using smart tag technology provided by 2007 Office system applications. Once such content is recognized, interesting actions can be performed on that information. In a server-side scenario, recognized information can be extracted and used to update the LOB data or start a workflow. In the client-side scenario, recognized information can be used to present a context-sensitive user interface using a CTP or the Ribbon. For example, in a proposal document, a customer name is recognized because it is bound to a "Customer Name" content control. The CTP then shows detailed customer information and order history from an LOB application. Another example is the recognition of a product SKU as a smart tag using regular expressions. The user can view product details and drawings by selecting appropriate smart tag menu options.

Complementary Document Workflow

Businesses often augment LOB processes with document exchanges outside the LOB system. Examples include sales pipeline forecasting, budgeting, proposal generation, and incident management. These exchanges are often ad hoc and take place through e-mail. With complementary document workflows, enterprises can better control and monitor the document-related processes that need to occur and can ensure that the processes are audited and meet compliance requirements. For cases with potentially significant variation in how information workers handle different types of information, best practices can be built into document handling routines through the use of workflows. You can combine the complementary document workflow pattern with the intelligent document pattern to enhance the underlying business process contained within an LOB system.

LOB-Initiated Document Workflow Pattern

Businesses often use information in an LOB system to generate documents that need to be reviewed, approved, and possibly edited. For example, if a report needs to be regularly reviewed for compliance reasons, the report can be generated and published to an Office SharePoint Server 2007 repository to track reviewing. The Office SharePoint Server 2007 document workflow will ensure that the review occurred and raise exceptions if proper procedures and timelines are not followed. One way to achieve more control over these generated documents is for the LOB system to publish the document to an Office SharePoint Server 2007 document library with an associated workflow. For instance, a system might publish a financial report that requires review by an auditor and approval by the controller to Office SharePoint Server 2007, and then Office SharePoint Server 2007 can manage the approval workflow, a process summarized in Figure 1-14.

Figure 1-14   Publishing to a document library in Office SharePoint Server 2007 can be the first step in initiating a workflow.

Alternatively, a default document type such as an Office InfoPath 2007 form can be associated with a document library. A workflow can be triggered by something as simple as adding a document to a document library, as shown in Figure 1-15.

Figure 1-15   A workflow can also be triggered by a simple event, such as adding a document to a document library.

Cooperating Document Workflow Pattern

In more complex scenarios, a series of interactions might take place between documents and LOB systems. An example is illustrated in Figure 1-16. For example, when performing sales pipeline forecasting, a company's management chain often needs to do different levels of review, roll-up, and so on. Additionally, at each stage in the process, certain actions might not be permitted. For instance, after a forecast has been submitted for roll-up, the forecast might no longer be editable. As the sales forecast moves through stages of refinement, intermediate results may be published to the LOB system so that management can extract rolled-up views of their organization. To achieve this scenario, a cooperating workflow could be created in Office SharePoint Server 2007, following either of two approaches to achieve integration with the LOB system. In the first approach, you can combine the LOB-initiated workflow pattern with an intelligent document pattern. With this composite pattern, the document contains LOB data, and an LOB add-in to the 2007 Office system client (such as Office Word 2007 or Office Excel 2007) interacts with the back-end system using the data embedded within the document.

The workflow provides logic while the intelligent document provides the interaction mechanisms to the LOB system based on its current state. The disadvantage of this approach is that the overall state is not as easily tracked because it is shared between the intelligent document interactions on the client and the workflow state on the server.

A second approach is to develop a workflow specific to the problem domain that interacts with the LOB system and enriches the workflow executing on Office SharePoint Server 2007, as illustrated in Figure 1-17.

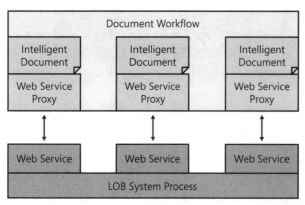

Figure 1-16   The cooperating document workflow pattern.

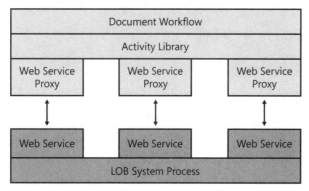

Figure 1-17   Developing a custom workflow to solve specific business scenarios.

Not all functionality, however, can be delivered on the server side and achieve as rich an interaction as with intelligent documents, but you can use the two approaches in conjunction. For instance, a sales pipeline forecasting spreadsheet could enforce some of the rules and manipulations based on the LOB information embedded in the intelligent document, and once the pipeline is approved, the server-side Office SharePoint Server 2007 workflow could extract the information from the Office Excel 2007 document and publish the results back to the LOB system. Figure 1-18 shows a simplified view of sales pipeline forecasting in which Office Excel 2007, an Office SharePoint Server 2007 workflow, and LOB processes are used in conjunction.

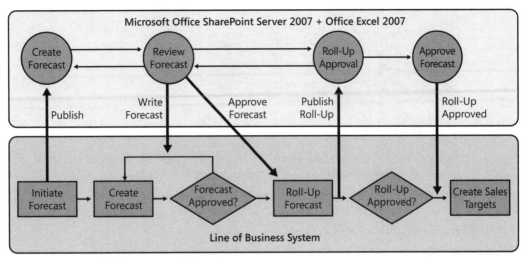

Figure 1-18   A sales forecast workflow.

Discovery Navigation Pattern

Search is becoming more pervasive in businesses. Search engines such as Microsoft Office SharePoint Server for Search are also integrating the ability to index LOB entities. Actions can be associated with these entities in the form of URLs. When an entity is included in the results of a search by an information worker, these actions are presented, serving as a launch point for initiating LOB operations. This type of approach is more consistent with how users often want to work. Rather than open a specific application, users prefer to find the information they need to act on or review and then choose the work they need to accomplish in that particular entity. For entities that information workers often use in an LOB system, making the information searchable within Office SharePoint Server 2007 and attaching actions that launch the LOB application enhance usability and increase usage.

The BDC is used for integrating content from LOB systems into the search index, as illustrated in Figure 1-19. Capabilities are supported for incremental index updates as well.

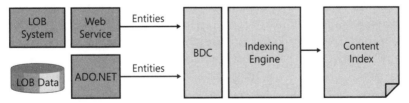

Figure 1-19   You can use the BDC to integrate content from LOB systems into the search index.

After data is indexed, searches can result in the discovery of related LOB data, and navigation into LOB applications can be initiated from the results page, as shown in Figure 1-20. Custom tabs in the search center results can categorize the results for your application as well.

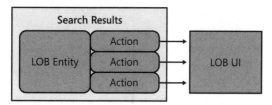

Figure 1-20   Once data is indexed, searches can result in the discovery of related LOB data, and navigation into LOB applications can be initiated from the results page.

Through the use of search properties, a single entity can be mapped to multiple LOB systems as long as the entity contains sufficient information for populating the parameters for the LOB system URL.

Collaborative Site Pattern

Although traditional LOB systems such as customer relationship management (CRM), enterprise resource planning (ERP), and product life-cycle management (PLM) are good at enforcing and executing structured business processes, they fall short at facilitating the unstructured human collaboration that precedes the structured LOB business process. In many cases, unstructured collaboration requires the participation of users who have no need for the LOB system. Traditionally, such collaboration takes place through e-mail. But as team size, the amount of information, and process timeframes increase, this method becomes ineffective and can lead to errors and delays. The collaborative site pattern addresses this situation.

Office SharePoint Server 2007 provides a team site template that can be used to collaborate on a specific business problem. A team site can provide document libraries, discussions, task lists, a team calendar, and tools for project management among many other collaboration features. The site can be secured to restrict access to only certain users.

The collaborative site pattern utilizes a dedicated team site to collaborate on a specific LOB entity or process such as sales opportunities, service requests, budgeting, and forecasting. In other words, there is one team site per LOB entity or process, as required. The context of the LOB business entity can be used to provision the team site and populate site contents. A link between the LOB business entity and the team site is maintained so that users can navigate from the LOB application's user interface to the Office SharePoint Server 2007 team site. Richer user experiences can be offered by embedding elements of the team site's user interface in the LOB user interface to facilitate collaboration in context. Users who do not have access to the LOB system can collaborate by accessing the team site through a Web browser. These users might need the context of the LOB system business object within the team site to effectively contribute to the content, which can be achieved by bringing LOB data to the surface through a Web Part. The Web Part can use either the direct integration pattern or the mediated integration pattern to access LOB data.

For example, the collaboration site pattern can be used in a CRM application to manage sales opportunities. If a particular sales opportunity is large and requires many people from different groups—such as sales, engineering, and legal—to collaborate on it, an Office Share-Point Server 2007 team site can be created for collaborating on that specific opportunity. Because the CRM system maintains a list of team members, it automatically grants those members access to the team site. The CRM user interface displays the URL for the team site so that users can navigate to the site while viewing the opportunity in the CRM. Team members from the engineering and legal departments who do not have access to the CRM system can open the team site in a Web browser and contribute to the content. Because team members need some context about the sales opportunity—for example, customer information and opportunity size—a CRM Web Part is added to the team site to show that information from the CRM system.

Composite User Interface Pattern

Users often need to access and gather information from multiple LOB systems to compose a complex business document. In other cases, information such as customer data can be related to multiple LOB systems. Situations such as these require the composition of multiple application user interfaces. A pattern such as the composite user interface pattern allows developers to build a solution—independent of other LOB applications—that lets a user compose data from multiple LOB applications in a container such as a 2007 Office system document or a Web page on an Office SharePoint Server 2007 site.

Office Client–Based Composite User Interface

This pattern uses the 2007 Office system client application shell as a container for user interface composition. A set of Ribbon elements (tabs, groups, and controls) and custom task panes are implemented for each LOB system. The Ribbon groups and controls are placed on a custom tab or on one of the built-in tabs. When a user initiates actions with the LOB system through a Ribbon element, the corresponding task pane is displayed and presents the LOB data relevant to the action selected. For example, while working on a proposal document, a user might click a Product Catalog button on a Siebel CRM tab that displays a task pane for viewing product catalog information within Siebel. Then the user can click on a View Inventory button on an SAP tab to view product inventory information in an SAP task pane. When adding functionality with custom Ribbon elements and custom task panes, the standard conventions of Office should be followed for consistency. In particular, a CTP should become visible as a result of a user gesture such as clicking a button on the Ribbon, and the user should close the CTP when the work is complete. (See Figure 1-21.) Automatically showing and hiding the custom task pane can be confusing and should be avoided.

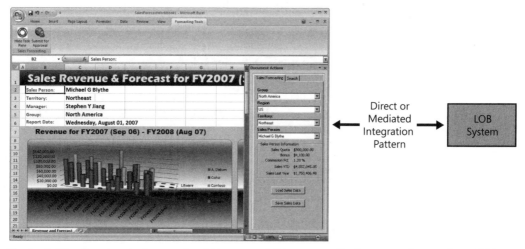

Figure 1-21   A custom task pane should become visible as a result of a user action, such as clicking a button on the Ribbon.

This pattern can be combined with the intelligent document pattern to provide a context-sensitive user interface. In this variation, when a user selects the content of the document that is recognized as LOB-relevant information, the corresponding LOB Ribbon user interface elements and CTP are made visible. This pattern can also use contextual tab sets and context menus to provide LOB actions relevant to recognized data. For example, when a user selects a product diagram in a document, Office Word 2007 displays the Picture Tools contextual tab set. An SAP PLM add-in could recognize the picture as a product diagram and add an SAP PLM custom tab to the tab set. A user could click a View Product Data button on that tab to view product data from the PLM system in a CTP. A Siebel CRM add-in also recognizes the same picture and adds a Siebel CRM custom tab to the Picture Tools tab set. The user can click the View Product Promotion button on the Siebel CRM tab to view promotional data in a Siebel CTP.

Composite Web User Interface

This pattern uses a Web page on a SharePoint site as a container for UI composition. It makes use of the Office SharePoint Server 2007 Web Part infrastructure to bring data from multiple LOBs into a single Web page. The Office SharePoint Server 2007 Web Part infrastructure is built on the ASP.NET Web Part framework. Office SharePoint Server 2007 provides built-in Web Parts such as BDC Web Parts, Excel Services Web Parts, filter Web Parts, and many others. An ASP.NET Web Part can use the direct integration pattern, and a BDC Web Part can use the mediated integration pattern to access LOB data. Office SharePoint Server 2007 allows end users to compose custom Web pages by selecting Web Parts from a gallery and connecting them together to build a composite UI. When two Web Parts are connected, one Web Part can send data to another Web Part, which can change its content based on the data received. One Web Part can send data to more than one Web Part. This connection capability is what enables UI composition.

Analytics

The analytics pattern is a specialized composite Web UI focused on presenting a data analysis dashboard to the end user. It makes use of Excel Services and Excel Services Web Parts provided by Office SharePoint Server 2007. Users such as financial analysts, business planners, and engineers use Office Excel 2007 heavily for data analysis and visualization. They can create complex Office Excel 2007 workbooks using formulas, tables, PivotTables, and charts, and can use a data connection to an LOB system to populate the content. These Office Excel 2007 workbooks can be published to Office SharePoint Server 2007 and their output can be viewed through the Excel Service Web Part. Excel Services Web Parts can be connected to other Web Parts, such as a data-filtering Web Part, BDC Web Part, and ASP.NET Web Parts to create an analysis dashboard.

Another important Web Part provided by Office SharePoint Server 2007 is a key performance indicator (KPI) Web Part. It allows users to define a KPI based on data in any Office SharePoint Server 2007 list, including a BDC list. A BDC list presents data from an LOB system and the KPI Web Part renders the indicators based on that real-time data, as illustrated in Figure 1-22.

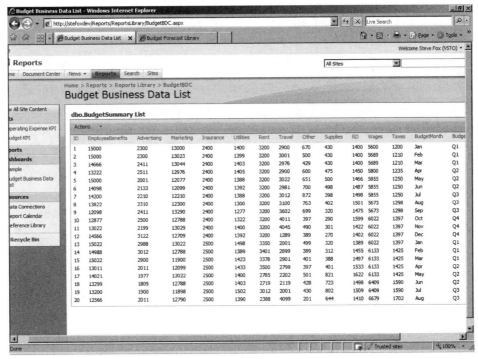

Figure 1-22   A BDC list presents data from an LOB system and the KPI Web Part renders the indicators based on that real-time data.

Application-Generated Tasks and Notifications

Many LOB applications assign tasks and generate notifications for end users. These tasks and notifications can be viewed and updated when a user logs into the LOB application. Because an organization generally uses more than one LOB application, managing tasks and responding to notifications across these applications becomes cumbersome, often resulting in poor task management and delayed responses. This problem can be alleviated by delivering LOB tasks and notifications to Office Outlook 2007. Several patterns implement such functionality, depending on the complexity and richness of the desired solution.

Simple Task and Notification Delivery

In this pattern, an LOB system delivers tasks and notifications to users as Office Outlook 2007 tasks and e-mail messages. This flow of information is one way; in other words, if a user makes any changes to the tasks and messages in Office Outlook 2007, those changes are not sent back or reflected in the LOB system. The details of a task and notification are embedded in the body of the item. HTML can be used to format the content in the item, including links to the LOB application, where a user can obtain more information and take appropriate actions.

In a "push" variant of this pattern, the LOB system delivers tasks and e-mail messages to Microsoft Exchange Server. Users can use Office Outlook 2007, Microsoft Office Outlook Web Access (OWA), or a Pocket Outlook (Smart Phone/Pocket PC) client to read and manage the information, as shown in Figure 1-23.

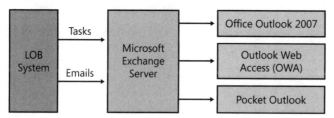

Figure 1-23   An example of the simple task and notification delivery pattern.

In a "pull" variant of this pattern, an Office Outlook 2007 add-in pulls task and notification data from the LOB system and creates Office Outlook 2007 tasks based on that information. Alternatively, an LOB system can make task and notification information available as an RSS feed, and users can subscribe to it using Office Outlook 2007. This approach works well with notifications but might not work as well for tasks because users do not have a task management experience (such as changing due date, priority, or status) with an RSS feed. (See Figure 1-24.)

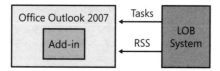

Figure 1-24   A LOB system can make task and notification information available as an RSS feed.

Task Synchronization

In this pattern, an LOB system sends tasks to users through Exchange or Office Outlook 2007, and the tasks are synchronized bidirectionally. That is, the LOB system can update the task that was sent previously to a user's inbox, the user can update the task in Office Outlook 2007, and the changes are propagated to the LOB system. For example, let's say an LOB system creates a workflow task and sends it as an Outlook task to a user. When this user completes the task, she marks the task "Complete" in Office Outlook 2007. The task status change is propagated to the LOB system, and the LOB system takes appropriate action.

There are two variants of this pattern based on the synchronization choice.

Direct task synchronization   In this variant, tasks are synchronized by Office Outlook 2007 and the LOB system communicating directly with each other. An Office Outlook 2007 add-in is responsible for synchronizing the tasks in the LOB system and Office Outlook 2007. In a push scenario, an LOB system sends tasks and updates to Exchange Server. When the Office Outlook 2007 client receives these tasks and updates, it creates a new task or applies updates to the existing task. The same add-in detects whether a user makes changes to the task in Office Outlook 2007 and propagates those changes to the LOB system. The Office Outlook 2007 add-in needs to handle conflict resolution and offline scenarios. (For example, a user might update the Office Outlook 2007 task while the LOB system is not accessible.)

Mediated task synchronization   In this variant, Office SharePoint Server 2007 acts as a mediator between the LOB system and Office Outlook 2007 to provide task synchronization. It uses two features provided by Office SharePoint Server 2007 to simplify synchronization logic: the ability to synchronize a SharePoint task list with Office Outlook 2007 tasks and its event mechanism, which can call custom code when the contents of the task list are modified. In this pattern, the LOB system publishes tasks to a Office SharePoint Server 2007 task list, which can be a team task list shared by all team members. Because a team task list is shared, the LOB system should assign tasks to team members by setting the Assigned To property for the task. Alternatively, the LOB system can publish tasks to individual users' personal task lists. The Office SharePoint Server 2007 task list is replicated to and kept in sync with Office Outlook 2007 tasks through native synchronization capability. When a user updates the task in Office Outlook 2007, the changes are pushed automatically to Office SharePoint Server 2007, which raises an event indicating that the change has occurred, which allows custom code to update the LOB system. Office SharePoint Server 2007 and Office Outlook 2007 handle task synchronization, conflict resolution, and offline mode. The solution provider is responsible for implementing the logic to push LOB tasks to the Office SharePoint Server 2007 task list and handling task list change events raised by SharePoint to update the LOB system. A schematic of this scenario is shown in Figure 1-25.

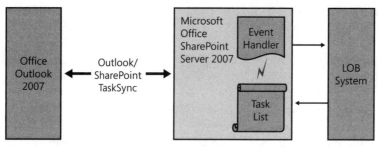

Figure 1-25   Microsoft Office SharePoint Server 2007 and Office Outlook 2007 handle task synchronization, conflict resolution, and offline mode, and the solution provider implements logic to complete the operation.

Intelligent Tasks and Notifications

Information workers need to take action based on the tasks or notifications sent by an LOB system. Usually this activity involves logging on to the LOB system, finding the required information, and updating it. This scenario can be optimized by allowing users to take such actions in Office Outlook 2007 within the context of a task or an e-mail item. For example, when a manager views an e-mail message sent by a human resources system to approve the vacation request for an employee, an Office Outlook 2007 custom task pane could show the employee's current vacation balance and the organization's vacation policy. The Outlook Ribbon could provide controls for approving or rejecting the request. When the manager clicks Approve, the HR system is updated. Some of the scenarios in Duet (a product developed by SAP and Microsoft) are based on this pattern.

The key concept in this pattern is recognizing the context and data embedded in a task or an e-mail message. The content recognition can be enabled through a variety of methods: custom properties, smart tags, content parsing, and regular expressions. After the context (for example, a vacation request) and embedded data (for example, an employee ID) are recognized, the relevant LOB data and actions can be presented through the Outlook Ribbon and a custom task pane.

Form-Based Tasks and Notifications

This pattern is a variant of the intelligent tasks and notification pattern described earlier. It uses an Office InfoPath 2007 form as an attachment to the e-mail message. The LOB system populates the Office InfoPath 2007 form template and e-mails the form to the user. The user opens the message and fills out the form. Office InfoPath 2007 facilitates data validation, custom calculations, and logic. In addition, an Office InfoPath 2007 custom task pane can present additional LOB data for context. The user submits the form data to the LOB system through a Web service call. For example, a project management system can e-mail a project time card form to a user at the end of the work week. Certain fields like employee information and project information are already populated in the form. The user opens the form in the message. He can view project details such as estimated hours, remaining hours, and hours reported in the prior week in the Office InfoPath 2007 custom task pane. The employee enters the number of hours worked each day, the Office InfoPath 2007 form validates the input, and the form's data is submitted to the project management system.

This pattern benefits from the integration of Office Outlook 2007 and Office InfoPath 2007. An Office InfoPath 2007 form can be sent through e-mail without requiring a separate deployment of the form template because the template is embedded in the message. The attached form can be previewed in the Office Outlook 2007 reading pane. Also, forms can be organized in Office Outlook 2007 folders and the form data can be presented as table columns of the folder view.

A variant of this pattern uses Office Forms Server, which is part of Office SharePoint Server 2007. Forms Server lets users fill out forms in a Web browser, even an HTML-enabled mobile device. In this pattern, the Office InfoPath 2007 form is posted to the forms library in the user's personal site, and the URL of the form is e-mailed to the user. The user then navigates to the form using a Web browser, and the Office InfoPath 2007 form is rendered in a browser without requiring the Office InfoPath 2007 client to be on the user's computer. The user fills out the form in the browser and submits the data to the LOB system. This pattern extends the reach to users and organizations that do not use Office InfoPath 2007. For example, the project time card example could be extended to include partners and contractors. The project management system can post the Office InfoPath 2007 time card form to the forms library on an Office SharePoint Server 2007 extranet site, and then a contractor can fill out and submit the time card using a Web browser.

Sample Office Business Application: From Budget File to Budgeting Application

In this section, I'll describe a sample OBA and the processes it helps manage. This example is intentionally simple for illustrative purposes. (You can find a similar and more complete budgeting OBA in the next chapter.)

A common task within an enterprise is verifying budget status before approving a workflow-generated purchase order. A sales director and a merchandise planner can execute this process by using a single Office Excel 2007 document to store data and Excel Services to maintain it. Through this approach, they have a definitive version of the data, and the budget plan can be shared from the server with other people in the organization who need to review or use the information.

The Office Excel 2007 workbook file can be stored in a document library on an Office SharePoint Server 2007 site. A workflow can be associated with this document library, with custom business logic that executes whenever the workbook is saved. For example, the workflow could run validation rules on a worksheet; apply approval policies to the data; cleanse, validate, or filter the data; or update an LOB or other back-end system. An OBA can range from a solution that requires little or no coding to a highly complex integration project involving

LOB systems and custom development that makes use of 2007 Office system APIs. For example, the budgeting data could be exposed through the BDC (and would then be available in all stages of the expense approval), to LOB system processes, and to the entire enterprise. The Open XML file format could provide document tagging and inspection, database integration, and content auditing. Adapters, hosted in either BizTalk Server or Office SharePoint Server 2007, could be used to abstract details from the LOB system and allow interaction with business data and processes. Figure 1-26 illustrates the workflow and technologies involved in an OBA such as this example.

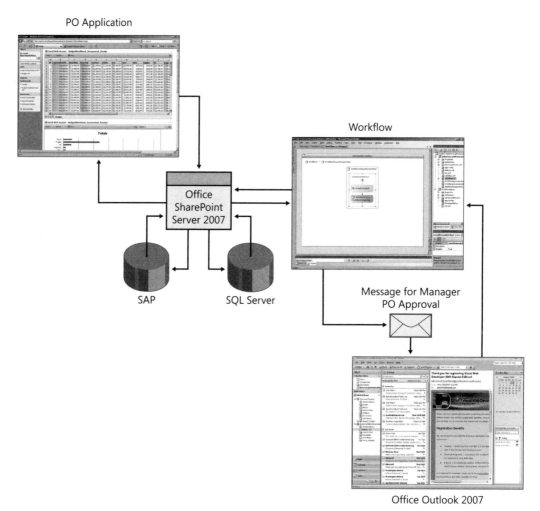

Figure 1-26   An Office Business Application that transforms the use of a budget file to a budgeting application.

To design and implement an OBA such as this one, you would follow steps such as these:

1. Create an Office Excel 2007 file that contains the budget numbers and purchase order information using the metadata.

2. Create an Office SharePoint Server 2007 portal and publish the file to Excel Services within the portal. The document will reside within a document library. Excel Services allows multilevel permissions to be applied to the file. For example, users might be allowed to view the file's contents in a browser but not be granted permission to open the file in their Office Excel 2007 client. Or, users might be able to see only the numbers in the Office Excel 2007 client but not have access to any of the formulas being used in the document.

3. Create personalized sites for the controller and buyer within the portal and provide links to the Office Excel 2007 file on each of the sites. These users will see only those files they are interested in. Because the file is being hosted in Excel Services, all users receive the same copy of the file.

4. Using the Microsoft .NET Framework 3.0 and Visual Studio 2005, develop a workflow that takes the contents of the Excel file and saves it to a database. Use the OpenXml libraries (under *System.IO.Packaging*) available in the .NET Framework 3.0 to get the Office Excel 2007 data. Because the workflow will be hosted in Office SharePoint Server 2007, at run time it has access to the attributes of the file—in other words, the stream for the file, which has been modified; the user who last modified the file; or the library where the file resides. The workflow can also perform more complex functions such as creating an Office SharePoint Server 2007 task for a set of users, sending an e-mail message to the users with the details of the task, and so on. Alternatively, to support communication across partners, the workflow could also send the data externally to a trading partner. As a final step, you can create a strongly named assembly containing the workflow and install it in the local .NET Global Assembly Cache.

5. Create an associated form using InfoPath. This form will be used to accept user data when the workflow is associated with the document library. Create an initiation form if required. The initiation form might be used to accept user data when the workflow starts execution. Install the workflow in the Office SharePoint Server 2007 portal as a feature and associate it with the document library that contains the Office Excel 2007 file. Configure the workflow such that whenever any changes are made to the file and saved, the workflow will be executed.

6. At the back end, create a data warehouse based on the schema that matches the Office Excel 2007 spreadsheet metadata. Using SQL Server Integration Services, copy data from the database to the data warehouse in a scheduled or on-demand manner. Create a SQL Server Analysis Services cube using the warehouse.

7. Create a PivotChart in an Office Excel 2007 file and link it to the cube. Publish the Office Excel 2007 file to Excel Services. Finally, use the Excel Web Renderer Web Part to display the chart to users of the portal. Alternatively, using BDC metadata, declare an entity for each row in the database. Use BDC Web Parts to display lists of the entities, allow users to search the database, etc. The specification can also be used to create a parent-child relationship between entities; for example, a purchase order can contain line items. Because the metadata is in XML, it does not require users to be aware of any programming language to make changes.

What's Next

The remaining chapters of this book provide examples and descriptions of Office Business Applications that make use of the application patterns, technologies, and platform capabilities described in this chapter. In the next chapter, you'll see an example of a budgeting application that makes use of the BDC and workflows. In Chapter 3, "Managing Sales Forecasting with an Office Business Application," you'll see an example of a custom task pane and data integration. Later chapters demonstrate more complex workflows, document assembly, use of the Open XML format, and more, including the architecture for a business intelligence solution that is built on the OBA platform.

Chapter 2
Managing and Automating the Budget Approval Process

—Steve Fox, Microsoft Corporation

Managing the workflow required to review and approve a budget is a necessary function for many organizations today. The documents used to create, approve, monitor, and track budgets are among the types of documents that organizations do not often store centrally, build and format consistently, or distribute according to processes that the organization has established. The lack of controls such as these often results in disparate budget-related documentation that lives in various parts of the organization—locally on employee hard drives, in hard copies, as e-mail attachments, and so on. This situation not only raises obvious problems for managing the review process—such as not having a current, versioned document available to the review team—but it can also lead to other problems, such as local and network resources housing the same file or files in different locations, which can lead to an increased and redundant load across valuable organizational hardware. While the latter might be considered a maintenance issue, the former can lead to inaccuracies and additional resource time to review and approve a budget, directly affecting the health of business decisions.

The advent of Office Business Applications (OBAs) provides a way to better manage processes such as budget review and approval. You can manage, review, and centrally edit budget-related documents on a Windows SharePoint Services site; Web Parts can host business data that can inform budgetary decisions; and client-side extensibilities can add budget-specific functionality to the budget approval workflow. Taken together, these capabilities offer significant benefits to the OBA developer, the end user, and the organization.

Take the following scenario, for example: The owner of a budget might use different tools to pull together budget data—e-mail, data from back-end databases (or line-of-business systems such as SAP or PeopleSoft), and so on. The budget owner will then use Microsoft Office Excel 2007 to create a draft budget, attach the worksheet to an e-mail message, and send it to his manager. This message begins processes related to reviewing and iterating over the document—steps that might or might not be part of a formal review process. After the budget owner and manager agree on the budget, the manager or business owner will send that information through e-mail to her manager in the original Office Excel 2007 format or as a Microsoft Office Word 2007 document that contains a summarized executive view. Creating and sending the summary in Office Word 2007 might require additional changes and time to edit the document, further protracting the budget review process. Figure 2-1 illustrates this scenario.

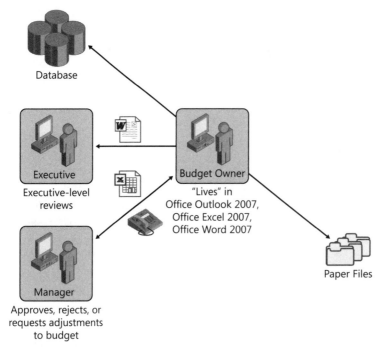

Figure 2-1   A budget approval process that does not rely on an OBA.

If we take the scenario shown in Figure 2-1 and develop it as an OBA, the technology that manages the budget approval process changes, as does the gain in efficiencies along the way. Thus, the way in which we map the scenario changes (and subsequently the way in which each participant in the workflow interacts). Figure 2-2 provides an overview of the budget approval process developed as an OBA.

In the OBA scenario, the budget owner now uses a SharePoint site as his starting point. The budget owner creates a content type based on an Office Excel 2007 budget template. The template contains a Microsoft Visual Studio Tools for Office (VSTO) add-in that extends the functionality of the Office Excel 2007 document. Through customizations to the Ribbon and a custom task pane, the budget owner can load centrally managed line items for the budget and, for example, automatically generate an executive report. SharePoint workflow manages the routing of the budget: After the budget owner creates the budget, a notification is sent to the owner's manager, who can then review and approve the budget. The approval process is managed through a custom e-mail message kicked off by a SharePoint workflow, and the budget owner can assign a specific due date to the review and approval of the budget.

Using a combination of these technologies, you can also build and deploy a similar OBA in your organization. That said, the rest of this chapter will discuss specific parts of the preceding scenario in more detail.

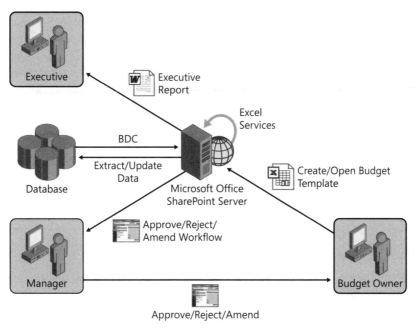

Figure 2-2   A budget approval process that relies on an OBA.

More Info   To learn more about Visual Studio Tools for Office, see the VSTO Developer
Portal on MSDN: *http://msdn2.microsoft.com/en-us/office/aa905533.aspx.*

Building Your OBA

In the remainder of this chapter, I'll discuss three main areas:

- Creation of the Office Excel 2007 budget template
- Building the SharePoint budget site
- Creating the SharePoint workflow

The budget workflow application described in this chapter incorporates attributes of two of
the OBA application patterns defined in Chapter 1. It reflects the document integration
pattern through the add-in that integrates with the budget data (or to an LOB system) and the
composite interface pattern through the customized 2007 Office system client and SharePoint
dashboard that act as entry points to a Microsoft SQL Server database (or, again, by extrapo-
lation, to data stored in an LOB system).

After you complete this chapter, you will have gained enough information to not only be
excited about going out and building your own OBA (and maybe one that can manage your
own budget process), but also to understand how.

Required Software

Before you begin building your own budget approval application, you'll need to set up and configure an environment. This chapter does not describe the installation and configuration of an environment but assumes that your environment is set up and configured correctly. You will need the following prerequisites for your environment:

- Windows Server 2003

- The Microsoft .NET Framework (version 2.0 and 3.0)

- Microsoft Office SharePoint Server 2007

- The 2007 Microsoft Office system

- 2007 Office System XML Code Snippets

- MSXML 6.0 parser

- Visual Studio 2008 Professional Edition (which includes Visual Studio Tools for Office version 3.0)

- Microsoft Exchange Server 2007

- Windows SharePoint Services 3.0 SDK

- Microsoft Office SharePoint Designer 2007

Note   The application discussed in this chapter was developed using a beta release of Visual Studio 2008 (formerly codenamed Orcas). Some changes might be required to the code if you use the samples shown in this chapter.

Creating the Excel Budget Template

The first step in developing the budget workflow application is to create the budget template. You can create the template as an Excel 2007 workbook or directly in Visual Studio 2008 through a VSTO document-level Excel project. I built the budget template in Excel 2007 and then imported it into a VSTO project. To do this, open Visual Studio 2008, and then click File, New, Project. Choose C# (or Visual Basic), Office, 2007, Excel Template. This command will invoke the new Excel project. During the process, the wizard prompts you to create a new document or copy an existing document. (See Figure 2-3.) If you created a template, click Browse and then click OK to load the Excel 2007 template as the default project template.

After you create your project, you can add more functionality to your template by using VSTO 3.0. For example, you can extend the Office Fluent user interface with your own set of Ribbon elements (new tabs, buttons, and so on), or you can build custom task panes that host user controls, Web service calls, or bindings to data sources (or all of the aforementioned). Note that you can also format the Excel workbook within the VSTO project because Visual Studio integrates the menus for Visual Studio and Office Excel 2007.

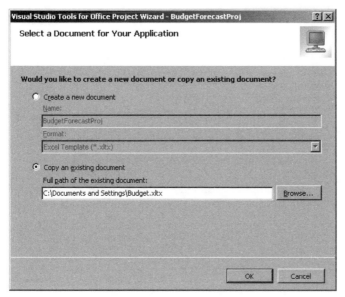

Figure 2-3   The VSTO Office Project Wizard opening an existing Excel 2007 template.

Customizing the Ribbon

In this application, I built some controls into the Ribbon and built a custom task pane to help manage data integration. The Ribbon control was built using the VSTO Ribbon Designer, a drag-and-drop designer (new to VSTO 3.0) that allows you to drag the controls you want from the toolbox, drop them into groups on the surface of the designer, and then add event handlers to the controls by double-clicking them. To create the Ribbon, right-click the solution and select Add New Item. In the Add New Item dialog box, select Ribbon (Visual Designer). (VSTO also gives you the option of creating a Ribbon using raw XML and "call-backs," a way of tying events to the XML.) Figure 2-4 illustrates the Add New Item dialog box with the appropriate item selected.

With the Ribbon shell now created, you can add specific controls to the Ribbon. For example, I created a new tab called Budget, added three groups to that tab, and then added Ribbon elements to each one of the groups. Figure 2-5 illustrates these elements.

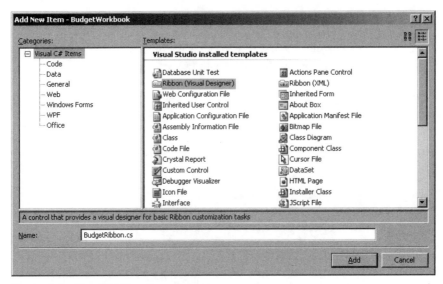

Figure 2-4   The Add New Item dialog box.

Figure 2-5   Custom Budget Ribbon elements.

When I added these controls, I accepted most of the default properties. The properties I changed are listed in Table 2-1.

Table 2-1   Properties Changed in Building the Budget Ribbon

Parent Element	Child Element	Child Element	Properties Changed
Budget Tab			*Name*: tabBudget
			Label: Budget
	Task Pane Group		*Name*: grpTaskPane
			Label: Task Pane
		Hide/Show Checkbox	*Name*: chkbxTaskHide
			Label: Hide/Show
	Reporting Group		*Name*: grpReporting
			Label: Reporting
		Create Chart Button	*Name*: btnCreateExecReport
			Label: Create Chart
			OfficeImageID: CreateFormPivot-Chart

Table 2-1   Properties Changed in Building the Budget Ribbon

Parent Element	Child Element	Child Element	Properties Changed
	Currency Exchange		*Name*: grpCurrencyExchange
			Label: Currency Exchange
		Chinese Yen	*Name*: btnCHNCurExchange
			Label: > Chinese Yen
			OfficeImageID: AccountingFormat
		Canadian Dollars	*Name*: btnCANCurExchange
			Label: > Canadian Dollars
			OfficeImageID: AccountingFormat
		Euros	*Name*: btnEUROCurExchange
			Label: > Euros
			OfficeImageID: AccountingFormat

Before I discuss the event-handling code that was added to the Ribbon elements, let's review an additional component that was added to the Excel template: a customized actions pane used to manage the integration with the data source. Customized actions panes are another VSTO feature that enable you to customize the 2007 Office system task pane. You can add user controls, WinForm controls, WPF controls, and Web service calls (among other integrations) to the custom task pane. And although I integrated the example discussed in this chapter with a small SQL Server database, you could also use Microsoft Office Access 2007, larger-scale SQL Server databases, SharePoint lists, or other technologies, such as SAP or PeopleSoft data sources.

Customized Actions Pane

To add the actions pane, I first created a user control. To add a user control to your project, right-click the project, select Add New Item, User Control, and then provide a name for the user control. In my project, I called the user control DataLoadControl. At this point, Visual Studio displays an empty user control in designer mode. You can add controls to the design surface of the user control that will manage your data source integration. In my user control, I added a number of controls and accepted most of the default properties. Figure 2-6 provides a snapshot of the user control that I used in my example.

When you are developing in VSTO, custom task panes are different from customized actions panes. The custom task panes are associated with application-level add-ins—add-ins that load when the host application loads. (For example, the custom task pane loads every time I open Office Word 2007.) Customized actions panes are task panes that are associated with document-level customizations—or customizations that load when the host document loads (for example, an actions pane that loads every time I open a specific Office Word 2007document).

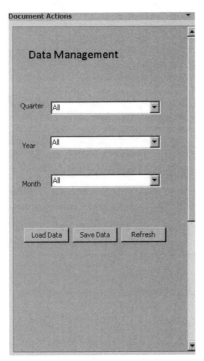

Figure 2-6   Budget user control for a custom task pane.

Table 2-2 lists the controls I added along with the properties that I changed.

Table 2-2   User Control and Properties

Control	Properties Changed	Description
Label	*Name:* lblGeneralLabel *Label*: Data Management *Font*: Calibri, Bold, 14	Title label
Label	*Name*: lblQuarter *Label*: Quarter:	Label for the Quarter combo box
Combo Box	*Name*: cmboBoxQuarter *Collection Items*: Q1, Q2, Q3, Q4	Combo box that lists the available calendar quarters
Label	*Name*: lblYear *Label*: Year:	Label for the Year combo box
Combo Box	*Name*: cmboBoxYear *Collection items*: 2005, 2006, 2007	Combo box that lists the available years
Label	*Name*: lblMonth *Label*: Month:	Label for the Month combo box
Combo Box	*Name*: comboBoxMonth *Collection items*: Jan, Feb, Mar, Apr, May, Jun, Jul, Aug, Sep, Oct, Nov, Dec	Combo box for the available months

Table 2-2   User Control and Properties

Control	Properties Changed	Description
Button	*Name*: btnAddData *Label*: Add Data	Button to load data per combo box selections and then add the data to the Excel template
Button	*Name*: btnSaveData *Label*: Save Data	Button to save any changes from the spreadsheet to the database
Button	*Name*: btnReset *Label*: Refresh	Button to reset the selected items in the combo boxes to null

The user control must now be added to the project, essentially by using the *ActionsPane* object to instantiate an instance of an actions pane and then adding the user control you created to that instance. Listing 2-1 illustrates how to create and add a custom actions pane to the Office Excel 2007 template. Specifically, the instantiation of the *dataCtrl* object and the sample code within the *Startup* method (which invokes any code when the host application loads the Office Excel 2007 document-level customization) are key in creating and adding the control to the actions task pane.

Listing 2-1   Adding an actions pane.

```
namespace BudgetForecast
{
    public partial class ThisWorkbook
    {
        private DataLoadControl dataCtrl;

        private void ThisWorkbook_Startup(object sender, System.EventArgs e)
        {
            this.dataCtrl = new BudgetUserControl();
            this.ActionsPane.Controls.Add(this.dataCtrl);
        }

        …

    }
}
```

Adding Events to the Custom Ribbon

You can now also add event handlers to each of the controls (both the controls you added to the Ribbon and those you used to build the actions pane) to trigger specific events, either against the customized actions pane or against data within the Office Excel 2007 spreadsheet. To do this, double-click each of the controls and add your event handlers to event methods that are created for you by Visual Studio. For example, the following code sample enables you to hide and show the custom task pane from the check box control (*chkbxTaskHide*).

...

```
        private void chkbxTaskHide_Click(object sender, RibbonControlEventArgs e)
    {
            if (Globals.ThisWorkbook.TaskPaneVisible == true)
            {
                Globals.ThisWorkbook.TaskPaneVisible = false;
                chkbxTaskHide.Label = "Show Task Pane";
            }
            else
            {
                Globals.ThisWorkbook.TaskPaneVisible = true;
                chkbxTaskHide.Label = "Hide Task Pane";
            }

            return;
    }
```

...

Note that the *chkbxTaskHide_Click* event uses a property called *TaskPaneVisible*, which it sets to True or False. This property hides or shows the actions pane (*DataLoadControl*) and is set through the Boolean *TaskPaneVisible* class, which I've added to the *ThisWorkbook* class, the core class for the VSTO add-in that contains the startup and shutdown methods. The *TaskPaneVisible* method sets a Boolean to True or False depending on whether the task pane is displayed.

```
        public bool TaskPaneVisible
        {
            get { return Application.CommandBars["Task Pane"].Visible; }
            set
            {
                if (value == false)
                {
                    Application.CommandBars["Task Pane"].Visible = false;
                }
                else
                {
                    Application.CommandBars["Task Pane"].Visible = true;
                }
            }
        }
```

Another customization to the button is the ability to create a chart. Functionality such as this can be a bit tricky, depending on whether you want to build the chart directly from SQL statements, dynamically create the cell range, or hard-code the cell range that you want to use to create the chart. The following code illustrates how to create a chart using a hard-coded cell range. The chart I created displays the totals for each of the budget line items. You could apply the same technique to other parts of the data that you want to display as well.

The actual event handler associated with the Create Chart button (btnCreateChart) is the *btnCreateChart_Click* event, which contains one method call, the *CreateChart* method.

```
private void btnCreateChart_Click(object sender, RibbonControlEventArgs e)
    {
        CreateChart();
    }
```

Listing 2-2 shows the *CreateChart* method call that then creates the chart from the data in the range. In this code sample, I've created an instance of a worksheet using the *active* worksheet and then added a chart to that worksheet. I've then taken a range of data from the budget spreadsheet and used the *ChartWizard* method to build a chart (of type *xl3DBar*).

Listing 2-2   Chart creation code.

```
//Ensure your references are added to the project file.
using Excel = Microsoft.Office.Tools.Excel;
using ExcelIO = Microsoft.Office.Interop.Excel;
    ...
    public void CreateChart()
    {
        //Create an instance of the worksheet.
        Excel.Worksheet bdgtWkSheet =
            (Excel.Worksheet)Globals.ThisWorkbook.ActiveSheet;
        //Create an instance of the chart and add to the worksheet.
        Excel.Chart bdgtChart =
            (Excel.Chart)Globals.ThisWorkbook.Charts.Add(Type.Missing,
            bdgtWkSheet, Type.Missing, Type.Missing);
        //Assign cell range to the data in the active spreadsheet.
    ExcelIO.Range bdgtCellRange =
            (ExcelIO.Range)bdgtWkSheet.Application.get_Range("A1", "B5");
        //Build the chart using the chart wizard.
            bdgtChart.ChartWizard(bdgtCellRange, ExcelIO.Constants.xl3DBar,
          Type.Missing,ExcelIO.XlRowCol.xlColumns, 2, 2, false, bdgtWkSheet.Name,
          Type.Missing, Type.Missing, Type.Missing)
    ...
    }
```

You could optionally add formatting to the chart; however, if you used only the preceding code, the *ChartWizard* method would build a basic 3D bar chart for you.

The final part of the Ribbon extensibility is the Currency Exchange button group. I added this set of buttons for a couple of reasons. First, given the global nature of projects and budget management, I wanted the ability to express my budget in different currencies. Second, I wanted to illustrate the ability to call a Web service from the Ribbon that will affect changes within the budget spreadsheet. For this example, I used a free Web service from *http://www.xmethods.com/ve2/Directory.po,* specifically the Currency Exchange Rate Web service. Because free Web services come and go quickly, you could use this or another Web service, either one from a third party or one that you create yourself.

Before you can use a Web service in your code, you need to add a reference to it. To do this, follow these steps (which are specific to the previously mentioned Web service):

1. In Visual Studio, right-click References and select Add Service Reference.

2. Click Advanced and then click Add Web Reference.

3. In the URL field, enter the WSDL reference for your Web service (e.g., *http://www.xmethods.net/sd/2001/CurrencyExchangeService.wsdl*) and then click Go.

4. When the Web service loads successfully, enter **wsCurExchange** in the Web Reference name field and then click Add Reference.

Now you need to add event handlers to each of the buttons that take a certain range within the budget template and convert the currency value in that range to the currency you selected. I used buttons to represent three different currency exchanges, but you could just as easily use other ways of implementing the currency exchange—a drop-down list or another type of control, for example. Again, the goal of this example is to illustrate how and what you can do, as opposed to recommending specific design considerations for your architecture. To add the event handlers, I've associated a specific currency parameter with each of the buttons that will be used to calculate the exchange rate, which will then be applied to a recalculation within the spreadsheet. For example, the following code sample shows that when I click the btnCANCurExchange button, I create a new string parameter called *Canada* that is passed to the *getNewCurrencyRate* method.

```
private void btnCANCurExchange_Click(object sender, RibbonControlEventArgs e)
{
    //Set currency input parameter to "Canada" and call currency exchange
        method.
    string curExchangeTo = "Canada";
    getNewCurrencyRate(curExchangeTo);
}
```

In the *getNewCurrencyRate* method call, I've used the *curExchangeTo* parameter as one of the inputs for the *getRate* Web service method call. In the following code sample, I've initialized the variables that will be used in the currency exchange (*getRate*) call and then instantiated the Web service so that we can actually call the *getRate* method.

```
public void getNewCurrencyRate(string curExchangeTo)
{

    //Initialize variables to be used in the Currency Rate method call.
    string curExchangeFrom = "USA";
    float exchRate;

    //Create an instance of the Currency Rate Web service and call getRate
        method.
    CurrencyExchange.wsCurExchange.CurrencyExchangeService curExchange = new
        CurrencyExchange.wsCurExchange.CurrencyExchangeService();
    exchRate = curExchange.getRate(curExchangeFrom, curExchangeTo);
    ...

}
```

The preceding code will provide the exchange rate that you need to recalculate your budget totals in another currency, here specifically applied to the Canadian exchange call. You can also use the *getNewCurrencyRate* method with each of the other buttons, alternatively passing in the respective string parameter for that button. After you have the value of the exchange rate, you can apply this value as you see fit to your totals, reformatting your spreadsheet by adding a new column beside a totals column, for example, that has the U.S. budget line-item value expressed in the selected currency.

Because you will likely want to design your own Ribbon elements and event handlers, the preceding examples are not comprehensive. They should, however, provide you with a starting point for understanding how to build your custom Ribbon and add event handlers to the Ribbon elements.

Adding Events to the Actions Pane

Let's now discuss the event handlers that are associated with the controls on the actions pane. I've added a number of different controls to the budget approval application, specifically our DataLoadControl user control, which includes the following:

- Combo boxes to capture user input. This input will be used to generate the SQL queries.
- Buttons that load or save data to and from the SQL database or reset the user selections within the combo boxes to null.

The goal of the DataLoadControl user control is quite simple: to capture user feedback with which to generate a SQL query and populate the budget with the appropriate data from the SQL Server database. A number of key variables are required for our application. Listing 2-3 illustrates the initialization of a number of these. This code sample should give you an idea of the types of variables that you would need to develop an application such as the example described in this chapter.

Listing 2-3   Variable initialization.

```
public partial class DataLoadControl : UserControl
{
    ...

    //User input variables from combo boxes that will be used for SQL query
    //generation.
    string bdgtQuarter;
    string bdgtMonth;
    string bdgtYear;

    //Objects to hold/manage the data from SQL.
    SqlDataAdapter sqlDataAdptr = null;
    DataSet bdgtDataSet = null;
    System.Data.DataTable bdgtDataTable = null;

    //Objects that will be used to insert data into budget template.
```

```
Excel.Worksheet bdgtWrkSheet = null;
Excel.Range rngData = null;
Excel.Range rngBudgetData = null;

...

}
```

The *btnLoad_Click* event manages the translation of the user input from the combo boxes and creates the WHERE condition for the SQL query that is passed to the *GetBudgetData* method. The first part of this code (shown in Listing 2-4) illustrates how to set the user input to null values (which will subsequently generate a WHERE condition for the SQL query on that user parameter—such as *Quarter*, *Month*, or *Year*) or will pass the user selection that will then be used to build a WHERE condition for the SQL query. The second part of the *btnLoad_Click* event handles the creation of the WHERE conditions. That is, if a user selects one of the collection items in the combo boxes, the selection will become part of the WHERE condition that will be created in the *GetBudgetData* method. The third part of the *btnLoad_Click* event calls the methods that generate the SQL query, call the SQL Server database, and load the data into the budget template. Note that in the following code, you'd need to add your own error handling to ensure that exceptions are trapped and managed appropriately. You might also want to investigate the use of LINQ as an alternate way to build and execute SQL queries.

Listing 2-4 Load data event.

```
private void btnLoad_Click(object sender, EventArgs e)
{
    //Part 1: Transform the user input into nulls if they select 'All' in the
    //combo box. If they select 'All', then the string is set to null.
    //If not, then the string is set to the user selection that is used
    //to create a WHERE condition for the SQL query.
    if (this.cmboBoxQuarter.SelectedItem.ToString() == "All")
    {
        bdgtQuarter = "";
    }
    else
    {
        bdgtQuarter = "(BudgetQuarter LIKE '" +
            this.cmboBoxQuarter.SelectedItem.ToString() + "')";
    }

    if (this.cmboBoxYear.SelectedItem.ToString() == "All")
    {
        bdgtYear = "";
    }
    else
    {
        bdgtYear = "(BudgetYear LIKE '" +
            this.cmboBoxYear.SelectedItem.ToString() + "')";
    }

    if (this.cmboBoxMonth.SelectedItem.ToString() == "All")
```

```
    {
        bdgtMonth = "";
    }
    else
    {
        bdgtMonth = "(BudgetMonth LIKE '" +
            this.cmboBoxMonth.SelectedItem.ToString() + "')";
    }

    //Part 2:Builds out the WHERE condition and accounts for differences
    //across the cases in the user selections.
    string whereClauseQuarter = "WHERE " + bdgtQuarter;
    string whereClauseYear = "AND " + bdgtYear;
    string whereClauseMonth = "AND " + bdgtMonth;

    if (whereClauseQuarter == "WHERE " && whereClauseMonth == "AND " &&
        whereClauseYear == "AND ")
    {
        whereClauseQuarter = "";
        whereClauseYear = "";
        whereClauseMonth = "";
    }

    if (whereClauseQuarter == "WHERE ")
    {
        whereClauseQuarter = "";
        whereClauseYear = "WHERE " + bdgtYear;
        whereClauseMonth = "AND " + bdgtMonth;
    }

    //Insert other WHERE conditions here to build out your SQL queries.

    ...

    //Part 2:With the SQL WHERE clause created, you can get the data and then
    //insert into the spreadsheet.

    GetBudgetData(whereClauseQuarter, whereClauseYear, whereClauseMonth);
    CreateBudgetWorksheet();
    InsertBudgetData();
    FormatBudgetWorksheet();
}
```

Note the four key method calls in the *btnLoad_Click* event:

- *GetBudgetData(string whereClause, string whereClause, string whereClause)*
- *CreateBudgetWorksheet()*
- *InsertBudgetData()*
- *FormatBudgetWorksheet()*

The *GetBudgetData* method (Listing 2-5) passes the WHERE conditions that are generated from the user input. The method then creates the SQL query and a connection to the SQL database and issues the SQL query against that database.

Listing 2-5   *GetBudgetData* method.

```
public void GetBudgetData(string whereClauseQuarter, string whereClauseYear,
    string whereClauseMonth)
{
    SqlConnection sqlCnn;
    ...
    if (bdgtDataSet == null)
    {
        bdgtDataSet = new DataSet();
    }
    else
    {
        bdgtDataSet.Tables.Remove(bdgtDataTable);
    }

    sqlCnn = new SqlConnection("Server=ORGBUDGET;" + "Database=Budget;" +
        "integrated security = true");
    string strSQL = "SELECT * FROM BudgetSummary " + whereClauseQuarter +
        whereClauseYear + whereClauseMonth + "ORDER BY ID";

    SqlCommand sqlCmd = new SqlCommand(strSQL, sqlCnn);

    sqlDataAdptr = new SqlDataAdapter(sqlCmd);
    sqlDataAdptr.Fill(bdgtDataSet);
    bdgtDataTable = bdgtDataSet.Tables[0];

    SqlCommandBuilder cmdBldr = new SqlCommandBuilder(sqlDataAdptr);
    sqlDataAdptr.UpdateCommand = cmdBldr.GetUpdateCommand();
    ...
}
```

The second method call, *CreateBudgetWorksheet,* creates a range in the budget worksheet, ensures that the range is clear, and then creates column headings using the data in the data table. The code is shown in Listing 2-6.

Listing 2-6   Formatting the budget spreadsheet.

```
public void CreateBudgetWorksheet()
{
        //Create a new worksheet object for the Budget worksheet.
        Excel.Worksheet bdgtWrkSheet =
            (Excel.Worksheet)Globals.ThisWorkbook.Worksheets["Budget"];

        //Set the range for where you'll add the SQL data.
        rngBudgetData = (Excel.Range)bdgtWrkSheet.Cells[2, 1];
        rngBudgetData.CurrentRegion.Clear();
```

```
//Add SQL data into data table.
int i = 0;
Excel.Range rng;

foreach (DataColumn col in bdgtDataTable.Columns)
{
    i++;
    rng = (Excel.Range)bdgtWrkSheet.Cells[1, i];
    rng.Value2 = col.ColumnName;

    ...
}
}
```

The third method, *InsertBudgetData*, shown in Listing 2-7, takes the data from the data table, iterates through the data that is passed, and then inserts the data into the budget template.

Listing 2-7   *InsertBudgetData* method.

```
public void InsertBudgetData()
{

    int i, j = 0;

    DataRow bdgtDataRow;

    if (bdgtDataTable != null)
    {
        for (i = 0; i <= bdgtDataTable.Rows.Count - 1; i++)
        {
            bdgtDataRow = bdgtDataTable.Rows[i];
            for (j = 0; j <= bdgtDataTable.Columns.Count - 1; j++)
                rngBudgetData.get_Offset(i, j).Value2 =
                    bdgtDataRow[j].ToString();
        }
    }
    rngData = rngBudgetData.CurrentRegion;
    ...

}
```

The final method, *FormatBudgetWorksheet*, performs some minor formatting on the columns in the spreadsheet. You could add additional formatting here for individual cells, or you could customize the template within Excel 2007 or the VSTO project. Either way, Excel 2007 provides some really nice formatting options with which you can present the data in a structured and intuitive fashion. Here is the code for *FormatBudgetWorksheet*.

```
private void FormatBudgetWorksheet()
{
    rngData.Columns.NumberFormat = "0";
    rngData.Columns.AutoFit();
    ...
}
```

While the connection to your database is open—in our case the SQL Server budget database—you can also save any of your changes back to the server. You could design this operation in a couple of ways, depending on how you've developed your application so far. One way is to iterate through the rows and update the data table. For example, the following line of code illustrates how you could use the *bdgtDataTable* object to update the changed values in the budget spreadsheet. This line of code would need to be embedded in an iterative statement that walks through each row of the *bdgtDataTable* object to ensure that each cell within the table is updated. In this method, I've passed the method the data table as an object, and the method iterates through using the table and updates each of the rows and columns in the table.

```
private void updateBudgetTable(object dataTable)
{
    ...

    bdgtDataTable.Rows[Row][Col] = bdgtRange.Value2;
    ...
    updateSQLBudgetTable(bdgtDataTable);

}
```

After the data table is updated, you can then pass the *bdgtDataTable* to an update method that uses the data table to synchronize the changes with the SQL Server database. While the preceding example is one way of managing updates in a spreadsheet, you can also use the ListObject control to push and pull data directly from SQL Server into (and from) the spreadsheet. You might find better performance using the list object.

More Info   For more information on the ListObject, see *http://msdn2.microsoft.com/en-us/library/2ttzcbhb(VS.80).aspx.*

The *btnRefresh_Click* method is attached to the Refresh button and simply resets the selected items in the combo boxes. Alternatively, you could set the defaults to "All" and not allow nulls. Note that what is not shown here is the fact that you would need some degree of event handling for null values for selected items in the combo box.

```
...
    private void btnRefresh_Click(object sender, EventArgs e)
    {
        ...
        this.cmboBoxQuarter.SelectedItem = null;
        this.cmboBoxYear.SelectedItem = null;
        this.comboBoxMonth.SelectedItem = null;
        ...
    }
...
```

The Completed Budget Template

At this point, we have created an Office Excel 2007 budget template (shown in Figure 2-7), imported it into a new VSTO project, created a customized actions pane that is integrated with the data source, and added some custom Ribbon extensibility into the project as well. We've also added some customizations to the formatting of the template: namely, using the conditional formatting option for dollar-value data to provide visual indicators for the data and adding a small summary table to the bottom of the template. You should customize your application to meet the needs of your organization or to your liking.

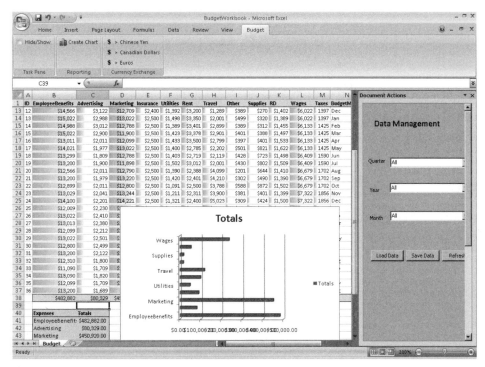

Figure 2-7   The completed sample budget template.

This approach will provide you with a number of important client-side 2007 Office system customizations and get you on your way to developing a useful (and maybe your first) OBA. I say "get you on your way" because when building OBAs, you must realize that the client-side portion of the OBA is but one part of the story; that is, while your end users will have the budget template VSTO customizations on their 2007 Office system client, you will also want to have a server-side component to your OBA (or an integration with an LOB system through the client). That said, let's look at some aspects of our budget approval application and its relationship to Windows SharePoint Services version 3 and Microsoft Office SharePoint Server 2007.

Building the SharePoint Budget Dashboard

In this section, the description of including server-side components in an OBA primarily involves Windows SharePoint Services technology. You can, however, also build custom Web services or more complex business logic into either the client-side components (for example, custom Web service calls from a custom task pane) or Windows SharePoint Services capabilities (for example, displaying LOB data in Business Data Catalog Web Parts). Thus, your OBA will not necessarily stop at the implementation of only the 2007 Office system client and SharePoint technologies; moreover, you can extend an OBA to integrate with LOB systems such as SAP, Microsoft Dynamics, or PeopleSoft. VSTO and Windows SharePoint Services support both of these approaches.

While the integration of LOB systems into the 2007 Office system is an exciting and growing area of business application development, it is out of scope for this chapter. What we'll cover in this chapter is native to the 2007 Office system technology; that is, developing components within our SharePoint budget site that will help provide different views into the data for the budget approval workflow application. Specifically, we will integrate the template as a content type within a document library and create a budget dashboard that aggregates information about the budget.

Integrating a Content Type in a Document Library

Building the custom Office Excel 2007 template that is bound to your enterprise data source is one thing. It's another to ensure that your organization has access to the template and can use it. You can use a SharePoint site to ensure that your budget template is available by creating a document library for your budget reports and then creating a content type with which budget owners can create and consume the template you've created.

> **Note** This section assumes that you have already set up a SharePoint site.

To create the document library, first open the budget site. To create a document library, click Document Center, Site Actions, Create, and then select the Document Library option. The page you see prompts you to provide a name, description, and other properties for your document library. Be sure to select Microsoft Office Excel Spreadsheet as the document template, as shown in Figure 2-8.

I named my document library Budget Library, and·I'll store my budget template here. Although it is outside the scope of this chapter, you can also create a content type for the Office Excel 2007 spreadsheet. Thus, when a user opens the document library, she can click New, and in the drop-down menu she'll see an option to choose the customized budget template, which she can then go ahead and use. You can use the content library to store the budget documents and start your workflow, but having a centralized view into the key metrics associated with the budget data—that is, a dashboard—also helps.

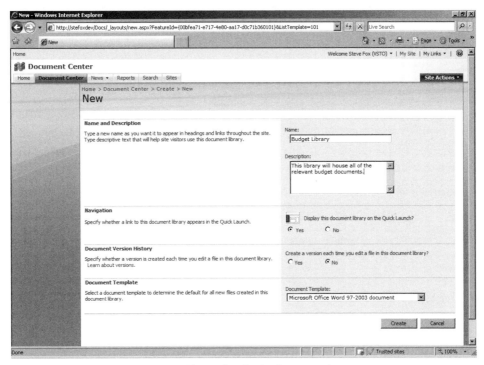

Figure 2-8   Creating a document library for the budget template.

Quick Overview of Content Types

A content type is a means of associating metadata and properties with a specific type of content and making that information available in a list or library in a SharePoint site. Content types also let you separate the definition of a type of content from the location in which the content is stored in SharePoint, because lists and libraries can be set up to support more than one content type. (In Windows SharePoint Services 2.0, metadata was associated with a particular list, rather than the items a list might contain.) Imagine that you want to store the Office Excel 2007 worksheets you use for tracking expense budgets and sales forecasts in the same document library—called Financial Reporting—but you want to collect different metadata about each of these document types. You might also need to assign different workflows to the two types of documents, which content types also support. You could create a content type for each of these types of documents but maintain the relationship between the documents by storing them in a common folder.

You can create content types at the site level or the list level. Content types created at the site level are available across the entire site (and the site's children). Content types created at the list level relate only to that list. You can also modify site-level content types for use in a specific list. For example, in the budget workflow application discussed in this chapter, I associated the customized Office Excel 2007 template to the Budget Library as a specific content type. This way, users can create a new instance of the budget template from SharePoint. Windows SharePoint Services stores a copy of the site-level content type in the list so that the original is not affected by the modifications.

Event handlers that you register for a content type provide a specific behavior you want to support. For example, take a content type such as Budget Template, which you might add to the Financial Reporting document library. You can create event handlers and register them at the level of this content type so that all documents based on Budget Template receive specific processing. When someone uses this content type, he immediately also gets the behavior attached to the list or library.

Collections of content types are represented in the SharePoint object model through the *SPContentTypeCollection* class. This class can be accessed from an *SPList* object or an *SPWeb* object depending on whether the collections are site-level content types or list-level content types.

More Info   For detailed information about creating and managing content types, see the Windows SharePoint Services SDK, which is available at *http://msdn2.microsoft.com/en-us/library/ms441339.aspx*.

A dashboard aggregates key data, content, and information through lists, charts, graphs, and other key metrics. The goal of the budget dashboard is to display key insights that help the budget review team make informed decisions about the budget. For the budget review application, I used three main Microsoft Office SharePoint Server technologies: key performance indicators (KPI), Excel Services, and the Business Data Catalog (BDC).

Key Performance Indicators

KPIs provide a way to monitor and track important metrics for an organization and convey current performance against that metric. The goal of a KPI is to provide a quick summary by which users can gauge the KPI data listed on the dashboard to understand how individuals, teams, or an organization as a whole is progressing toward a goal. KPIs are straightforward to create and can be generated manually or linked to a SQL Server Analysis Services 2005 cube, an Office Excel 2007 workbook, or a SharePoint list.

KPIs are measured through indicators. The two primary indicators that drive KPIs are an *indicator value* and an *indicator goal*. The indicator value represents the value for the metric that you are measuring; the indicator goal is the baseline metric value against which you are measuring the indicator value. For example, in the case of the budget review application, we might want to associate and understand specific levels of accuracy for our budget forecast with line items in the budget to avoid having the forecast fall short of the actual spend. Let's say the budget to be spent on Research and Development is $5,000 (indicator value) in January, yet the actual amount spent was $7,500. Management likely provides some leeway, perhaps $500 (indicator goal), but any actual amount spent over $5,500 would be flagged in the KPI list as a serious overspend.

To create a KPI, log onto the SharePoint site as an administrator and then click the Reports tab to view the Report Center. Now follow these steps:

1. Click Site Actions, click Site Settings, and then click Modify All Site Settings.

2. In the Site Administration group of the Site Settings page, click Site Libraries And Lists.

3. Click the Create The New Content link at the top of the Site Libraries And Lists page.

4. In the Custom Lists column, select KPI List.

5. Name the list **Demo KPI List**.

6. Click Create.

Figure 2-9 shows a screenshot of the New KPI List creation page.

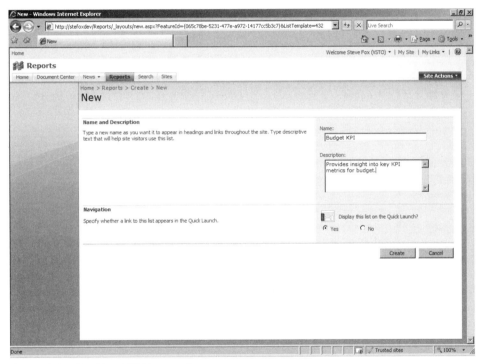

Figure 2-9 The New KPI List creation page.

At this point, you can enter a list of KPI metrics, including some metadata and the sources for their values. (I used the Excel workbook as the source of the KPI metrics.) To do this, follow these steps:

1. In the KPI list view, click New, Indicator Using Data In Excel Workbook. You'll then be prompted to provide a name, description, comments, indicator value source, and rules for the status icons.

2. In the Workbook URL field, browse to the location of your spreadsheet and then select the specific cell addresses for the indicator value and goal and warning values.

3. Click OK.

Figure 2-10 illustrates the information you'll need to complete to provide some additional information about your KPI.

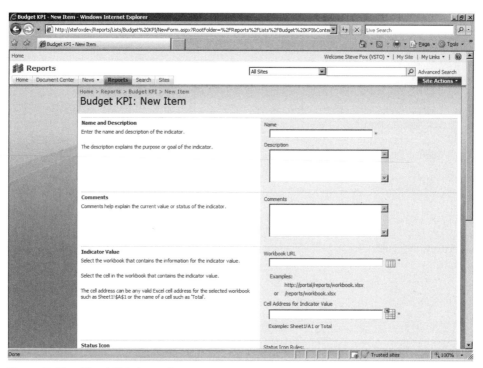

Figure 2-10   New KPI information.

For the budget review application, I added an Overall Expenses KPI and a breakdown of the budget line items. This way, I can see the overall status of the budget KPI and the specific expense categories that make up the budget. Thus, any item whose variance is high is flagged appropriately in the KPI list. Figure 2-11 provides an overview of the KPI list I created for the budget application.

KPIs come in a couple of different flavors. The KPI that I created for my application is mapped to the cells in my budget template, where the data is further mapped to the SQL Server database. This means that the KPIs are always mapped to data that is centrally stored and managed. Conversely, KPIs can also be manually created, and with the manual KPI lists there are no dependencies on other files; however, the link to "real-time" business data updates does not exist, and some management of the list is required.

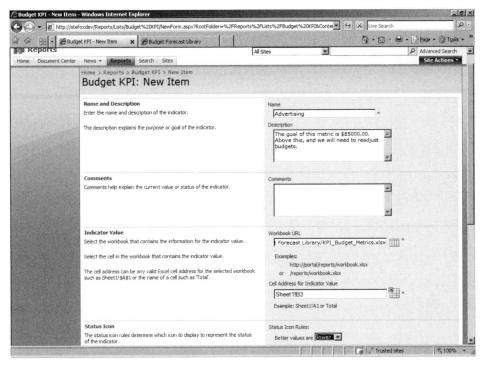

Figure 2-11   Budget KPI list.

Excel Services

At this point, we have a customized Excel budget template that includes Ribbon customizations and a custom actions pane, a document library, a content type for the budget template, and a budget dashboard that includes some KPIs for quick views of the status of budget metrics. Another SharePoint technology that you can incorporate in a budget approval application is Excel Services.

Excel Services is a server-side technology that shipped with Microsoft Office SharePoint Server 2007. Excel Services enables you to calculate workbooks that are created in the Office Excel 2007 client on a server and then distribute the workbook through either a browser-based interface or a Web service. In our example, Excel Services lets us extend the Office Excel 2007 client to the server and bring elements of our budget spreadsheet (created on the client) to the budget dashboard.

You can use Excel Services independent of an OBA. For example, Excel Services is a way to extend spreadsheets to the server and provide an organization with a view of your spreadsheets. You can also incorporate Excel Services as a key part of an OBA, as we are doing in this example. Some of the benefits of Excel Services are as follows:

- You don't have to distribute your spreadsheet; moreover, you can provide a server-side view of it.

- The spreadsheet you provide a view of is always updated to reflect the spreadsheet to which it is mapped. In other words, you don't need to manage multiple documents.

- You can display specific elements of the spreadsheet, such as charts or graphs, to provide visibility into those areas without bringing the entire Office Excel 2007 document to the surface.

- You can view the spreadsheet in the context of, or alongside, other business intelligence elements within a dashboard.

For our application, we will use Excel Services to do three primary things for us:

- Provide a browser-based view into our budget worksheet for quick viewing on our dashboard

- Provide a view into a budget summary chart that provides key information about the total expense line items that make up our budget

- Provide a view into a budget expense breakdown pie chart that provides a view into how much each of the individual expenses constitutes the overall budget

One thing to note here is that while we'll be able to load the preceding items as Excel Services Web parts, we will not be able to load the VSTO customizations into the browser. These customizations—along with graphics, macros, external data queries, and restricted workbook settings—are not supported by the current release of Excel Services.

To provide a browser-based view of the budget spreadsheet, we'll create a Web Part as an element of our budget dashboard. The Web Part will be an Excel Services Web Part, which will enable us to associate the Web Part with a specific budget spreadsheet. As with the KPIs, we will associate our Excel Services Web Part with the budget template I created earlier to not only display the worksheet (in other words, the tables in the budget spreadsheet), but also the charts that we've created. To do this, we first need to publish the elements of our budget spreadsheet to Excel Services and then create a Web Part within Office SharePoint Server 2007 to point to those specifically published elements.

To publish the Office Excel 2007 budget spreadsheet to the server, follow these steps:

1. Navigate to the document library where you uploaded the budget. If you've been following along with the example in this chapter, the name of the document library is Budget Library.

2. Right-click the budget spreadsheet file (or click the down arrow to the right of the file) and select Edit in Microsoft Excel.

3. In the budget spreadsheet, click the Office button, click Publish, and then click Excel Server Options. This will open the Excel Server Options dialog box, where you can publish the entire spreadsheet to the server or just specific parts.

4. In the Sheets drop-down box, select All Sheets.

5. Click Save, and then save the spreadsheet back to the server.

At this point you can create a Web Part and reference the sheet or sheets you just published to the server. To do this, follow these steps:

1. Open your SharePoint site and navigate to the Reports Center (click Reports).

2. Click Site Actions, and then click Edit Page.

3. When the page loads in edit mode, click Add A Web Part.

4. From the list of Web Parts, choose Excel Web Access and then click Add. This will add an editable Web Part to the site.

5. On the Web Part, click the link Click Here To Open The Tool Pane. This will open the Excel Web Access tool pane, where you can configure the Web Part to point to your specific spreadsheet and elements within your spreadsheet.

6. In the Workbook field, navigate to the appropriate workbook and click OK.

7. If you want to display a specific element (such as a chart) within the workbook, in the Workbook field, enter the name of the element (**Chart 1**, for example).

8. Click OK.

The Web Part should now load whatever you configured for display within the Web Part tool. For example, Figure 2-12 shows the entire workbook as published through Excel Services.

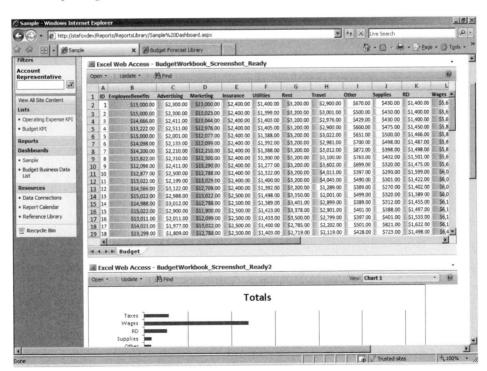

Figure 2-12   Excel Services displaying entire spreadsheet.

More Info   To learn more about using Excel Services in your applications, refer to the Excel Services Information Center Portal on MSDN at *http://msdn2.microsoft.com/en-us/office/bb203828.aspx*.

Using the Business Data Catalog

The Business Data Catalog (BDC) is essentially an abstraction layer between a SharePoint Web Part and an LOB data source. The following services within Office SharePoint Server 2007 are supported through the BDC:

- **Business Data List Web Part**   The most commonly used Web Part. It displays data (or more precisely, a list of instances for a specific entity) that is registered in the Business Data Catalog.

- **Business Data Related List Web Part**   Displays related data that has associated data registered in the Business Data Catalog.

- **Business Data Item Web Part**   Displays details for a particular entity instance.

- **Business Data Actions Web Part**   Displays the actions that can be performed for a specific entity instance.

- **Business Data Item Builder Web Part**   A normal SharePoint page on which details are displayed through a programmatic call and passing of query string information and identifier information.

In the budget workflow application, I used the BDC to display a listing of the data from my LOB data source. In other words, I used the Business Data List Web Part and simply listed the data within the small database I had created for the application. I could perform this operation because the data source was fairly small, consisting of 15 elements within a single table called BudgetSummary—thus the display of the data did not clutter the Web Part. While the data schema itself is not likely to reflect an organization's data schema, for our application it provides a SQL Server data source that we can integrate into the workflow application. It also provides a simple schema, and when viewing the application definition file (ADF), which maps the data schema to the SharePoint Web Part, having a simpler schema helps you digest the elements of the ADF. Figure 2-13 provides an overview of the BudgetSummary table.

Now that you have a sense of what's in the database, I'll describe how to translate and map this schema to the BDC, which is done through the ADF. The ADF is essentially an indication of how the data within your database (in this case the BudgetSummary table within the Budget database) is mapped to the SharePoint Web Part (in this case the Business Data List Web Part), as well as a representation of any methods you want to call against that data. The ADF is an XML file that uses the bdcmetadata.xsd XML schema, which can be found in the c:\Program Files\Microsoft Office Servers\12.0\bin folder. You cannot load the data within Office SharePoint Server 2007 without the ADF.

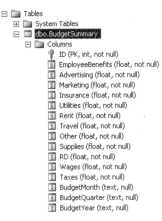

Figure 2-13   Budget data schema.

Listing 2-8 provides an overview of the BudgetSummary ADF file. Our ADF file is fairly straightforward. It not only reflects the simple schema for the BudgetSummary database, but it also reflects that there is only one method that we will issue against the BudgetSummary from within our Web Part—essentially a "SELECT * FROM BUDGETSUMMARY" SQL call that will get all the data from all the elements.

Listing 2-8   Sample application definition file for a budget database.

```
<?xml version="1.0" standalone="yes"?>
<LobSystem xmlns:xsi="http://www.w3.org/2001/XMLSchema-instance"
    xsi:schemaLocation="http://schemas.microsoft.com/office/2006/03/
    BusinessDataCatalog BDCMetadata.XSD"
    xmlns="http://schemas.microsoft.com/office/2006/03/BusinessDataCatalog"
    Type="Database" Version="1.0.0.0" Name="tempdbLOBSystem">
  <Properties>
    <Property Name="WildcardCharacter" Type="System.String">%</Property>
  </Properties>
  <LobSystemInstances>
    <LobSystemInstance Name="tempdbInstance2">
    <Properties>
    <Property Name="DatabaseAccessProvider"
      Type="System.String">SqlServer</Property>
    <Property Name="AuthenticationMode" Type="System.String">PassThrough</Property>
    <Property Name="rdbconnection Data Source"
      Type="System.String">STEFOXDEV\BDC</Property>
    <Property Name="rdbconnection Initial Catalog"
      Type="System.String">Budget</Property>
    <Property Name="rdbconnection Integrated Security"
      Type="System.String">True</Property>
    </Properties>
    </LobSystemInstance>
  </LobSystemInstances>
  <Entities>
    <Entity EstimatedInstanceCount="0" Name="dbo.BudgetSummary">
      <Identifiers><Identifier Name="[ID]" TypeName="System.Int32" />
```

```
    </Identifiers>
    <Methods>
      <Method Name="Getdbo.[BudgetSummary]">
        <Properties>
          <Property Name="RdbCommandText" Type="System.String">Select[ID],
            [EmployeeBenefits],[Advertising],[Marketing],
            [Insurance],[Utilities],[Rent],[Travel],[Other],
            [Supplies],[RD],[Wages],[Taxes],[BudgetMonth],
            [BudgetQuarter],[BudgetYear] From dbo.[BudgetSummary]
          </Property>
          <Property Name="RdbCommandType" Type="System.Data.CommandType">Text
          </Property>
        </Properties>
        <Parameters>
          <Parameter Direction="Return" Name="dbo.[BudgetSummary]">
            <TypeDescriptor TypeName="System.Data.IDataReader, System.Data,
              Version=2.0.3600.0, Culture=neutral,
              PublicKeyToken=b77a5c561934e089"
              Name="dbo.[BudgetSummary]DataReader" IsCollection="true">
            <TypeDescriptors>
            <TypeDescriptor TypeName="System.Data.IDataRecord, System.Data,
              Version=2.0.3600.0, Culture=neutral,
              PublicKeyToken=b77a5c561934e089"
              Name="dbo.[BudgetSummary]DataRecord">
            <TypeDescriptors>
            <TypeDescriptor TypeName="System.Int32" IdentifierName="[ID]"
              Name="ID" />
            <TypeDescriptor TypeName="System.Double" Name="EmployeeBenefits" />
            <TypeDescriptor TypeName="System.Double" Name="Advertising" />
            <TypeDescriptor TypeName="System.Double" Name="Marketing" />
            <TypeDescriptor TypeName="System.Double" Name="Insurance" />
            <TypeDescriptor TypeName="System.Double" Name="Utilities" />
            <TypeDescriptor TypeName="System.Double" Name="Rent" />
            <TypeDescriptor TypeName="System.Double" Name="Travel" />
            <TypeDescriptor TypeName="System.Double" Name="Other" />
            <TypeDescriptor TypeName="System.Double" Name="Supplies" />
            <TypeDescriptor TypeName="System.Double" Name="RD" />
            <TypeDescriptor TypeName="System.Double" Name="Wages" />
            <TypeDescriptor TypeName="System.Double" Name="Taxes" />
            <TypeDescriptor TypeName="System.String" Name="BudgetMonth" />
            <TypeDescriptor TypeName="System.String" Name="BudgetQuarter" />
            <TypeDescriptor TypeName="System.String" Name="BudgetYear" />
            </TypeDescriptors>
            </TypeDescriptor>
            </TypeDescriptors>
            </TypeDescriptor>
          </Parameter>
        </Parameters>
        <MethodInstances>
          <MethodInstance Name="dbo.[BudgetSummary]Finder" Type="Finder"
            ReturnParameterName="dbo.[BudgetSummary]"
            ReturnTypeDescriptorName="dbo.[BudgetSummary]DataReader"
            ReturnTypeDescriptorLevel="0" />
        </MethodInstances>
      </Method>
```

```
<Method Name="dbo.[BudgetSummary]SpecificFinder">
  <Properties>
    <Property Name="RdbCommandText" Type="System.String">Select [ID],
      [EmployeeBenefits],[Advertising],[Marketing],[Insurance],
      [Utilities],[Rent],[Travel],[Other],[Supplies],[RD],
      [Wages],[Taxes],[BudgetMonth],[BudgetQuarter],[BudgetYear]
      From dbo.[BudgetSummary] Where ([ID]=@ID)
    </Property>
    <Property Name="RdbCommandType" Type="System.Data.CommandType">Text
    </Property>
  </Properties>
  <Parameters>
    <Parameter Direction="In" Name="@ID">
      <TypeDescriptor TypeName="System.Int32" IdentifierName="[ID]"
        Name="[ID]" />
    </Parameter>
    <Parameter Direction="Return" Name="dbo.[BudgetSummary]">
      <TypeDescriptor TypeName="System.Data.IDataReader, System.Data,
        Version=2.0.3600.0, Culture=neutral,
        PublicKeyToken=b77a5c561934e089"
        Name="dbo.[BudgetSummary]DataReader" IsCollection="true">
      <TypeDescriptors>
      <TypeDescriptor TypeName="System.Data.IDataRecord, System.Data,
        Version=2.0.3600.0, Culture=neutral,
        PublicKeyToken=b77a5c561934e089"
        Name="dbo.[BudgetSummary]DataRecord">
      <TypeDescriptors>
      <TypeDescriptor TypeName="System.Int32" IdentifierName="[ID]"
        Name="ID" />
      <TypeDescriptor TypeName="System.Double" Name="EmployeeBenefits" />
      <TypeDescriptor TypeName="System.Double" Name="Advertising" />
      <TypeDescriptor TypeName="System.Double" Name="Marketing" />
      <TypeDescriptor TypeName="System.Double" Name="Insurance" />
      <TypeDescriptor TypeName="System.Double" Name="Utilities" />
      <TypeDescriptor TypeName="System.Double" Name="Rent" />
      <TypeDescriptor TypeName="System.Double" Name="Travel" />
      <TypeDescriptor TypeName="System.Double" Name="Other" />
      <TypeDescriptor TypeName="System.Double" Name="Supplies" />
      <TypeDescriptor TypeName="System.Double" Name="RD" />
      <TypeDescriptor TypeName="System.Double" Name="Wages" />
      <TypeDescriptor TypeName="System.Double" Name="Taxes" />
      <TypeDescriptor TypeName="System.String" Name="BudgetMonth" />
      <TypeDescriptor TypeName="System.String" Name="BudgetQuarter" />
      <TypeDescriptor TypeName="System.String" Name="BudgetYear" />
      </TypeDescriptors>
      </TypeDescriptor>
      </TypeDescriptors>
      </TypeDescriptor>
    </Parameter>
  </Parameters>
  <MethodInstances>
    <MethodInstance Name="dbo.[BudgetSummary]SpecificFinder"
      Type="SpecificFinder" ReturnParameterName="dbo.[BudgetSummary]"
      ReturnTypeDescriptorName="dbo.[BudgetSummary]DataReader"
      ReturnTypeDescriptorLevel="0" />
```

```
            </MethodInstances>
          </Method>
        </Methods>
      </Entity>
    </Entities>
  </LobSystem>
```

> **Note** While it would be useful to review the details of the ADF, we do not have the space to do it here. Other resources, however, provide great detail about each element in the ADF XML file. For example, for more detailed information about the BDC, go to *http://msdn2.microsoft.com/en-us/library/ms499729.aspx*. A recent Microsoft Press book by Patrick Tisseghem, *Inside Microsoft Office SharePoint Server 2007*, provides very useful information about the ADF and the BDC.

At the time of this writing, some home-grown tools do exist that allow you to create an ADF that corresponds to a particular database; however, not all these tools have been widely adopted or tested. In some cases these tools work well, and in others they don't. For the budget workflow application, I used an unreleased Microsoft tool (as part of a test group) as opposed to hand-crafting the ADF from scratch. This approach worked quite well for the simple BudgetSummary schema. As you can imagine, hand-crafting an ADF file can be quite an effort if your data schema is complex and the methods you want to implement against that schema are many.

With the ADF created, the next step in our application's development is to import the ADF file into SharePoint so that we can display the budget data in our Web Part. Once we've imported the ADF file, we can then build and configure our Business Data List Web Part, which will use the imported ADF file to display the budget data.

To import the ADF, navigate to the Shared Services Provider administration site. In the Business Data Catalog section, click Import Application Definition. In the Import Application Definition dialog box, click the Browse button to browse to the location of the ADF file you want to import. (See Figure 2-14.) Note that if you have not validated your ADF XML file against the bdcmetadata.xsd file format, the validation will be performed during the import process. To avoid errors at this point, I would recommend importing the bdcmetadat.xsd file into Visual Studio (or an equivalent XML editor) and validating the file before importing it. If any errors are raised, an error message will prompt you with the problematic line number in your ADF XML file. (If no errors occur, the file will be successfully imported.)

After you've successfully imported the ADF, you will be able to view the entities. To do this, click the appropriate link under Entities and then click your newly imported ADF. I gave my example the name BudgetSummary, as shown in Figure 2-15.

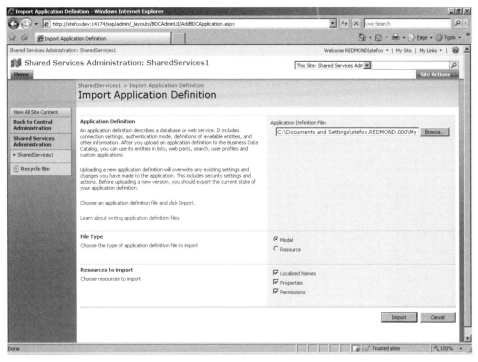

Figure 2-14   Import Application Definition dialog box.

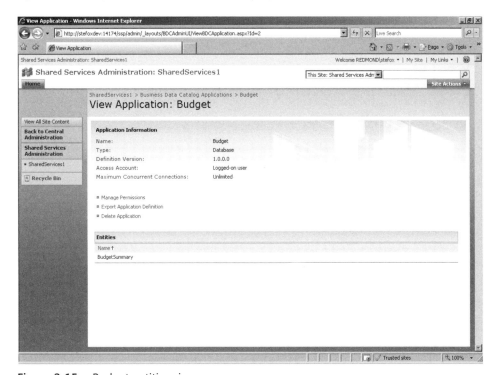

Figure 2-15   Budget entities view.

Clicking this link provides a detailed view of the entities that exist within the entity you just imported. Figure 2-16 provides an overview of this view.

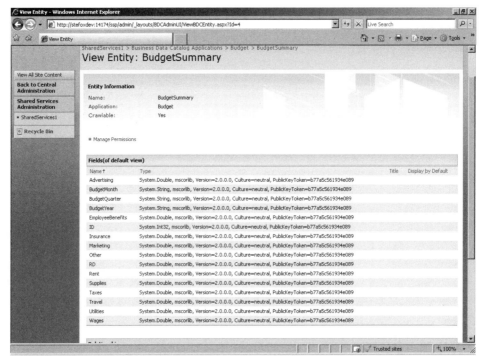

Figure 2-16   List view of the budget entities.

With the ADF file successfully imported, you'll want to create a new page on your dashboard for displaying the data from the BDC connection to (in our case) the budget database. For this, we create a new Business Data List Web Part and configure that Web Part to display the newly imported BDC entity.

To create a new Business Data List Web Part, click the page on which you want to add the Web Part. Click Actions, click Edit Page, and then click Add A Web Part. This command invokes the Add Web Parts dialog box (shown in Figure 2-17), in which you will find the Business Data List Web Part. Select the Business Data List and then click Add.

With the Business Data List Web Part added to your page, you need to configure the Web Part to display the data from the BudgetSummary database. Click the Open The Tool Pane link in your empty Web Part and then use the Business Data Picker to select the appropriate ADF file. (In our case, I associated the BudgetSummary ADF file with the Business Data List Web Part.) Click OK in the Business Data Type Picker, and then click Apply in the tools pane to load the entity into the Business Data Catalog Web Part. Figure 2-18 illustrates this process.

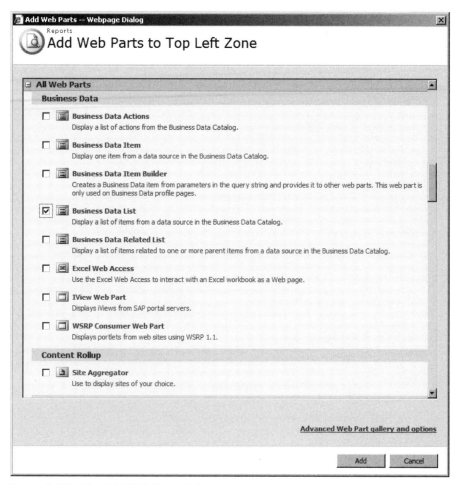

Figure 2-17   The Add Web Parts dialog box.

With the Business Data List Web Part added to your dashboard (see Figure 2-19), you will now have multiple views into the data on your dashboard. And while you may only want some of these views, the goal of showing you Excel Services, KPIs, and the BDC is to illustrate that you can provide different views for different audiences and for different purposes. Ultimately, requirements may dictate what views you will design into your OBA; however, knowing what options you have is half the battle. I encourage you to experiment with the functionality of not only those technologies discussed in this section, but also others that are available in SharePoint.

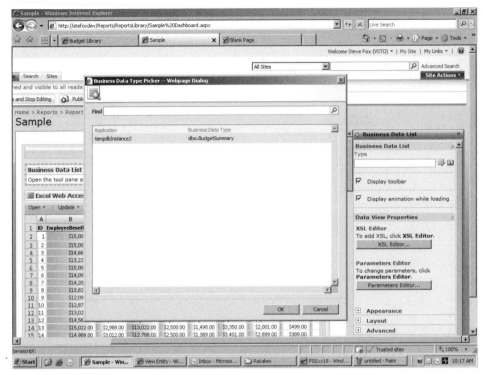

Figure 2-18   Selecting the entity for display in the Web Part.

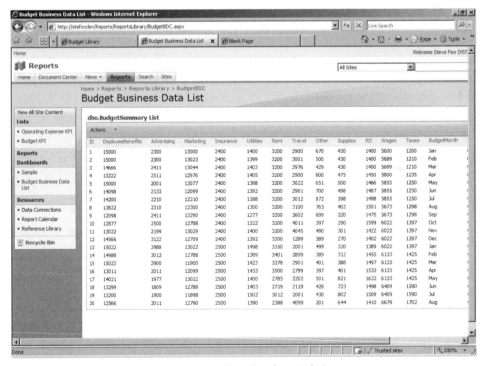

Figure 2-19   Budget data in the Business Data Catalog Web Part.

We'll now turn to the final part of the chapter: the incorporation of SharePoint workflow into our budget application.

Creating the SharePoint Workflow

SharePoint workflow is a technology that helps manage the business process of approving the budget within the approval team. If you remember our original diagram (Figure 2-2) that showed how we wanted to architect the workflow of the budget approval application, you'll remember that our approval process has three parts: approve, reject, and request amendments. You'll also remember that the two main actors in the approval process are the budget owner and the manager. The fact that we have an approver and a budget owner is reflective of the workflow around which the budget application is built.

You create your workflow through the workflow settings within SharePoint. You can create the workflow so that it is triggered by an event such as a change to a document (in our case the budget template); the workflow can also be triggered manually. Having the workflow trigger when the document is saved (or alternatively, having a manual trigger in the Ribbon, such as a Submit Workflow button) is a great way to automate the creation of the approval workflow.

For the budget approval application, we're fortunate to have a default workflow, called Approval, that ships with SharePoint. We're going to create a new instance of this workflow and associate it with our budget forecast document. To do this, we must first create a new content type, which you can do through the Site Settings page. For the budget workflow application, I created a content type called Budget Forecast and then added some metadata to the content type so that when the user invokes the content type from the document library, the Document Information Panel will be populated with the associated metadata. Figure 2-20 shows the settings for the Budget Forecast content type.

I've also already associated the content type with a Budget Library document library that we created earlier so that when a user clicks New in the document library, the Budget Forecast content type is one of the available options, as shown in Figure 2-21. Further, the content type that loads is the one with our VSTO customizations, so any modifications we have are tied back to a central data source.

With all the preceding elements created, we can now create the workflow piece of the application. To create the workflow, click Workflow Settings on your new content type and then click Add Or Change A Workflow. On the next page, select Add A Workflow. You can now enter information about that workflow. For my application, I selected the Approval workflow template, provided a name, and left the other defaults selected. Figure 2-22 shows the new workflow definition.

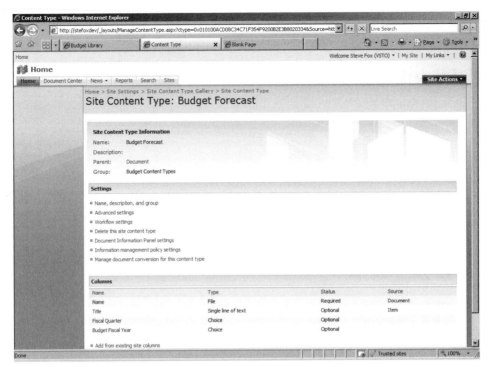

Figure 2-20   Settings for the Budget Forecast content type.

Figure 2-21   Budget Forecast content type in document library.

After creating the workflow, click Next to add permissions and delegates for the task approvers within the workflow. After you've completed this step, click OK, which completes the creation of the Approval workflow.

Depending on how you set up your workflow, it will be triggered through saving a document to the server or triggered manually when a user initiates the workflow through the document library menu. For example, Figure 2-23 illustrates how you can access the workflow by clicking a specific document in the document library.

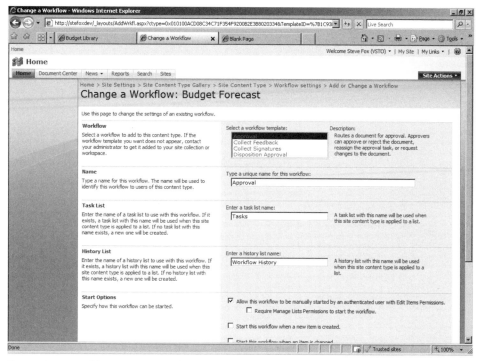

Figure 2-22   Adding a new workflow.

Figure 2-23   Initiation of the workflow through the document library.

Whether you invoke the workflow manually or through a trigger that you associate with the document (such as when a user saves the document), once you've made this association you can see the progress of the workflow in the workflow column. For example, Figure 2-24 shows a status of In Progress for the approval workflow on the Budget_2007_Forecast.xlsx document—a document created by a budget owner with our earlier VSTO customizations in it.

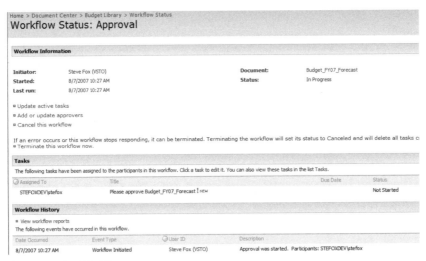

Figure 2-24   Workflow status.

To view the exact status of the workflow task, you can click the status entry, which will take you to the Workflow Status page, shown in Figure 2-25. On the page, you can note the owner of the task, the status, and a link to select the task, which in our case is to approve the budget forecast.

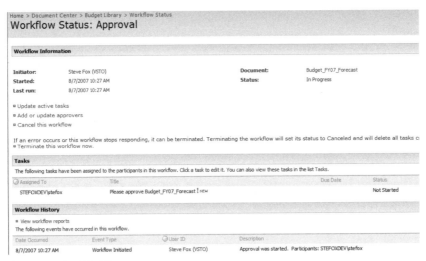

Figure 2-25   Workflow status page.

Clicking the Please Approve link invokes the Approval workflow and displays a page that enables the approver to either approve or reject the forecast.

Now you may be asking yourself, what about the amend? And if you're going to use the default workflow that ships with SharePoint, you would not end the workflow until your workflow was approved and you would use Reject to trigger an amendment to the document. You might also build some deeper sophistication into the workflow by using VSTO's SharePoint workflow tools.

After the workflow is completed, the Approval workflow column will now read Approved, and if you want a detailed account of the task history within the workflow you click the status for the workflow status page.

In the preceding workflow, we used the out-of-the-box experience. However, as mentioned earlier you can also build customized workflow using VSTO 3.0. Using VSTO saves you quite a bit of time and brings some significant power to workflow customization—debugging, IntelliSense, and .NET to name but a few. Customization can arrive in many different forms as well, but one exciting way to customize your workflow (also another VSTO feature) is by automatically creating customized Office Outlook 2007 form regions that can then be used to host Windows Presentation Foundation (WPF) controls that provide some insight into the data. For example, in our case we could extract the saved forecast data for the next fiscal year and represent that graphically within the Office Outlook 2007 form region. Thus, when task mails are sent instead of the stock SharePoint mails, the custom workflow code creates a new type of Office Outlook 2007 message class that has customized components hosted on it and provides the ability to approve or reject straight from the message—as opposed to manually navigating to the SharePoint site. In this case, the customizations would not replace the out-of-the-box SharePoint experience but enhance it.

While our scenario included a budget owner and a manager to approve that budget, in reality the budget approval routing will likely entail multiple people for review but one person who is the point person in the management chain for budget approval. Therefore, workflow would not just be exchanged between two people. Moreover, the budget owner would be the principal actor in kicking off the workflow approval process, a review team would get issued some sort of review guidelines, and a manager would own ultimate approval of the budget. Thus, workflow can be quite complex, with activities involving multiple parties within an organization, and you'll need to think through this carefully as you design the workflow capabilities of your own OBA.

Summary

I hope you're beginning to realize the power of combining SharePoint technologies with VSTO customizations within the 2007 Office system environment. So far, we've created a fairly simple OBA that uses SharePoint as the central point of management for the budgets and we've customized the client to add some significant power to managing data in and out of the spreadsheet. And at its core, we've created an environment for the budget owner to create and manage a budget spreadsheet through a customized spreadsheet; we've created several views into that data where consumers of that data can quickly gauge progress and breakdowns of budget items; and we've created a workflow that ties it all together. Now imagine this environment where we extend beyond the 2007 Office system to integrate Web services to custom applications or to integrate LOB systems such as SAP, Microsoft Dynamics, or People-Soft through their native Web services: with that you have a very powerful information worker experience. That is, you've now created a fully functional, workflow-centric application that helps manage the process of creating (for example) a budget. Bear in mind that this application also provides visibility into the data so other reviewers can get insight into key areas of the data.

In closing, I encourage you to think about what we've walked through in this chapter, and even if you did not use the example code within the chapter, think of how you could architect your own OBA that utilizes the core 2007 Office system technology. OBA is a powerful idea, and the technology behind it is extremely potent—especially when you begin to take advantage of all of the functionality and features of the 2007 Office system client and Office Share-Point Server 2007.

Chapter 3

Managing Sales Forecasting with an Office Business Application

–Joanna Bichsel, Microsoft Corporation

Mya, a salesperson at Wide World Importers, needs to prepare her sales forecasts for the coming fiscal year. She launches her Web browser and opens the company's sales portal, in which a dashboard displays live sales data for the current fiscal year. The dashboard includes charts and tables with key performance indicators (KPIs) pulling data from a line-of-business (LOB) system that stores sales figures for each salesperson and customer across each region. This information is gathered by using Web Parts built into Excel Services in Microsoft Office SharePoint Server 2007 to publish Microsoft Office Excel 2007 charts and lists along with Business Data Catalog (BDC) List Web Parts to display the LOB data. The portal also relies on Enterprise Search, which enables employees to search indexed LOB data and retrieve information that they use to keep track of their customers and sales data and perform competitive sales forecasting analysis.

To start working on her sales forecasts for the next fiscal year, Mya opens the Sales Forecasts document library, which the Sales Portal home page is linked to. She creates a new sales forecast document based on a content type defined for that document library.

> **Note**   *Content types* are templates of any file type. Content types can have workflows associated with them, and they can host code, custom user interface elements, and other special behaviors. Multiple content types can be associated with a single document library. In this solution, the sales forecast content type is an Office Excel 2007 template linked to a custom workflow.

After Office Excel 2007 loads, a custom tab named Sales Forecasts is visible on the Microsoft Office Fluent user interface. The spreadsheet contains two charts, one for the current fiscal year and one for the projected fiscal year. Tables on the spreadsheet are linked to the charts. Mya clicks the Sales Forecasts tab, where two buttons appear. One button is used to display a document actions task pane that Mya can use to create her sales forecasts, and the other button submits her forecast for approval. The document actions task pane allows Mya to retrieve data from the LOB system and insert it in her forecasting spreadsheet. She is also able to query the Windows SharePoint Services database to retrieve supporting documents and open Web pages such as dashboards and document libraries in the sales reports portal. With these operations, she can perform research and analysis right from Office Excel 2007. Submitting the forecast for approval initiates a custom workflow that saves the data to the LOB system, saves the spreadsheet to the document library, and sends an e-mail message to Mya's manager.

All the features I've described here take advantage of the capabilities of Microsoft Visual Studio Tools for Office (VSTO). The new visual designer for the Ribbon makes customizing the user interface easy, and support for custom task panes provides seamless integration. The *ServerDocument* class in VSTO allows manipulation of custom XML cached data so you can pull the data from the Office Excel 2007 spreadsheet. Support for Windows SharePoint Services in VSTO, as well as its integration with Windows Workflow Foundation (WWF), gives developers the ability to create custom workflows through state machine workflow and sequential workflow project templates with custom workflow activities that you can tie together with custom code.

Figure 3-1 shows a high-level overview of the sales forecasting solution. From this scenario, you can see that a salesperson can work within the context of an application he knows well—in this case, Office Excel 2007. Everything is at the user's fingertips: access to LOB data, a calculation engine, graphical analysis, and an automatic workflow. There is no need to copy and paste information from multiple applications, no need to switch to an LOB application and perform complex queries, no need to send a submission e-mail in Microsoft Office Outlook 2007, and no need to manually save a document to the SharePoint document library. Efficiency is greatly improved when compared to traditional sales forecasting processes.

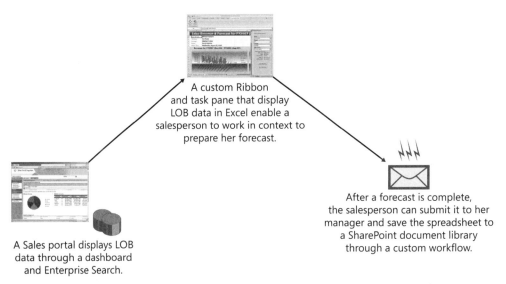

A custom Ribbon and task pane that display LOB data in Excel enable a salesperson to work in context to prepare her forecast.

After a forecast is complete, the salesperson can submit it to her manager and save the spreadsheet to a SharePoint document library through a custom workflow.

A Sales portal displays LOB data through a dashboard and Enterprise Search.

Figure 3-1 An overview of the sales forecasting solution.

For the developer, the time required to develop an enterprise application for a sales forecasting scenario is greatly reduced as a result of the expanded application programming interfaces (APIs) available from the services and features in Office SharePoint Server 2007 and tools such as VSTO. For example, the SOAP calls available from the Enterprise Search service allow developers to bring LOB data to the surface in the Office Excel 2007 client. Also, you only need to define the entities within your LOB data in an XML file to display them in SharePoint through the BDC. This requires no code—a far different requirement from the many lines of code that were previously needed to bring LOB data to a SharePoint site. By not having to focus on "plumbing" code, developers can create a true enterprise solution and spend time programming the business logic rather than the framework. The 2007 Microsoft Office system and VSTO are about efficiency and richness in enterprise solutions.

Software Requirements

Before you begin building your own sales forecasting application, you'll need to set up and configure an environment. This chapter does not describe the installation and configuration of an environment but assumes that your environment is set up and configured correctly. You need the following prerequisites for your environment:

- Microsoft Windows Server 2003

- Microsoft Office SharePoint Server 2007

- Microsoft Office Professional 2007

- Visual Studio 2008 Professional and Visual Studio Tools for Office 3.0

Note   The application discussed in this chapter was developed using a beta release of Visual Studio 2008 (formerly codenamed Orcas). Some changes might be required to the code if you use the samples shown in this chapter.

Solution Architecture

Figure 3-2 shows the detailed architecture of the sales forecasting solution. This solution generally follows the cooperating document workflow pattern that is described in Chapter 1, "Getting Started with Office Business Applications."

The sales forecasting solution uses Visual Studio as the development tool, integrated with VSTO. Using VSTO provides custom user interface development for the solution's document actions task pane and custom Ribbon (with visual designers), abstracted Open XML File Format manipulation with the *ServerDocument* class, and custom workflow project types for creating state machine diagrams with custom workflow activities. The solution was built using C# and Microsoft .NET Framework 3.5, which the latest version of VSTO is based on.

The sales reports portal is a solution built on Office SharePoint Server 2007, which is itself based on Windows SharePoint Services 3.0. The SQL Server AdventureWorks database (a sample database that ships with SQL Server) is used as the LOB database for this solution and connects to Windows SharePoint Services 3.0 through an OLEDB connection. Within Windows SharePoint Services 3.0, the solution's workflow features are based on the Windows Workflow Foundation. The sales forecast spreadsheet is a content type made available through the Sales Reports document library, and custom site templates based on Master Pages have been applied to make the site uniform across the sales portal.

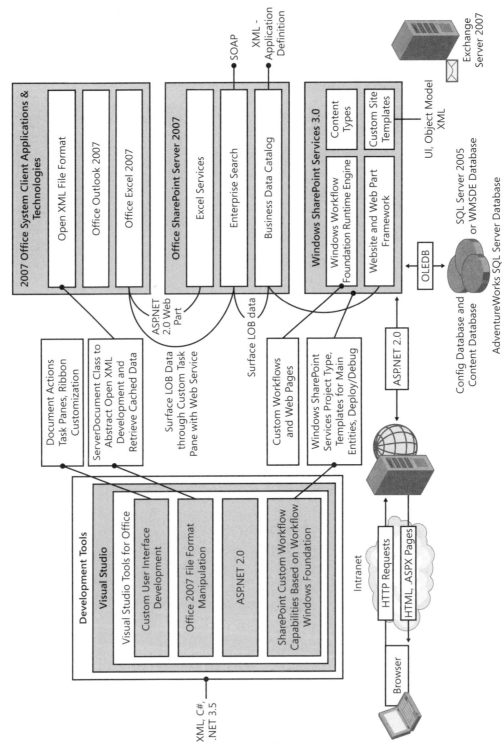

Figure 3-2 Sales forecasting solution logical architecture.

In Office SharePoint Server 2007, the BDC is used to display LOB data by using XML through an application definition file (ADF). This data is then displayed in the dashboard through Web Parts in lists and is indexed to make it available across the portal through Enterprise Search. The LOB data is also available through Enterprise Search by using the Web service that is associated with a document actions pane in Office Excel 2007, created using VSTO. Excel Services is used in the dashboard to show data pulled from sales forecasting spreadsheets in the form of charts, tables, and KPIs. These Excel Services Web Parts are just HTML and JavaScript hosted in an ASP.NET 2.0 Web Part, so there is zero footprint for the end user.

The 2007 Office system client that is used the most in this solution is Office Excel 2007. Office Outlook 2007 is used to view the e-mail message by the approver during the custom workflow, and when the workflow is assigned, the approver receives a task item in Outlook 2007. The sales forecasting spreadsheet is the centerpiece of the solution. For only the sales forecasting document (not for all instances of Office Excel 2007), we use project templates and classes available in VSTO to show the custom Ribbon and the custom task pane. The custom task pane has two tabs, one to load and save sales forecasting data into the spreadsheet via SQL queries and one to search the SharePoint portal by using the Enterprise Search Web service. The spreadsheet also has cached data. The *ServerDocument* class in VSTO can access this cached data during the workflow, when we send an e-mail message to the approver with the sales forecasting data. The *ServerDocument* class abstracts Open XML file format manipulation by allowing a developer to access the cached data as a business object.

Sales Forecasting Solution Walk-Through

In the following sections, I'll describe the operations of the sales forecasting solution in detail. You'll learn about how the solution integrates the sales portal dashboard; how it makes use of the BDC and content types; and how I developed the custom Ribbon, document actions pane, and workflow.

Sales Portal Dashboard

The home page of the sales forecasting solution is the Sales Reports home page, which acts as a dashboard for the sales department of Wide World Importers. From this page, users can quickly view charts of sales revenue by customer, filter lists of customer sales forecasts across fiscal year using KPIs, and view a list of sales by salesperson through the display of LOB data. This dashboard, shown in Figure 3-3, was created by assembling a series of Web Parts specific to Excel Services and the BDC, with no code required.

Figure 3-3   Sales forecasting dashboard.

Excel Services Web Parts

Excel Services allows you to publish a spreadsheet to a SharePoint site through Web Parts. It also provides Web services that you can use to create custom applications that make use of the Office Excel 2007 calculation engine in its full fidelity. Some of the advantages of using Excel Services through Web Parts include the following:

- There is zero footprint. The end user does not need to install anything, including ActiveX controls, nor does she need to have Office Excel 2007 on her computer.

- The author or publisher of the spreadsheet decides which part of the spreadsheet he wants to display. You no longer need to route a spreadsheet in e-mail, exposing everything in the workbook (all the worksheets, all the formulas behind the data, and the data connections, for example). Excel Services allows you to specify whether you want to show only a particular table, chart, range, or worksheet, or whether you want to show the whole spreadsheet.

- There is one version of the truth. Distributing spreadsheets in e-mail enables people who receive the spreadsheet to change the data and then forward the spreadsheet to other users. This haphazard approach can result in multiple versions of the same spreadsheet, which has caused serious compliance issues resulting in regulations such as Sarbanes-Oxley.

By uploading a spreadsheet to Excel Services, you don't need to distribute the spreadsheet by e-mail—it is saved in a central repository.

■ If users have Office Excel 2007 on their computers, the author/publisher has complete control over how the data is viewed when it is downloaded to client computers. The author/publisher can choose not to allow end users to download the spreadsheet or can grant permission to download the file as a regular spreadsheet or only as a snapshot. A snapshot looks like the original spreadsheet, with the same layout and formatting and the latest calculated data, but it doesn't include the formulas behind the data, it doesn't include the data connections, and it doesn't have any auxiliary worksheets that the author/publisher decided not to show in the Excel Services Web Part. This is another way that Excel Services helps protect your data.

■ For developers, the most significant advantage is no longer needing to understand the business model of the spreadsheet. With Excel Services, a financial analyst creates the business model in Office Excel 2007 and publishes the spreadsheet to the server. All the developer needs to do is access those Web services to use the business model. If the spreadsheet changes, the developer does not have to update the code, which was required in more traditional scenarios.

More Info   To learn more about using Excel Services in your custom applications and all the associated benefits, refer to the Excel Services Information Center on the Microsoft Developer Network at *http://msdn2.microsoft.com/en-us/office/bb203828.aspx.*

To create an Excel Services Web Part, you start out in the Office Excel 2007 client. To publish, click the Office button in Excel 2007, point to Publish, and then click Excel Services. You'll see a dialog box that provides options for publishing the spreadsheet. To show the entire workbook, you can just click Save, and the file will open in Excel Services in its own application page. In the Sales Forecasting solution, we only want to publish the Sales YTD chart and the CustomerSales table within the spreadsheet. You accomplish this by clicking the Excel Services Options, shown in Figure 3-4.

Use the drop-down list to select Entire Workbook, Sheets, or Items In The Workbook. In Figure 3-4, I've selected the third option. On the Show tab, I cleared the check box for All Charts and selected only the Sales YTD chart. Then I cleared the option for All Tables and selected only the CustomerSales table. You can also select named ranges, which are always better to use than regular ranges because if your data is moved, the named range moves along with the data and does not break your solution. There is also a Parameters tab so that you can make certain cells in your workbook editable, which is helpful in cases for which you want to turn the Excel Services Web Part into a modeling solution. For example, let's say that you work for a bank and create a dashboard for your mortgage specialists based on Office Share-Point Server 2007. You can upload a worksheet range to an Excel Services Web Part with embedded formulas and parameters, which the mortgage specialists can use so that they can perform calculations on the fly when meeting with their customers.

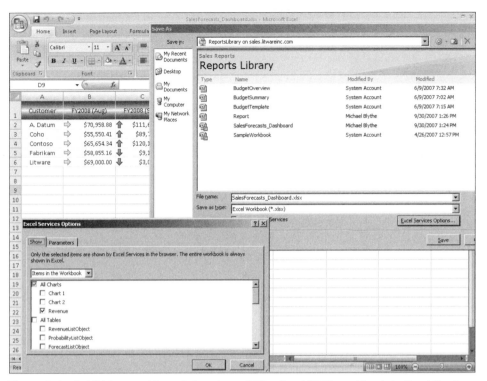

Figure 3-4   Publishing a table and chart in an Office Excel 2007 workbook to Excel Services.

To continue on with publishing the spreadsheet, after you click OK in the Excel Services Options dialog box, you return to the Save As dialog box. We can just click Save here. Because the option Open in Excel Services is selected, the file will automatically open in a dynamic SharePoint page–an Application page–with the spreadsheet rendered in straight HTML and JavaScript. There is a View drop-down list at the top right that you can use to switch between the chart and the table.

Now we want to create an Excel Services Web Part and point to the spreadsheet located in the document library. This operation will let us show both the chart and the spreadsheet in separate Web Parts. To start, return to the sales reports dashboard. In the top right, click Site Actions, Edit Page, which allows us to add Web Parts to the page. Clicking Add a Web Part displays a window that allows you to choose from many different Web Parts, one of which is Excel Web Access, located under All Web Parts. Select that Web Part and click Add. A hyperlink becomes available in the Web Part to open the tool panel. In the tool panel, enter the path to the workbook in the Workbook field. In the Sales Forecasting solution, the Named Item field had the value Sales YTD so that it pointed to the chart. Once you enter the Named Item field, you just need to click Apply. It's that easy. To add the table complete with KPIs, follow the same steps but enter your table name in the Named Item field in the tool pane. Notice that the KPIs, which are actually conditional formatting in Office Excel 2007, and the grid look like they do in the client, even though they are rendered only in HTML and JavaScript.

Business Data Catalog Web Parts

Just like the Excel Services Web Parts, the BDC Web Parts allow you to create components of a dashboard for analysis without writing any code. The BDC allows you to bring LOB data from any LOB application–Siebel, SAP, CRM, or others–into SharePoint. You can display the data in Web Parts, associate it with user profiles, index it for Enterprise Search, and make use of it through BDC Web services in custom applications–all without having to write any code.

> **More Info**   More detailed information about pulling LOB data into the BDC is available later in the chapter in the section "The Business Data Catalog." This section will only describe adding BDC Web Parts to a dashboard.

Two BDC Web Parts are included in the sales reports dashboard of the sales forecasting solution. Both are Business Data List Web Parts, but one allows users to query the sales results by fiscal year, while the other displays all the sales by a salesperson for the previous year and the current year to date.

To add the Business Data List Web Part for sales results by fiscal year, go to the dashboard, click Site Actions in the top right, click Edit Page, and then click Add A Web Part in whichever region you choose. Under All Web Parts, select the option for Business Data List and click Add. You will see a Web Part with a hyperlink that opens the tool pane. Open the tool pane and fill in the Type field by clicking the Browse button to the right (the book icon). From here, you can select from a list of entities that have been defined when you upload the application definition file to SharePoint 3.0 Central Administration. (To see how to do this, refer to the Business Data Catalog section later in this chapter.) For this particular Web Part, I selected the SalesbyYear Business Data Type, a business entity defined in the application definition file. Now just click OK, and then click OK again in the tool pane.

To add the second Web Part, I followed the same steps as for the first one, but instead of selecting the SalesbyYear Business Data Type, I selected SalesbySalesPersonName. Now, to change this Web Part from simply a search pane (like the first Web Part) to a list, return to the Web Part and click Edit View in the top right. Change the option Retrieve Items Specified By The User to Retrieve All Items, and then select the columns that you want to show. Click OK. When you check in the page and then publish it, you will see that the search query toolbar has disappeared.

The Business Data Catalog

As mentioned previously, the BDC allows you to display data from an LOB application such as SAP or Siebel in SharePoint without writing any code. As a result, this data is available through Web Parts, indexed as part of the Enterprise Search in your portal, available through lists and user profiles, and used in custom applications through the available Web services. End users no longer need to work in separate applications to retrieve data–applications that are often not intuitive, require a lot of training, and are usually limited to users in specific roles. Office SharePoint Server 2007, through the BDC, allows more users to view LOB data without switching contexts, as if it were regular data entered in SharePoint. The BDC provides support for the creation of dashboards as well as for bringing LOB data into the client through Web services.

The BDC makes use of standard .NET classes to interface with LOB systems, connecting with OLEDB and ODBC data sources using an ADO.NET interface or, if it's a traditional LOB system such as SAP, a SOAP interface. In the sales forecasting solution, the BDC connects to the AdventureWorks sample database through an ADO.NET interface. You need only describe the data source using an XML metadata file and define your business entities to connect to the BDC, which is why no code is required.

> **More Info**   For more detailed information on the architecture of the BDC, see *http://msdn2.microsoft.com/en-us/library/ms499729.aspx*. You can also learn more about the architecture of the BDC in Chapter 1.

The application definition file is an XML file that contains all the necessary information to connect to the LOB system and return the requested data. In the application definition file, you define business entities, which are like business objects with properties and methods. Application definitions follow the schemas defined in the bdcmetadata.xsd file located under Program Files\Microsoft Office Servers\12.0\Bin. Two application definition files in the sales forecasting solution have been imported into Office SharePoint Server 2007: AW_ActualSales.xml and AW_SalesForecasts.xml.

The first *property* element in the application definition is the wildcard character, which we define as the % symbol. The *property* element can be defined throughout the application definition, as shown here.

```
<Properties>
  <Property Name="WildcardCharacter" Type="System.String">%</Property>
</Properties>
```

In the *Properties* tag you'll also find the *AccessControlList* element, which exists for each entity. It specifies who has permission to access and work with the data.

```
<AccessControlList>
    <AccessControlEntry Principal="LITWAREINC\administrator">
      <Right BdcRight="Edit" />
      <Right BdcRight="Execute" />
      <Right BdcRight="SetPermissions" />
      <Right BdcRight="SelectableInClients" />
    </AccessControlEntry>
```

The *Entity* element is used to define the business entities, and it contains the definitions for the methods that return the information as well as the data types for each column. If we take the AW_SalesForecasts.xml as an example, you can see we have defined the entities *Forecasts-bySalesPersonName*, *ForecastbyYear*, *ForecastbyQuarter*, and *ForecastbyTerritory*. Listing 3-1 shows the *ForecastbyYear* entity (with the *AccessControlList* node collapsed).

Listing 3-1   The *Forecastbyyear* entity.

```xml
<Entity EstimatedInstanceCount="10000" Name="ForecastbyYear">
  <Properties>
    <Property Name="DefaultAction" Type="System.String">View Profile</Property>
    <Property Name="Title" Type="System.String">Forecasts by Year</Property>
  </Properties>
  <AccessControlList>…
  <Identifiers>
    <Identifier TypeName="System.Int32" Name="[FiscalYear]" />
  </Identifiers>
  <Methods>
    <Method Name="GetForecastbyYear">
      <Properties>
        <Property Name="RdbCommandText" Type="System.String">
        SELECT SUM(rawforecast) as TotalSales, FiscalYear FROM
          Sales.[SalesForecast]
        WHERE (FiscalYear &gt;= @MinFY AND FiscalYear &lt;= @MaxFY) GROUP BY
          FiscalYear
        </Property>
        <Property Name="RdbCommandType" Type="System.Data.CommandType,
          System.Data, Version=2.0.0.0, Culture=neutral,
          PublicKeyToken=b77a5c561934e089">Text</Property>
      </Properties>
  <AccessControlList>…
      <FilterDescriptors>
        <FilterDescriptor Type="Comparison" Name="FiscalYear" />
      </FilterDescriptors>
      <Parameters>
        <Parameter Direction="In" Name="@fiscalyear">
          <TypeDescriptor TypeName="System.Int32" IdentifierName="[FiscalYear]"
          AssociatedFilter="FiscalYear" Name="FiscalYear">
            <DefaultValues>
              <DefaultValue MethodInstanceName="ForecastByYear"
                Type="System.Int32">0</DefaultValue>
              <DefaultValue MethodInstanceName="ForecastByYearSpecific"
                Type="System.Int32">0</DefaultValue>
            </DefaultValues>
          </TypeDescriptor>
        </Parameter>
        <Parameter Direction="In" Name="@MinFY">
          <TypeDescriptor TypeName="System.Int32" IdentifierName="[FiscalYear]"
          AssociatedFilter="FiscalYear" Name="MinFY">
            <DefaultValues>
              <DefaultValue MethodInstanceName="ForecastByYear"
                Type="System.Int32">0</DefaultValue>
            </DefaultValues>
          </TypeDescriptor>
        </Parameter>
        <Parameter Direction="In" Name="@MaxFY">
```

```
        <TypeDescriptor TypeName="System.Int32" IdentifierName="[FiscalYear]"
         AssociatedFilter="FiscalYear" Name="MaxFY">
          <DefaultValues>
            <DefaultValue MethodInstanceName="ForecastByYear"
             Type="System.Int32">99999999</DefaultValue>
          </DefaultValues>
        </TypeDescriptor>
      </Parameter>
      <Parameter Direction="Return" Name="Forecasts">
        <TypeDescriptor TypeName="System.Data.IDataReader, System.Data,
         Version=2.0.3600.0, Culture=neutral,
         PublicKeyToken=b77a5c561934e089" IsCollection="true"
         Name="ForecastDataReader">
          <TypeDescriptors>
            <TypeDescriptor TypeName="System.Data.IDataRecord, System.Data,
             Version=2.0.3600.0, Culture=neutral,
             PublicKeyToken=b77a5c561934e089" Name="ForecastDataRecord">
              <TypeDescriptors>
                <TypeDescriptor TypeName="System.Decimal, mscorlib,
                 Version=2.0.0.0, Culture=neutral,
                 PublicKeyToken=b77a5c561934e089" Name="TotalSales">
                <LocalizedDisplayNames>
                  <LocalizedDisplayName
                   LCID="1033">Forecast</LocalizedDisplayName>
                </LocalizedDisplayNames>
                <Properties>
                  <Property Name="DisplayByDefault"
                   Type="System.Boolean">true</Property>
                </Properties>
                </TypeDescriptor>
                <TypeDescriptor TypeName="System.Int32, mscorlib,
                 Version=2.0.0.0, Culture=neutral,
                 PublicKeyToken=b77a5c561934e089"
                 IdentifierName="[FiscalYear]" Name="FiscalYear">
                <LocalizedDisplayNames>
                  <LocalizedDisplayName
                   LCID="1033">Year</LocalizedDisplayName>
                </LocalizedDisplayNames>
                <Properties>
                  <Property Name="DisplayByDefault"
                   Type="System.Boolean">true</Property>
                </Properties>
                </TypeDescriptor>
              </TypeDescriptors>
            </TypeDescriptor>
          </TypeDescriptors>
        </TypeDescriptor>
      </Parameter>
    </Parameters>
    <MethodInstances>
      <MethodInstance Type="Finder" ReturnParameterName="Forecasts"
       ReturnTypeDescriptorName="ForecastDataReader"
       ReturnTypeDescriptorLevel="0" Name="ForecastByYear">
<AccessControlList>…
      </MethodInstance>
```

```
                <MethodInstance Type="SpecificFinder" ReturnParameterName="Forecasts"
                    ReturnTypeDescriptorName="ForecastDataReader"
                    ReturnTypeDescriptorLevel="0" Name="ForecastByYearSpecific">
    <AccessControlList>…
                </MethodInstance>
            </MethodInstances>
        </Method>
        <Method Name="Sales.[FiscalYear]IDEnumerator">
            <Properties>
                <Property Name="RdbCommandText" Type="System.String">Select Distinct
                    [FiscalYear], [FiscalQuarter] from Sales.[SalesForecast]</Property>
                <Property Name="RdbCommandType" Type="System.Data.CommandType,
                    System.Data, Version=2.0.0.0, Culture=neutral,
                    PublicKeyToken=b77a5c561934e089">Text</Property>
            </Properties>
    <AccessControlList>…
            <Parameters>
                <Parameter Direction="Return" Name="[FiscalYear]s">
                    <TypeDescriptor TypeName="System.Data.IDataReader, System.Data,
                        Version=2.0.3600.0, Culture=neutral,
                        PublicKeyToken=b77a5c561934e089" IsCollection="true"
                        Name="Sales.[FiscalYear]s">
                        <TypeDescriptors>
                            <TypeDescriptor TypeName="System.Data.IDataRecord, System.Data,
                                Version=2.0.3600.0, Culture=neutral,
                                PublicKeyToken=b77a5c561934e089" Name="Sales.[FiscalYear]">
                                <TypeDescriptors>
                                    <TypeDescriptor TypeName="System.Int32"
                                        IdentifierName="[FiscalYear]" Name="FiscalYear" />
                                </TypeDescriptors>
                            </TypeDescriptor>
                        </TypeDescriptors>
                    </TypeDescriptor>
                </Parameter>
            </Parameters>
            <MethodInstances>
                <MethodInstance Type="IdEnumerator" ReturnParameterName="[FiscalYear]s"
                    ReturnTypeDescriptorName="Sales.[FiscalYear]s"
                    ReturnTypeDescriptorLevel="0" Name="[FiscalYear]EnumeratorInstance">
                    <AccessControlList>…
                </MethodInstance>
            </MethodInstances>
        </Method>
    </Methods>
    <Actions>
        <Action Position="1" IsOpenedInNewWindow="false"
            Url=http://moss:32901/ssp/admin/Content/ForecastbyYear.aspx?FiscalYear={0}
            ImageUrl="/_layouts/1033/images/viewprof.gif" Name="View Profile">
            <ActionParameters>
                <ActionParameter Index="0" Name="FiscalYear" />
            </ActionParameters>
        </Action>
    </Actions>
</Entity>
```

To upload the application definition to SharePoint, go to SharePoint Central Administration, click Shared Services Administration in the left navigation panel, select your shared service, and then, under the Business Data Catalog category, select Import Application Definition and browse to your application definition file. Figure 3-5 shows what the *Product* entity definition looks like after the application definition has been uploaded successfully.

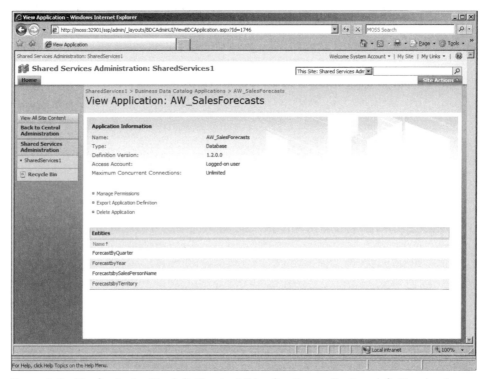

Figure 3-5   The *Product* entity definition is visible after the application definition has been uploaded into Office SharePoint Server 2007.

After you have successfully uploaded the application definition into Office SharePoint Server 2007, you can add BDC Web Parts, and Enterprise Search will index your LOB data. This also enables you to bring LOB data to the client through the BDC Web Services by using something such as a custom task pane.

More Info   For more information on the BDC, see the following references:

■ The BDC SDK at *http://msdn2.microsoft.com/en-us/library/ms563661.aspx*.

■ The BDC Information Center at *http://msdn2.microsoft.com/en-us/office/bb251754.aspx*.

Content Types

A content type is a new feature in Windows SharePoint Services 3.0. You can think of a content type as a template on steroids. These templates can be of any file type—Microsoft Office Word, Office Excel, PDF, and so on—and their goal is to be flexible enough to fit your business process. For example, in the sales forecasting solution, the Sales Forecasts document library has a content type called Sales Forecast: When a salesperson needs to create a new forecast, she just goes to the document library, clicks New, and then clicks Sales Forecast to work with the template. You could also have other content types of any file type in this document library to make your business processes as efficient as possible. For example, you could have an Executive Report content type based on an Office Word 2007 file or a PDF file. Content types don't pertain only to document libraries. You can also define them in lists and folders.

The powerful thing about content types is that you can create a rich template with event-driven custom code and user interface elements, content control connections to back-end data, rich metadata that improves search indexing of the document and controls data entry, document conversion, and associated information management policies. You can also associate one or more workflows with a content type that is initiated whenever a file is created or modified. In addition, content types are organized into hierarchies that allow one content type to inherit characteristics from another content type, improving efficiency in creating templates and increasing consistency in business processes.

The sales forecast content type is based on an Excel 2007 spreadsheet associated with the sales forecast approval workflow. It contains charts for the actual and projected fiscal year data and associated metadata that, when the spreadsheet is opened in Office Excel 2007, is editable in the Document Information panel. The Document Information panel is a feature in Office Word 2007, Microsoft Office PowerPoint 2007, and Office Excel 2007 that allows the author of a document to enter metadata associated with the document so that the metadata is stored in SharePoint but the user has the ease of entering the information through the client. The creator of the content type can specify which fields are required, thereby enforcing data entry of these fields, which is important to many organizations, especially for compliance reasons. The Document Information panel, shown in Figure 3-6, is based on a Microsoft Office InfoPath 2007 form, so you can easily customize it in Office InfoPath 2007.

This specific workbook has a document actions task pane associated with it that you use to insert fiscal year data and search server-side resources. The salesperson can also use a custom Ribbon tab to show or hide the document actions pane and then submit her sales proposal to her manager, thereby kicking off a workflow. More information about the actions pane and the custom Ribbon is provided later in this chapter in "Creating the Custom Ribbon."

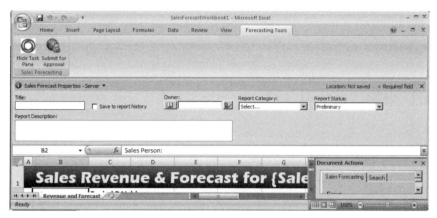

Figure 3-6 The Document Information panel in the Sales Forecast content type.

To create a site content type that you can use in document libraries, lists, and folders through-out a site, click Site Actions (in the top right), Site Settings, Modify All Site Settings. Under Site Collection Administration, click Go To Top Level Site Settings. Under Galleries, click Site Content Types. You'll see the page shown in Figure 3-7.

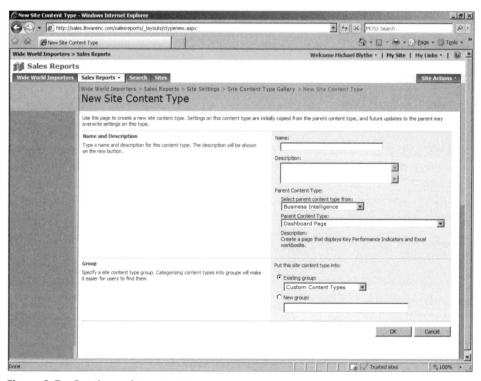

Figure 3-7 Creating a site content type.

First you define the parent content type and specify which group the new site content type belongs to. Next you define the properties associated with that content type, such as workflow and policy settings.

To view the Sales Forecast content type in the Sales Forecast document library, go to the Document library, click Settings, and then click Document Library Settings. You'll see a header for content types. Here you'll have the option to view content types, add from existing site content types, and change the order of content types shown on the New button and the default content type. Viewing the content type shows us the same page we used to define the properties for the site content type, which is shown in Figure 3-8.

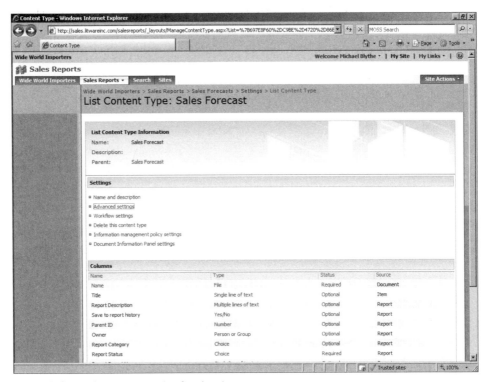

Figure 3-8   Defining properties for the site content type.

> **More Info**   For more information about content types, see the following resources:
>
> - Introduction to content types at *http://office.microsoft.com/en-us/sharepointserver/HA101495511033.aspx?pid=CH101779691033*.
> - Content types articles in the Windows SharePoint Services SDK at *http://msdn2.microsoft.com/en-us/library/ms479905.aspx*.

Creating the Custom Ribbon

In VSTO, you can create a custom Ribbon either through a visual designer or by assembling the XML directly (because the 2007 Office system user interface is based on XML). To create a custom Ribbon in VSTO, right-click your project, click Add, New Item, and then in the dialog box, under Visual C# Items (or Visual Basic Items if that is your preference), select Ribbon (Visual Designer). Click Add, and you will see a Ribbon canvas that has the built-in Add-Ins tab and a predefined group1. The sales forecasting solution has one group, called Sales Forecasting, and the tab is called Forecasting Tools. Two buttons appear in the group, which you can see in Figure 3-9.

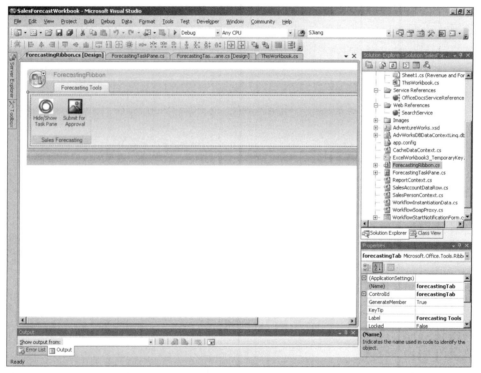

Figure 3-9   Custom Ribbon tab as shown via the visual designer in Visual Studio Tools for Office.

To change the Add-Ins tab to a custom tab, you need to go to the Properties window of the tab. Under *ControlId*, change *ControlIdType* from Office to Custom. To place buttons on a group in the visual designer, drag a button from the toolbox (under the Office Ribbon Controls section). You can see that several controls are available here, including a gallery that is a button that drops down a graphical array of images and controls—a very rich display of user interface. The first button image is referenced in the Resources file while the second and third buttons use images that ship with the 2007 Office system.

More Info   Hundreds of images shipped out of the box with 2007 Office system. You can use one of these icons to achieve the look and feel of the 2007 Office system without having to create your own. To view the icons so that you can then reference them easily in your code, download a handy Office Excel 2007 add-in from *http://www.sunflowerhead.com/ msimages/Office2007IconsGallery.zip*. (This add-in is not a Microsoft product and is not supported by Microsoft.)

For the sales forecasting solution, the *OfficeImageId* field in the Properties window for the Submit For Approval button is set to the image OutlookGlobe, which you can see in Figure 3-10. This is where you would reference the names of the out-of-the-box images.

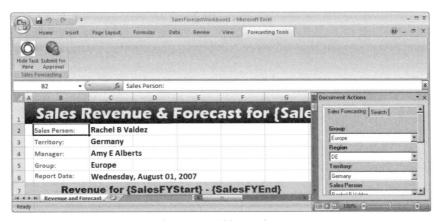

Figure 3-10   Forecasting Tools custom Ribbon tab.

After you have performed these basic tasks using VSTO, press F5 to build, debug, and install your Office Excel 2007 add-in. The custom Ribbon will load, and you are ready to work with your solution. Further on in the chapter, I will discuss what the code behind the Submit For Approval button does. Before I do that, however, I want to describe another important part of the sales forecasting solution—the document actions task pane—and how it hooks into the Show/Hide Task Pane button.

Document Actions Task Pane

Using VSTO, you can create a custom task pane (CTP) in Office Word 2007, Office Excel 2007, or Office PowerPoint 2007, or you can create a document actions task pane in Office Word 2007 or Office Excel 2007. Custom task panes are application-level, while document actions task panes (which I'll refer to as actions panes) are document-specific, meaning they are attached to a specific Office Word 2007 or Office Excel 2007 document or template. In essence, an actions pane is also a custom task pane but is specific to a certain document or spreadsheet, so I will use these terms a little interchangeably.

A CTP allows you to gain prime real estate on the screen so that end users can interact with your solution. It also gives you the flexibility to host managed controls, something that the Ribbon cannot do because a CTP is just a WinForm control. You can have multiple CTPs in an Office Word 2007, Office Excel 2007, or Office PowerPoint 2007 application and not have them overlap one another, as they did in previous versions of Microsoft Office, because of the multiple application spaces that exist for the CTPs. As a result, integration of CTPs with the Ribbon is not only nice, it is also necessary for clean-up reasons. Imagine a scenario in which a user has multiple add-ins installed and all of them have CTPs that are set to be visible when they load and their *Visible* property is never set to False. These task panes could cover the entire screen on the user's Office Word 2007 application window, for example, if the add-ins are not elegantly written to be hooked up to a button or a custom tab so that the CTP is triggered with a Show Task Pane command when the user decides to invoke the solution. For this reason, the Sales Forecasting tab has a button that presents the label Show Task Pane when the CTP's *Visible* property is set to False and presents the label Hide Task Pane when the *Visible* property is set to True.

To create a CTP, you only need to add a new user control to either an add-in project or an Office Word 2007 or Office Excel 2007 Document or Template project. To create an actions pane, you need to add an Actions Pane control to an Office Word 2007 or an Office Excel 2007 Document or Template project. After these steps, you need to add a few lines of code to turn the user control into a task pane. In the sales forecasting solution project, the actions pane is instantiated and added to the collection of actions pane controls in the startup method of ThisWorkbook.cs, which automatically causes it to become visible in the application upon loading.

```
public partial class ThisWorkbook
    {
        const int PAGESIZE = 5;
        private ForecastingTaskPane m_taskPane;

        private void ThisWorkbook_Startup(object sender, System.EventArgs e)
        {
            // Add and show the task pane.
            this.m_taskPane = new ForecastingTaskPane();
            this.ActionsPane.Controls.Add(this.m_taskPane);
        }
...
```

In the constructor for the forecasting Ribbon, the following code determines which label the button should show:

```
public ForecastingRibbon()
    {
        InitializeComponent();
        this.showHideTaskPaneButton.Label =
            (Globals.ThisWorkbook.TaskPaneVisible) ? "Hide Task Pane" : "Show
                Task Pane";
    }
```

To hook up the actions pane to the Show/Hide Task Pane button in the Ribbon, the following method exists behind the button in the *ForecastingRibbon* class:

```
private void ShowHideTaskPaneButton_Click(object sender, RibbonControlEventArgs e)
    {
        RibbonButton thisControl = (RibbonButton)sender;
        if (Globals.ThisWorkbook.TaskPaneVisible == true)
        {
            Globals.ThisWorkbook.TaskPaneVisible = false;
            thisControl.Label = "Show Task Pane";
        }
        else
        {
            Globals.ThisWorkbook.TaskPaneVisible = true;
            thisControl.Label = "Hide Task Pane";
        }

        return;
    }
```

Later in ThisWorkbook.cs, you can see the method that returns the Boolean value for whether the actions pane is visible to communicate with the Ribbon button so that we can change the label either to Hide or to Show.

```
public bool TaskPaneVisible
    {
        get { return Application.CommandBars["Task Pane"].Visible; }
        set
        {
            if (value == false)
            {
                Application.CommandBars["Task Pane"].Visible = false;
            }
            else
            {
                Application.CommandBars["Task Pane"].Visible = true;
            }
        }
    }
```

The actions pane has a control with two tabs. The first is used to populate the spreadsheet with data based on a specific territory, region, and user. The second tab is used to search the SharePoint repository (including the indexed LOB data) so that the salesperson can perform the analysis in context, without leaving Office Excel 2007.

Data Tab

Figure 3-11 shows the tab (labeled Sales Forecasting) used to populate the spreadsheet with data. While the BDC is able to bring LOB data to SharePoint as well as to your custom applications, it is currently not able to write that data back. If you want to bring LOB data into your application for read purposes, you would use the BDC Web services. If you require a read/write scenario, as this sales forecasting solution does, SQL queries are needed if you are using a SQL database. Otherwise, you would call Web Service methods to write back to your LOB system.

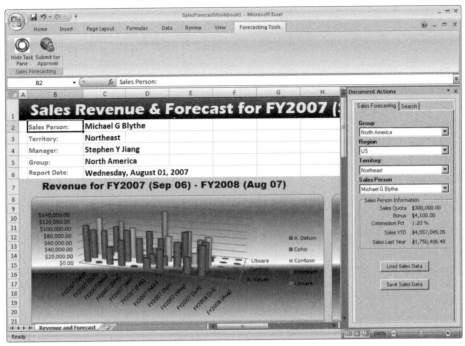

Figure 3-11 Controls on the Sales Forecasting tab in the document actions pane load and save LOB data to the sales forecasting spreadsheet.

When we load the task pane, we have cached data already stored in the task pane for the user. Here is the code that runs on loading the task pane:

```
private void ForecastingTaskPane_Load(object sender, EventArgs e)
    {
        if (Globals.ThisWorkbook.SalesForecastData.Employee.Count == 0 ||
            Globals.ThisWorkbook.SalesForecastData.SalesTerritory.Count == 0)
        {
            this.GetGeneralData();
        }
        else
        {
            Globals.ThisWorkbook.TaskPaneVisible = false;
            var territoryQuery =
                from AdventureWorks.SalesTerritoryRow salesTerritory
                in Globals.ThisWorkbook.SalesForecastData.SalesTerritory
                where salesTerritory.SalesTerritoryID ==
                    Globals.ThisWorkbook.SalesTerritoryID
                select salesTerritory;
            this.BindTaskPaneControls();
            territoryGroups.SelectedItem = territoryQuery.First().Group;
            territoryRegions.SelectedItem =
                territoryQuery.First().CountryRegionCode;
            territories.SelectedItem = territoryQuery.First().Name;
```

```
        salesPeople.SelectedItem =
          Globals.ThisWorkbook.SalesPersonContext.SalesPersonFullName;
        this.territoryGroups.Enabled = false;
        this.territoryRegions.Enabled = false;
        this.territories.Enabled = false;
        this.salesPeople.Enabled = false;
        this.loadSalesData.Enabled = false;
    }
    return;
}
```

We create a SQL query to run against the AdventureWorks database and bind the results to the *Group*, *Territory*, *Region*, and *Sales Person* controls in the task pane. After the user selects an item in the Group control, we enable the Region control and run a query to populate the drop-down list with a subset of the available regions. The same operation occurs with the *Territory* and *Sales Person* controls. After these controls have been selected, the user can click the button labeled Load Sales Data, which runs the code shown in Listing 3-2.

Listing 3-2   This code runs to load sales data.

```
private void LoadSalesData_Click(object sender, EventArgs e)
    {
        this.Cursor = Cursors.WaitCursor;

        try
        {
            // Set the cached properties on the main object
            Globals.ThisWorkbook.SalesPersonID =
              (int)this.salesPeople.SelectedValue;
            Globals.ThisWorkbook.SalesTerritoryID =
              (int)this.territories.SelectedValue;
            Globals.ThisWorkbook.ReportDate = DateTime.Today;

            // Get the data from SQL
            List<string> revenueDataHeaders;
            List<string> forecastDataHeaders;
            List<string> probabilityDataHeaders;
            List<string> rowHeaders;
            ReportContext reportContext;
            this.GetSalesForecastData(out reportContext,
                out revenueDataHeaders, out forecastDataHeaders, out
                probabilityDataHeaders, out rowHeaders);
            // Get the data contexts
            // Set the header values
            Globals.Sheet1.ReportDateRange.Value =
              reportContext.ReportDate.ToLongDateString();
            Globals.Sheet1.SalesFYStartRange.Value =
              reportContext.StartFiscalRange;
            Globals.Sheet1.SalesFYEndRange.Value =
              reportContext.EndRevenueRange;
            Globals.Sheet1.ForecastFYStartRange.Value =
              reportContext.StartForecastRange;
            Globals.Sheet1.ForecastFYEndRange.Value =
              reportContext.EndFiscalRange;
```

```
                  // Set the table column headers
                  SetDataHeaders(revenueDataHeaders,
                    Globals.Sheet1.RevenueDataHeaders);
                  SetDataHeaders(forecastDataHeaders,
                    Globals.Sheet1.ForecastDataHeaders);
                  SetDataHeaders(probabilityDataHeaders,
                    Globals.Sheet1.ProbabilityDataHeaders);
                  // Bind the data to the Excel sheet ranges
                  Globals.Sheet1.RevenueListObject.SetDataBinding
                    (Globals.ThisWorkbook.SalesForecastData.Revenue);
                  Globals.Sheet1.ForecastListObject.SetDataBinding
                    (Globals.ThisWorkbook.SalesForecastData.Forecast);
                  Globals.Sheet1.ProbabilityListObject.SetDataBinding
                    (Globals.ThisWorkbook.SalesForecastData.Probability);
              }
              finally
              {
                  this.Cursor = Cursors.Default;
              }

              return;
          }
```

Here we first set the cached properties for the workbook, which is very important for when we try to pull data out of the workbook through its cached properties. (See the section "Programming Against the New Open XML File Format" later in this chapter.) In the method *GetSalesForecastData*, we use stored procedures to pass in the *salesPersonID*, *salesTerritoryID*, and *ReportDate*. We get the sales forecast data from the customer accounts from AdventureWorks and then add the revenue, forecast, and probability data to their respective tables in the workbook. We set the header values of the spreadsheet as well as the column headers from the values returned from the *GetSalesForecastData* method. Then we bind the lists to the data tables.

After the salesperson has completed his forecasting data, he can save it back to the database by clicking Save Sales Data. This is different from the Submit button on the Ribbon because it does not kick off a workflow, nor does it save the workbook to the SharePoint document library. All it does is save the forecast data to the LOB system. Listing 3-3 shows the code.

Listing 3-3   The *SaveSalesData* code.

```
  private void SaveSalesData_Click(object sender, EventArgs e)
      {
          this.Cursor = Cursors.WaitCursor;

          try
          {
              const int DATA_MONTHS = 12;
              NamedRange forecastRange = Globals.Sheet1.ForecastRange;
              NamedRange probabilityRange = Globals.Sheet1.ProbabilityRange;

              for (int row = 2; row <= Globals.ThisWorkbook.PageSize + 1; row++)
              {
                  // Get the customer name and id
```

```csharp
Microsoft.Office.Interop.Excel.Range customerNameRange =
    (Microsoft.Office.Interop.Excel.Range)
    forecastRange.Cells[row, 1];
string customerName = customerNameRange.Value2.ToString();
var salesAccountId =
    from AdventureWorks.SalesAccountRow salesAccount
    in Globals.ThisWorkbook.SalesForecastData.SalesAccount
    where salesAccount.SalesAccountName == customerName
    select salesAccount.SalesAccountID;
// Get the data values
decimal[] forecastValues = new decimal[DATA_MONTHS];
decimal[] probabilityValues = new decimal[DATA_MONTHS];
for (int col = 2; col <= DATA_MONTHS + 1; col++)
{
    Microsoft.Office.Interop.Excel.Range dataValue =
        (Microsoft.Office.Interop.Excel.Range)
        forecastRange.Cells[row, col];
    forecastValues[col - 2] =
      decimal.Parse(dataValue.Value2.ToString());
    dataValue =
        (Microsoft.Office.Interop.Excel.Range)
        probabilityRange.Cells[row, col];
    probabilityValues[col - 2] =
      decimal.Parse(dataValue.Value2.ToString());
}


// Save the values to the database
ReportContext reportContext = new ReportContext();
// Get a structure that shows the fiscal year/fiscal month
// ranges
SortedDictionary<int, SortedDictionary<int, decimal>>
    fiscalRange =
    reportContext.CreateEmptyForecastRange();
int index = 0;
AdvWorksDBDataContextLinqDataContext databaseContext =
    new AdvWorksDBDataContextLinqDataContext();
foreach (KeyValuePair<int, SortedDictionary<int, decimal>>
    fiscalYear in fiscalRange)
{
    foreach (KeyValuePair<int, decimal> fiscalMonth in
        fiscalYear.Value)
    {
        decimal forecastValue = forecastValues[index];
        decimal probabilityValue = probabilityValues[index];

        int result =
            databaseContext.uspSaveForecast(
                Globals.ThisWorkbook.SalesPersonID,
                Globals.ThisWorkbook.SalesTerritoryID,
                salesAccountId.First(),
                new DateTime(fiscalYear.Key, fiscalMonth.Key,
                    1).AddMonths(-6),
                forecastValue,
                probabilityValue);

        index++;
    }
```

```
                }
            }
        }
        finally
        {
            this.Cursor = Cursors.Default;
        }

        return;
    }
```

Two named ranges have been created in the spreadsheet, the *forecastRange* and the *probability-Range*. We iterate through the rows of the *forecastRange*, retrieve the customer name and ID, and formulate a SQL query to retrieve the *salesAccountID* from the AdventureWorks database, which we need to save the data back to the database. We get the forecast and probability values for that customer for the past twelve months in *forecastRange* and *probabilityRange* and then save that data to the database.

Search Tab

To connect the *listView* control present in the tab control to the Enterprise Search Web service in Office SharePoint Server 2007, we need to add a Web reference to *http://<serverName>/_vti_bin/search.asmx*. After the proxy class is created, we can access the *Query* and *QueryEx* methods we need.

First, we define some important variables, as shown here:

```
private const string siteName = "http://litwareinc.com";
private const string keywordQueryTemplate = "<?xml version=\"1.0\"
    encoding=\"utf-8\" ?>"
    + "<QueryPacket xmlns=\"urn:Microsoft.Search.Query\" Revision=\"1000\">"
    + "<Query domain=\"QDomain\"><SupportedFormats>"
    + "<Format>urn:Microsoft.Search.Response.Document.
      Document</Format></SupportedFormats>"
    + "<Context><QueryText language=\"en-US\"
      type=\"STRING\">query_text_placeholder</QueryText></Context>"
    + "</Query></QueryPacket>";

private const string registrationString = "<RegistrationRequest
    revision=\"1\" xmlns=\"urn:Microsoft.Search.Registration.Request\"
    action=\"NEW\"/>";

private SearchService.QueryService searchService = null;
```

The constant *keywordQueryTemplate* contains the structure for a keyword query, and when *query_text_placeholder* is replaced with the keyword that the user enters in the text box, the XML will contain all the information needed for a query to execute. The variable *registration-String* is needed when calling the search Web service.

Next we access the *Query* and *QueryEx* methods in the code behind the Search button.

```csharp
private void btnSearch_Click(object sender, EventArgs e)
    {
        try
        {
            if (KeywordTextBox.Text.Trim().Length > 0)
            {
                // Step 1: Add a web reference to the Search web service and
                // rename it to SearchService
                // Step 2: Create an instance of the web service.
                searchService = new
                    SalesForecastWorkbook.SearchService.QueryService();

                // Step 3: fill out the url for the search web service
                searchService.Url = siteName + @"/_vti_bin/search.asmx";

                // Step 4: set the credentials.
                searchService.Credentials =
                    System.Net.CredentialCache.DefaultCredentials;

                // Step 5: Register to the Search web service.
                // The result is an xml string containing a Status node that
                // indicates SUCCESS
                // or another message indicating why the registration failed.
                string result = searchService.Registration(registrationString);

                // Step 6: replace the query_text_placeholder with the string in
                // the text box.
                string queryString =
                    keywordQueryTemplate.Replace("query_text_placeholder",
                        KeywordTextBox.Text.Trim());

                // Step 7: Execute the Query method. This method returns an xml
                // string containing the search result.
                string queryResults = searchService.Query(queryString);

                // Step 8: Execute the QueryEx method. This method accepts the
                // same xml querystring but the result is a dataset.
                DataSet resultDataset = searchService.QueryEx(queryString);

                // Step 9: DataBind the datagridview to the first table of the
                // dataset but only show the Title and Path columns
                ResultDataGridView.DataSource = resultDataset.Tables[0];
                ResultDataGridView.AutoGenerateColumns = true;
                ResultDataGridView.Columns.Clear();
                ResultDataGridView.Columns.Add("Title", "Title");
                ResultDataGridView.Columns["Title"].DataPropertyName = "Title";

                DataGridViewLinkColumn PathColumn = new
                    DataGridViewLinkColumn();
                PathColumn.HeaderText = "Link";
                PathColumn.DataPropertyName = "Path";
                PathColumn.TrackVisitedState = true;
                ResultDataGridView.Columns.Add(PathColumn);

                ResultDataGridView.AutoResizeColumns
```

```
                        (DataGridViewAutoSizeColumnsMode.AllCells);
                }
        }
        catch (Exception ex)
        {
                MessageBox.Show(ex.Message);
        }
    }
```

In step 4, when the code performs authentication, you can pass the credentials of the currently logged-on user, or you can create an instance of the *NetworkCredential* class. We receive an XML string denoting the status of the search service by calling the registration method on the *SearchService* class. Then we pass the *queryString* to the *QueryEx* method to retrieve the search results as a serialized *DataSet*. We could have also just passed the *queryString* to the *Query* method to retrieve the search results in XML format, but I wanted to retrieve the results as a dataset because I want to bind it to a *GridView* control. In step 9, the code binds the resulting *DataSet* object to the *GridView* control and displays two columns, one for the title and one for the path whenever the search results from the SharePoint repository are displayed. Because of the nature of the *GridView* control, a *Click* event still needs to be handled for the cell when a user clicks the hyperlink so that a browser process starts and the URL is passed in as a string. You can see an example of the results of the query in Figure 3-12.

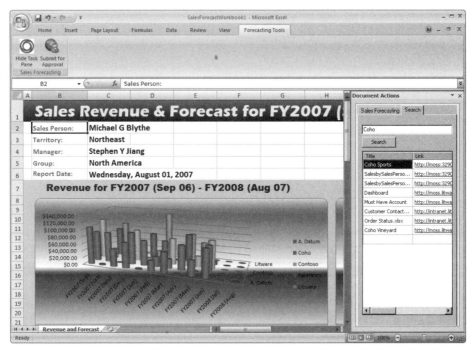

Figure 3-12   Search tab in the document actions pane returning results from the SharePoint Sales Reports portal.

The salesperson is now able to search for any relevant data that might exist in SharePoint about the customer she is analyzing as part of her fiscal year projections. For example, if the salesperson is trying to project the sales forecast for the customer Coho Vineyard, she can just go to the Search tab, type **Coho**, and find that there is a dashboard in Office SharePoint Server 2007 with this customer's statistics. Clicking that link takes the salesperson straight to the dashboard. Likewise, perhaps the salesperson would like to look at the Order Status.xlsx file that was one of the results from the search. Right from the task pane, the salesperson can open that spreadsheet, which is stored in the SharePoint repository. The salesperson has no reason to leave the application where she is working, and the sales forecasting process is made much more efficient.

Workflow

The sales forecasting solution includes a custom workflow for an approve/reject/make-changes scenario. An out-of-the-box Approval workflow template comes with Windows Share-Point Services, but this workflow was customized because we wanted to create a customized e-mail message with a particular set of activities. VSTO was used to create the custom workflow. If you are familiar with Visual Studio extensions for the Windows Workflow Foundation (VSeWWF), the latest version of VSTO incorporates VSeWWF and improves it by adding extra custom workflow activities.

To create a custom workflow, load Visual Studio, and then in the 2007 Office system node, select the SharePoint State Machine Workflow project template. At this point, you will be presented with a wizard in which you do the following:

1. Name the workflow and point to the URL for a local SharePoint site where you will debug the workflow.

2. Select the lists and libraries you want to associate the workflow with, as shown here.

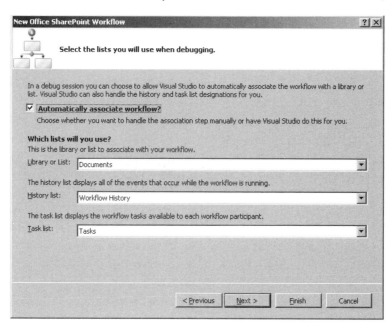

3. Specify the conditions for when the workflow is initiated. The choices are:

   a. Manually

   b. When an item is created

   c. When an item is changed

At this point, your project solution is created and you can start creating your custom workflow. Creating a custom workflow in Visual Studio is a combination of creating a state machine for your workflow by placing activities on a canvas, setting properties for these activities, and writing code behind them. Using the custom workflow activities available in the toolbox, you design your workflow by adding a wide variety of activities, such as state activities, event-driven activities, state-initialization activities, and state-finalization activities. Figure 3-13 shows a subset of the workflow activities available in the toolbox.

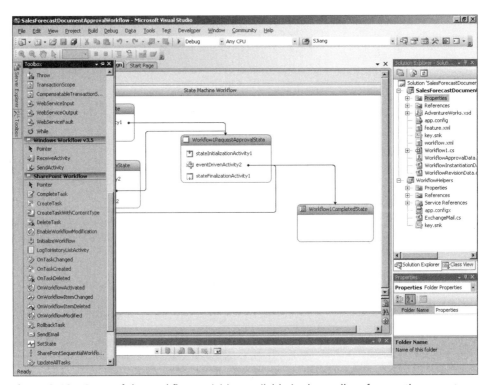

Figure 3-13   Some of the workflow activities available in the toolbox for creating a custom workflow in SharePoint.

Figure 3-14 depicts the state machine diagram for the sales forecasting solution.

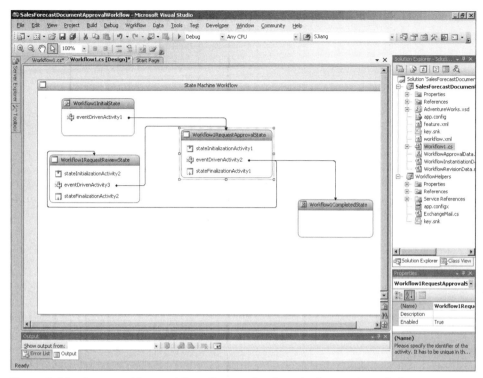

Figure 3-14   State machine workflow diagram for the sales forecasting solution.

Workflow1InitialState contains *eventDrivenActivity1*, which occurs after the Submit For Approval button is clicked on the custom tab in the Ribbon or the workflow is kicked off manually. *EventDrivenActivity1* contains an event called *onWorkflowActivated1* that retrieves the identities of the salesperson and his manager and sets their respective logon names as the originator and approving users and sets their e-mail addresses for the approval message that is sent. Next we transition into the *Workflow1RequestApprovalState*, which contains three high-level activities. Figure 3-15 shows a detailed view of the state machine diagram for the *stateInitializationActivity1*. You can see that the two activities here are essentially methods, themselves containing code.

In *createTask1*, we create an Approver task and set properties such as title, due date, and who the task is assigned to:

```
private void CreateApproverTask(object sender, EventArgs e)
    {
        this.approverTaskId = Guid.NewGuid();
        this.approverTaskProperties.Title = "Please approve this document";
        this.approverTaskProperties.AssignedTo = this.approverAccount;
        this.approverTaskProperties.Description = this.instructions;
        this.approverTaskProperties.TaskType = 0;
        this.taskDueBy = DateTime.Today.AddDays(5);
        this.approverTaskProperties.DueDate = this.taskDueBy;
```

```
this.approverTaskProperties.SendEmailNotification = false;
this.approverTaskProperties.ExtendedProperties["isApproved"] = "false";
this.approverTaskProperties.ExtendedProperties["isRejected"] = "false";
this.approverTaskProperties.ExtendedProperties["comments"] = "";
this.approverTaskProperties.ExtendedProperties["instructions"] =
    this.instructions;
}
```

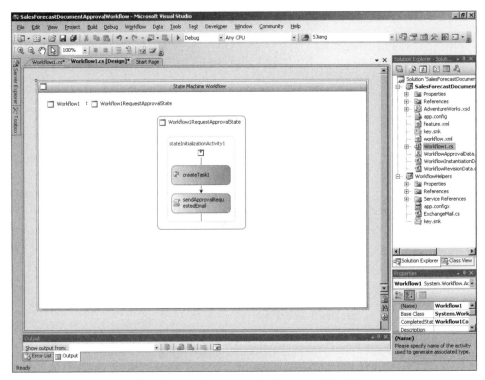

Figure 3-15   State machine diagram for *stateInitializationActivity1* in *Workflow1RequestApprovalState*.

The activity *SendApprovalRequestedEmail,* shown in Listing 3-4, defines the e-mail message to be sent to the approver, retrieves data from the sales forecasting workbook, and builds an attachment on the fly using Open XML. This method is especially interesting because it manipulates the Open XML file format to generate an attachment on the fly using the VSTO *ServerDocument* class.

Listing 3-4   The *SendApprovalRequestedEmail* activity.

```
private void sendApprovalRequestedEmail_ExecuteCode(object sender, EventArgs e)
    {
        // Define the subject
        this.emailSubject =
            string.Format(
                "{0} has requested approval for the document '{1}'",
```

```
              this.originatorName,
              this.workflowProperties.Item.Name);
// Define the body
this.emailBody =
     string.Format(
        "<html>" +
        "    <head>" +
        "        <meta http-equiv='Content-Type' content='text/html;
                    charset=utf-8'/>" +
        "        <style>" +
        "            table.mail" +
        "            {{border-style:none;" +
        "            border-collapse:collapse;" +
        "            font:8pt Tahoma;" +
        "            width:100%}}" +
        "            td.header" +
        "            {{background:#F8F8F9;" +
        "            border:1px solid #E8EAEC;" +
        "            padding:12pt 10px 4pt 10px}}" +
        "            td.body" +
        "            {{padding:12pt 10px 24pt 10px}}" +
        "            td.footer" +
        "            {{border-width:1px;" +
        "            border-style:solid none none none;" +
        "            border-color:#9CA3AD;" +
        "            padding:4pt 10px 4pt 10px}}" +
        "            a" +
        "            {{text-decoration:none}}" +
        "            div.title" +
        "            {{font:16pt Verdana}}" +
        "            div.headertext" +
        "            {{margin:5px 0px 0px 0px}}" +
        "            div.error" +
        "            {{font-weight:bold}}" +
        "            div.comment" +
        "            {{color:#9CA3AD}}" +
        "            span.wfname" +
        "            {{font:bold italic}}" +
        "        </style>" +
        "    </head>" +
        "    <body>" +
        "        <table cellpadding='2' cellspacing='0' class='mail'
                    dir='none'>" +
        "            <tbody>" +
        "                <tr class='header'>" +
        "                    <td class='header'>" +
        "                        <div
                            class='title'>{0}</div>" +
        "                        <br/>" +
        "                            <div
                            class='error'>Due by {1}</div>" +
        "                    </td>" +
        "                </tr>" +
        "                <tr class='body'>" +
        "                    <td class='body' valign='top'>" +
```

```
                "                        <div>{2}</div>" +
                "                    </td>" +
                "                </tr>" +
                "                <tr class='footer'>" +
                "                    <td class='footer'>" +
                "                        <div class='comment'>" +
                "                            To complete this task:" +
                "                            <br/>" +
                "                            <ol>" +
                "                                <li>" +
                "                                    Review <a href='{3}'
                                                    target='_blank'>" +
                "                                        {4}" +
                "                                    </a>." +
                "                                </li>" +
                "                                <li>Perform the specific
                                                    activities required for this
                                                    task.</li>" +
                "                                <li>" +
                "                                    <a href='{5}'
                                                    target='_blank'>Edit this
                                                    task</a> to resubmit the
                                                    document for approval." +
                "                                </li>" +
                "                            </ol>" +
                "                        </div>" +
                "                    </td>" +
                "                </tr>" +
                "            </tbody>" +
                "        </table>" +
                "    </body>" +
                "</html>",
        //Properties.Resources.ChangesRequestedMessageTemplate,
                this.emailSubject,
                this.taskDueBy.ToShortDateString(),
                this.instructions,
                string.Format(
                    "{0}/{1}",
                    this.workflowProperties.Web.Url,
                    this.workflowProperties.Item.Url),
                this.workflowProperties.Item.Name,
                string.Format(
                    "{0}/_layouts/WrkStat.aspx?List={1}&WorkflowInstanceID={2}",
                    this.workflowProperties.Web.Url,
                    this.workflowProperties.ListId.ToString("B"),
                    this.workflowProperties.WorkflowId.ToString("B")));
        // Define the email message
        // If you want to see the real message change the first parameter to
        // "IPM.Note"
        MessageType message =
            ExchangeMail.CreateMessage("IPM.Note.Forecast",
                this.emailSubject,
                BodyTypeType.HTML,
                this.emailBody,
                this.originatorEmail,
```

```
          new string[] { this.approverEmail },
          SensitivityChoicesType.Normal);
//// Create the message request but don't send it yet
CreateItemType emailRequest =
    ExchangeMail.CreateEmailRequest(MessageDispositionType.SaveOnly,
        DistinguishedFolderIdNameType.sentitems, message);
//// Create the message
ExchangeMail emailService =
    new ExchangeMail(new
        Uri("https://mail.litwareinc.com/ews/exchange.asmx"));
CreateItemResponseType createResponse;
emailService.CreateEmail(emailRequest, out createResponse);
ItemIdType messageId = null;
messageId = ExchangeMail.ValidateResponse(createResponse);
// Get the cached data items we need in order to run the SQL Query
// to build one of the attachments
ServerDocument serverDocument = new
  ServerDocument(this.workflowProperties.Item.File.OpenBinary(),
  ".xlsx");
CachedDataHostItem hostItem = serverDocument.CachedData.HostItems
  ["SalesForecastWorkbook.ThisWorkbook"];
CachedDataItem salesPersonIdData = hostItem.CachedData["SalesPersonID"];
CachedDataItem salesTerritoryIdData =
  hostItem.CachedData["SalesTerritoryID"];
CachedDataItem reportDateData = hostItem.CachedData["ReportDate"];
XmlSerializer serializer = new
  XmlSerializer(Type.GetType(salesPersonIdData.DataType));
int salesPersonId = (int)serializer.Deserialize(new
  StringReader(salesPersonIdData.Xml));
serializer = new
  XmlSerializer(Type.GetType(salesPersonIdData.DataType));
int salesTerritoryId = (int)serializer.Deserialize(new
  StringReader(salesTerritoryIdData.Xml));
serializer = new XmlSerializer(Type.GetType(reportDateData.DataType));
DateTime? reportDate = (DateTime?)serializer.Deserialize(new
  StringReader(reportDateData.Xml));
// Get the data from SQL and populate the internal DataSet
AdventureWorks dataSet = GetDocumentData(salesPersonId,
  salesTerritoryId, reportDate.Value);
const int pageSize = 5;
const int pageNumber = 1;
DataView salesForecastView = FilterSalesForecastData(dataSet, pageSize,
  pageNumber);
Uri spreadSheetUri =
    new Uri(
        string.Format(
            "{0}/{1}",
            this.workflowProperties.Web.Url,
            this.workflowProperties.Item.Url));
Uri reportUri =
    new Uri("http://sales.litwareinc.com/salesreports/
    Sales%20Forecast%20Word%20Documents/Forms/AllItems.aspx");
CreateAttachmentType attachmentToCreate = null;
using (MemoryStream stream = new MemoryStream())
{
```

```
                    GenerateCustomXml(
                        stream,
                        dataSet,
                        salesForecastView,
                        reportDate.Value,
                        spreadSheetUri,
                        reportUri,
                        this.instructions);
                    stream.Position = 0;
                    StreamReader reader = new StreamReader(stream);
                    attachmentToCreate =
                        ExchangeMail.CreateFileAttachmentRequest(
                            messageId, "salesdata", "salesdata", "text/xml",
                                "salesdata.xml",
                                Encoding.UTF8.GetBytes(reader.ReadToEnd()));
                }
                // Add attachments
                CreateAttachmentResponseType attachmentResponse;
                emailService.AddAttachment(attachmentToCreate, out attachmentResponse);
                ExchangeMail.ValidateResponse(attachmentResponse);
                // Get the current message state
                messageId =
                  emailService.GetCurrentMessageItemId(attachmentToCreate.ParentItemId);
                // Send the message
                SendItemResponseType sendResponse;
                emailService.SendEmail(messageId, out sendResponse);
                ExchangeMail.ValidateResponse(sendResponse);

                return;
            }
```

Once we finish defining the e-mail message, we use the *ServerDocument* class to retrieve the cached data in the sales forecasting spreadsheet. The *ServerDocument* class allows you to use the Open XML file formats to manipulate the cached data in either an Office Word 2007 file or an Office Excel 2007 file without having to work with the low-level XML. It allows you to define the text within a document—the content in the raw XML tags—as business objects so that you are working with them as properties of classes in a way that gives your data context. If you've ever worked with Open XML, you know that you need to use objects such as *XPath-Navigator* to traverse the nodes and retrieve the information. The code is intensive, validation of the code is difficult, and corruption of files occurs frequently. Working with the *Server-Document* class is a much cleaner and easier way to work with Open XML.

 More Info More discussion about Open XML, the VSTO *ServerDocument* class, and an explanation of this particular code snippet appears in the following section.

What we basically do in the preceding code with the *ServerDocument* class is retrieve the cached data from the sales forecasting spreadsheet to create SQL queries so that we can generate an XML document on the fly with all the sales forecasting data. This document will then be attached to the e-mail message. This XML file will be used to populate the contents of the e-mail message with the forecasting information so that the receiver of the e-mail message does not need a connection to the database to view the e-mail's content.

Figure 3-16 shows the details of the state machine diagram for *eventDrivenActivity2*.

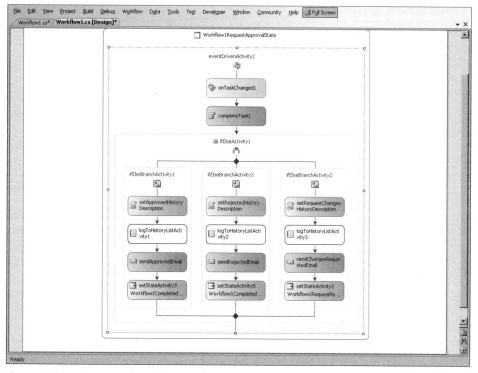

Figure 3-16   State machine diagram for *EventDrivenActivity2*.

Once we send the e-mail message, we hit *eventDrivenActivity2* because we are waiting for the approver to either accept, reject, or request changes to the sales forecast. We make sure to log whatever the result is in the Workflow History list and then send the e-mail back to the salesperson. If we either accept or reject the sales forecast, the workflow is complete. If the approver requests changes, the workflow returns to the *Workflow1RequestReviewState*. In the initialization activity of this state, we create a review task with the title stating that the document has been rejected. *EventDrivenActivity3* in *requestReviewState* looks very much like the *requestApprovalState*, as you can see in the state machine diagram shown in Figure 3-17.

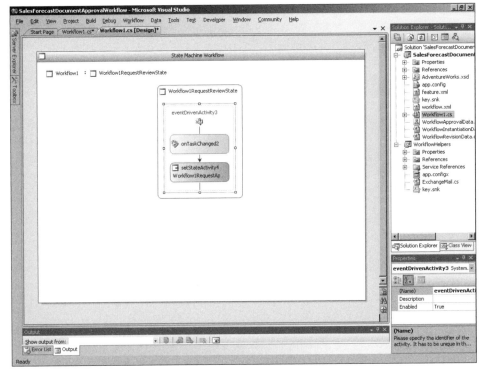

Figure 3-17   State machine diagram for *eventDrivenActivity3* in the *WorkflowRequestReviewState*.

The method *onTaskChanged2* has no code because the salesperson just needs to click the Submit button again and the workflow moves back to the initial reviewer state. At this point, we transition back to *Workflow1RequestApprovalState* and then to *workflowCompletedState*.

Programming Against the New Open XML File Formats

In the 2007 Office system, Word, Excel, and PowerPoint files now act as containers because they are actually compressed zip files. (Just try changing the extension to .zip, and you'll see what I mean.) To an end user, the file still looks like a single item, but to a developer the file is a package of parts, segmented in a logical tree structure and tied together by relationships that you can navigate through. No longer do you have the black box that the binary file format was in previous versions.

Open XML Benefits

So knowing about this new format, what are some of its benefits?

- **Interoperability**   Because of the open standard of the Ecma Open XML file formats, you can perform operations such as generating files from 2007 Office system documents on a non-Microsoft platform. One example is file format manipulation on the Linux platform. Because the file is only XML, an Office Word 2007 document can be programmatically manipulated and, by using XSLT, converted to HTML and published. At the same time, development teams can make use of the J2EE framework by working with the straight XML.

- **Mitigation of file corruption**   Because we now have a segmented architecture, if a part becomes corrupted, the other parts of the package should still be safe. For example, if your style part is corrupted, you will still be able to open your document–it just won't look as nice. Also, corruption tends to occur as a result of truncation. Because we are no longer working only in a binary format, you can mitigate data loss by putting the most important information at the top of the XML files in the package parts.

- **Security**   Security is greatly improved as a result of the segmented architecture. Macros now have their own parts within the package, and it is easy to separate this portion from the content to better manage security issues. This is why we have the new file formats, such as .xlsm, .pptm, and .docm, as well as the template macro-enabled versions. All these file types contain macros.

- **Digital signatures**   Now you have more power over what you sign within a document. You can digitally sign the packages using x.509 certificates, and you can sign all parts of the package, including even the digital signatures themselves. Imagine that as part of a custom workflow that is initiated when a document changes, the workflow's code could crack open the file, review which portions have changed, and then require digital signatures on only those document parts that changed (such as the macro parts if the macros were changed). This separation of the document allows for further granularity in security and certification. There are some very interesting scenarios here.

Open XML Abstraction with VSTO

VSTO abstracts working with Open XML so that you never have to go through the XML and navigate through the tree structure. Support for the 2007 Office system file formats with the *ServerDocument* class enables abstract manipulation of the cached data in the file. Rather than dealing with straight XML, you can work with the business objects to manipulate data within 2007 Office system files, reduce the amount of code you need to write, and avoid dealing with the file corruption issues that you encounter when working with straight XML.

In the sales forecasting solution, Open XML file format manipulation is performed using VSTO to pull cached data out of the sales forecasting spreadsheet to create an XML e-mail attachment on the fly during the custom workflow. The e-mail message sent to the approver can therefore display the sales projections from the database in an offline scenario. This operation is performed by referencing high-level business objects such as *SalesPersonID* and *ReportDate* in a few lines of code rather than having to navigate through all the nodes in the document parts to get to the actual data. This task would normally require a more significant amount of code and be much more complex and error-prone. In the sales forecasting solution, we cached the data and made it available to the *ServerDocument* class by defining it as public and caching in the *ThisWorkbook* class. You can see this implementation in the following code:

```
[Cached()]
public int SalesPersonID = 0;
[Cached()]
public int SalesTerritoryID = 0;
[Cached()]
public DateTime? ReportDate;
[Cached()]
public AdventureWorks SalesForecastData = new AdventureWorks();
[Cached()]
public SalesPersonContext SalesPersonContext = new SalesPersonContext();
```

We access this data in the spreadsheet during the custom workflow. Here is that part of the code again, which retrieves the cached data from the sales forecasting spreadsheet:

```
// Get the cached data items we need in order to run the SQL Query
// to build one of the attachments
ServerDocument serverDocument = new
  ServerDocument(this.workflowProperties.Item.File.OpenBinary(),
  ".xlsx");
CachedDataHostItem hostItem = serverDocument.CachedData.HostItems
  ["SalesForecastWorkbook.ThisWorkbook"];
CachedDataItem salesPersonIdData = hostItem.CachedData["SalesPersonID"];
CachedDataItem salesTerritoryIdData =
  hostItem.CachedData["SalesTerritoryID"];
CachedDataItem reportDateData = hostItem.CachedData["ReportDate"];
XmlSerializer serializer = new
  XmlSerializer(Type.GetType(salesPersonIdData.DataType));
int salesPersonId = (int)serializer.Deserialize(new
  StringReader(salesPersonIdData.Xml));
serializer = new
  XmlSerializer(Type.GetType(salesPersonIdData.DataType));
int salesTerritoryId = (int)serializer.Deserialize(new
  StringReader(salesTerritoryIdData.Xml));
serializer = new XmlSerializer(Type.GetType(reportDateData.DataType));
DateTime? reportDate = (DateTime?)serializer.Deserialize(new
  StringReader(reportDateData.Xml));
```

In the first line of code, we use the *workflowproperties* object to return a byte array from the sales forecast spreadsheet, and we indicate that it is of file type .xlsx. We pass both the byte array and the string ".xlsx" to the parameters of the *ServerDocument* constructor. We need to work with a VSTO workbook to use the *ServerDocument* class, and because the Sales-ForecastWorkbook is a VSTO solution, it has a class called *ThisWorkbook*. The latter is our *HostItem*. Now we create *CachedDataItems* for all that cached data that we defined previously in the *ThisWorkbook* class and retrieve the values. The rest of the code in the method uses those values to serialize the XML data from the database into an XML file and then attach that file to the e-mail message. That code can be seen in the "Workflow" section earlier in the chapter.

Summary

The sales forecasting solution draws together the platform capabilities of the 2007 Office system products and technologies with Visual Studio 2008 as the development tool, integrated with VSTO. For developers, this OBA solution showed how Rapid Application Development was enabled through features such as Excel Services and development tools such as VSTO. The Service Oriented Architecture of the 2007 Office system platform was easily translated to a custom application centered on consuming services from Office SharePoint Server 2007, such as Enterprise Search, which pulled LOB data through from the Business Data Catalog. VSTO provided visual designers for creating the custom user interface and the ability to create custom workflows via state machine diagrams. All of this resulted in a solution that enables users to work within one product while accessing data from multiple systems.

Chapter 4

Provisioning and Securing a Virtual Learning Workspace

–Adam Buenz, Windows SharePoint Services MVP

The Office Business Application (OBA) presented in this chapter consists of several moving pieces that form a framework for building, securing, and extending virtual learning workspaces (VLWs) that are appropriate for universities and academic institutions that deploy the Microsoft Office SharePoint Server 2007 or Windows SharePoint Services 3.0 platform. The virtual workspaces are designed to help students collaborate and communicate on academic assignments. VLWs demonstrate techniques and strategies that can be applied as academic institutions develop and depend more on Web technologies to provide a backbone for connecting students with other students, as well as with instructors and faculty.

Several key elements make up the VLW application, split between three main concepts: automated site provisioning, automated site security provisioning and enforcement, and VLW student-interaction enhancement. The first of these, automated site provisioning, is demonstrated through the use of custom reusable workflow activities. These activities provide building blocks for constructing complete Microsoft Windows SharePoint Services functionality that implements the workflow capabilities of the Windows Workflow Foundation. These activities also introduce some high-level programmatic tasks related to the Windows SharePoint Services security model. Concepts behind the security model will become increasingly important when we explore how to provision Windows SharePoint Services security objects through a SharePoint Feature Receiver.

We will then explore how to build a permission classification workflow that abstracts securable object functionality built into Windows SharePoint Services to easily classify assignment permissions without the intervention of any principals. An implementation of this custom workflow streamlines permissions assignments, removing the need to make any assumptions about the knowledge level of the solution's users and thereby increasing overall usability.

You'll next see how to use a Feature Receiver to provision the content repositories and the security objects required for students to interact with the workspace. The Feature Receiver demonstrates how to provision security concepts such as SharePoint groups and SharePoint roles, as well as document libraries that are based on built-in document content types and custom content types that can be defined in code or in XML files.

In the last sections of the chapter, we'll explore how to extend the site framework by facilitating user activities that are characteristic of a collaborative academic environment. You'll see examples of mechanisms for submitting assignments to VLW libraries and for capturing metadata related to document modifications that provide ease of use to students and provide administrators with insight into assignments students submit. You will also see how to expose some of the extended SharePoint security framework by exploring how to display and manipulate Active Directory information from managed code within a Web Part. You'll see, for example, how to manipulate Active Directory objects such as a directory services password for self-service options that increase environment security by decreasing the possibility of brute-force and human-guessing attacks.

Together these separate pieces form the structure of the VLW solution and allow a SharePoint architect to craft a zero-touch site and security provisioning framework that can provide a large student-user base with intuitive mechanisms for automated site provisioning and security–functionality tailored around the use of individual assignment documents stored in a document library within a VLW.

Figure 4-1 shows an overview of the VLW application. In the sections that follow, I'll describe the different components of this solution in more detail.

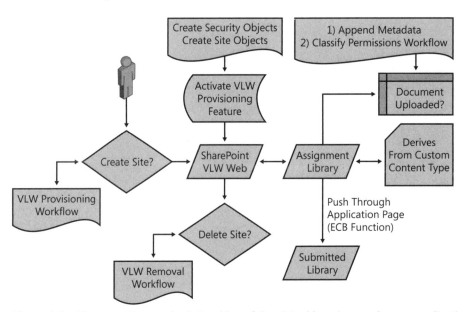

Figure 4-1   The operations and relationships of the virtual learning workspace application.

Software Requirements

You need Microsoft Visual Studio 2005 or later to work with the VLW code files, except for the XML files, most of which are related to deployment and activation mechanisms through the use of the SharePoint Features and solution framework. To use the Visual Studio 2005 designer for the Windows Workflow Foundation to explore the custom activities and opening projects such as the classify permissions workflow (which is based on the sequential workflow project template), you need to download and install the extensions for the Windows Workflow Foundation. If you don't have the extensions installed, you can download the released version from *http://www.microsoft.com/ downloads/details.aspx?familyid=5d61409e-1fa3-48cf-8023-e8f38e709ba6&displaylang=en.*

Workflow templates for use with SharePoint sites are available in the 2007 Microsoft Office System Starter Kit: Enterprise Content Management Starter Kit, which you can download from *http://www.microsoft.com/downloads/details.aspx?FamilyID=38ca6b32-44be-4489-8526-f09c57cd13a5&DisplayLang=en,* and the WSS 3.0 Starter Kit: Workflow Developer Starter Kit for Windows SharePoint Services 3.0, which is available for download at *http://www.microsoft.com/downloads/details.aspx?FamilyID=5ddf902d-95b1-4640-b9e4-45440dc388d9&DisplayLang=en.* (Both starter kits provide the same base templates.)

Building the VLW Workflow Activities

One of the more abstract concepts presented in this application is the building blocks for custom workflows, which are also known as *workflow activities.* Each of the activities in the solution—one to create a site and one to delete a site—inherits from the *Activity* base class from the *System.Workflow.ComponentModel* namespace, which provides the classes and interfaces required to build custom workflows and activities. Rather than inserting code into a workflow itself, it is often advantageous to build reusable actions that you can place into a workflow model so that the behavior the code performs is generically packaged and usable in a variety of workflow circumstances. In addition to having a reusable package, which can be essentially compared to a Microsoft .NET custom control, a developer using the activity is not limited to working with the workflow designer in Visual Studio (provided by the workflow extensions). A developer can also, through the use of a custom .actions file, expose the activity and make individual, unbundled workflows that can be bound to list instances through SharePoint Server 2007 Designer.

Packaging the code with an activity does not limit a developer to a one-time instantiation of the code and only requires that the developer understand the visual surface of the Visual Studio workflow designer, which provides a simple drag-and-drop experience. This also allows an IT professional to use the activity without knowing the underlying plumbing of the custom activity.

A custom activity functions much like a user control within a typical Web development environment, where the plumbing that is offered is hidden from the user but parameters that the user chooses—either supplied by the environment or as literal values—can be assimilated and consumed by the custom activity. The user does not have to know what is actually occurring in the workflow even though the execution, actions, and results are evident when it runs.

To expose the activities on the Visual Studio workflow design surface, you can create a new workflow project (such as a project based on a sequential workflow), and then add the Create or Delete VLW activity Visual Studio projects. Visual Studio will detect the presence of these custom activities. After you've taken these steps, you'll notice that the activities are exposed in the Visual Studio toolbox as components that you can drag onto the workflow designer's surface. You provide the required arguments that are consumed in the property panes. After placing the activities in the design pane in whatever order and with whatever steps you want, you need to set the parameters so that the relevant methods within an activity have the required parameters when the activity is executed.

> **Note**   This is not the only approach that you can take to expose your custom activities within the Visual Studio toolbox. If you would rather manually add the components to the toolbox, you can right-click the toolbox and add a reference to the activity assembly files under the Activities tab.

You can combine custom activities with other out-of-the-box SharePoint activities, for example the popular SendMail activity. In a combination such as this, e-mail messages can be sent when the activity is run successfully so that the message's recipient is aware that a new site has been created. As you will see shortly, within the custom site creation and site deletion activities, I've used such a default activity, specifically the LogToHistoryList activity, which provides the option of writing an entry to the history list of the workflow instance.

You can see the parameters that the activities use in the properties pane of the Visual Studio workflow design surface when you select the activity, which accepts parameters similar to a user control. After you set the properties, you can deploy the workflow consuming the custom activities as a bundled solution, activated most often through the use of a SharePoint Feature and deployed through a bundled SharePoint solution file (.wsp) so that associated files are distributed across a SharePoint server farm through the relevant SharePoint timer jobs.

Activities for Creating and Deleting Sites

The create VLW activity generates a new SharePoint Web (an *SPWeb* object) controlled through the parameters supplied by the SharePoint administrator or SharePoint workflow designer. In this activity, you can see examples of programmatic site provisioning and how to leverage workflows within SharePoint for automating business tasks. The parameters required for the site to be provisioned are similar to the arguments required when you create a typical SharePoint site with code; however, because we are building a zero-touch framework, they are supplied instead to the activity through parameters, either when the activity is added to the workflow design surface or through the SharePoint .actions file *<Parameters>* element. The custom activity uses the following parameters:

■ **URL of the parent web**   This parameter provides guidance to the activity that will be consumed in a workflow about where the subweb (*SPWeb* object) will be created. This string is required to set the site context appropriately, similar to setting up a site context reference with a statement such as

```
using (SPSite site = new SPSite("http://server")
```

The *using* statement allows the code to adhere to proper object disposal standards. The *using* statement also ensures that resources are cleaned up in the most timely manner possible.

- **Template ID**   Because provisioning a new *SPWeb* object requires a template on which provisioning is modeled, a template ID is required that will determine elements such as the site's style, images to support its design, Web Part pages, Web Parts, and types of various custom functionality. Within the create VLW activity, a custom method (*HarvestWebTemplate*) retrieves the templates that are applicable to site creation. You will see that this method iterates through an *SPWebTemplateCollection,* which inherits from *SPBaseCollection,* to select a template for use during the site provisioning process.

- **Site title**   You use this parameter to set the title of the site so that it is familiar to users navigating to it and using it. This property cannot be set blank and cannot contain the characters that SharePoint does not allow. (You can find this list of characters at *http://www.microsoft.com/technet/windowsserver/sharepoint/V2/fsdoclib.mspx#EMCAC*). The most common of these illegal characters are #, %, &, *, {, }, \, :, <, >, ?, /, and +. If necessary, you can use *SPUrlUtility.IndexOfIllegalCharInUrlLeafName* to strip out illegal characters, which allows you to build an index that you can use with a *Remove* method against the new SharePoint site's name to handle illegal characters.

- **URL of the site being created**   This parameter determines where the Web will be created within the Windows SharePoint Services environment. This parameter is required to set the location where the Web will be created and is a site-relative URL.

- **Site description**   This parameter describes the VLW to be created, passed in as a literal string value. This value will typically be decorated by the administrator in a fashion that accurately describes the purpose of the VLW being created. You can use replacement variables to make this process more intelligent or automated in a site provisioning design pattern.

- **Administrator of the site**   For the site being created, this parameter indicates the relevant administrative value equivalent to an *SPUser* object. People often find that this property should be the SharePoint service account because it will gain full control over the SharePoint site being created, thereby providing a good fallback account. It is important to note that no matter what, some object has to have full control over the SharePoint site, as is the case with all SharePoint securable objects. It is often best not to use the application pool account for this administrative account because if you use impersonation in later development efforts, such as an event receiver, in which you harness current SharePoint user objects (through a statement such as *SPUser curUser = web.CurrentUser*), you might need to make dual site references to get the appropriate impersonated context and be sure that you are getting the original user reference and not the reference to the application pool account.

The code that defines the create VLW activity includes relevant security attributes so that it can run with elevated privileges, which is why the method that does the actual processing is abstracted from the main execution method, an approach that is meant to alleviate any security issues that might arise with the code running under a context in which it would otherwise not be able to perform actions. The structure presented increases readability, as opposed to using a delegate call with inline code containing the relevant execution method. Using the approach I've taken, the subset of code that executes runs instead under the context of the SharePoint system account. When you are establishing your site reference, you can also pass in an *SPUserToken* binary object representing a token that identifies the authentication process (such as the identification information and the relevant domain membership) applied to a user as an argument. You can perform this operation through a principal object such as the application pool account by using the static *WindowsIdentity.Impersonate* overload and passing in the *System.IntPtr.Zero* as a token. Instead of an orthodox *using* statement when establishing site context, you can do something like the following (after instigating the relevant impersonation code):

```
SPUserToken token = SPWeb.AllUsers[WindowsIdentity.GetCurrent().Name].UserToken;
```

After the SharePoint user token has been established, you can continue by establishing the site context and using the token as a parameter, which opens the site context under the account that has been called for impersonation. After you have established the new site reference with the use of this token, you can create objects within the context of the impersonated user, as shown here:

```
new SPSite(Site, token)
```

The Delete VLW activity allows a site to be deleted in whatever manner the workflow designer chooses, depending on where the activity block is placed in context with other activities and workflow logic on the workflow design surface. The designer can opt for the activity to branch with whatever logic the designer decorates the workflow with. The delete activity is slimmer than the site creation activity. It requires fewer parameters because we are targeting an *SPWeb* object for removal, which makes objects such as a site administrator declaration unimportant. The only parameter required for the Delete VLW activity is the URL of the Web object to be deleted. You will notice that this value is passed to establish the site context in a manner similar to the approach used in the site creation activity because we have to reference the parent site collection.

A Look at clsCreateVLW.cs

The file clsCreateVLW.cs includes references that are needed for activity development support, including *System.Workflow.ComponentModel* and *Microsoft.SharePoint.Workflow*. In the first part of the code, we declare the namespaces that we will use:

```
using System;
using System.Collections;
using System.ComponentModel;
using System.Workflow.ComponentModel;
using System.Workflow.ComponentModel.Compiler;
```

```
using Microsoft.SharePoint;
using Microsoft.SharePoint.Administration;
using Microsoft.SharePoint.Utilities;
using Microsoft.SharePoint.Workflow;
using Microsoft.SharePoint.WorkflowActions;

namespace oba.Workflows
{
}
```

Next, we declare our main activity class, inheriting from the Windows Workflow Foundation *System.Workflow.ComponentModel.Activity* base class. When you inherit in this way, you are in essence designing a base activity for consumption within your workflow because the activity is a building block for a complete workflow solution. This activity can be made use of either in the workflow designer in Visual Studio or in SharePoint Designer (with some other modifications, such as creating an .actions file so that SharePoint Designer is aware of the parameters that are going to be used when binding the workflow to a specific list instance). Following the namespace references, class declaration, and inheritance decorations, the code defines several properties that correspond to the parameters used to create the site that were discussed previously.

```
public class clsCreateVLW : Activity
    {
        public static DependencyProperty vlwWebAdministratorProperty;
        private ActivityExecutionContext ExecContext;
        private string vlwDescription;
        private string vlwParentWeb;
        private string vlwSite;
        private string vlwTemplateID;
        private string vlwUrl;
        private string vlwWebTitle;
```

Execution Parameters

Some of the direct context (execution parameters such as those for getting the Web object or list context) are commented out in the class file. Although these parameters are special and specific to getting the context of the workflow execution, the activities are presented generically in the code and therefore don't consume these properties. These parameters allow you to perform operations such as accessing the current workflow context instance, the list bound to the workflow's GUID, and the corresponding list GUID for which the workflow is associated. These objects would be important if you tailored the activities to be associated with a list item. For example, you would use create an *SPList* object by using a statement such as the following to get the list that is associated with the workflow:

```
SPList list = __Context.Web.Lists[new Guid(__ListId
```

The way that the templates are harvested (which is discussed shortly) could be modified by a statement such as

```
SPWebTemplateCollection templates = __Context.Site.GetCustomWebTemplates.
```

You would also get the specific *SPListItem* object to which the workflow is associated through a statement such as

```
SPListItem Item = list.Items[__ListItem - 1]
```

You could then add the site by using the same execution parameters:

```
SPWeb newVLWFromList = __Context.Web.Webs.Add(<parameters>).
```

You can use the same approach when executing the VLW delete method. However, you would use the *Webs.Delete* method. The activities presented in this chapter are kept as generic as possible, but you could extend them to create sites by simply altering these properties.

We next declare a static constructor for the activity class that will be used to initialize some class members. I've taken this approach because when the activity class is called the first time, the static data members will be initialized. This is helpful when building activities for use with a SharePoint site because it is common that the value of one static member depends on the value of another static member that has already been declared within the activity class. Because we are not instantiating any member fields, we can leave the instance constructor empty. The Common Language Runtime (CLR) will create a blank constructor when the code is initialized anyway, so we can just as well provide our class with a constructor for clarity and for readability of the code.

```
static clsCreateVLW()
{
    vlwWebAdministratorProperty =
    DependencyProperty.Register("vlwWebAdministrator", typeof(string),
      typeof(clsCreateVLW));
// These execution parameters are related to the section that
// was previously discussed
    //__ContextProperty = DependencyProperty.Register("__Context",
    //    typeof(WorkflowContext), typeof(clsCreateVLW));
    //__ListIdProperty = DependencyProperty.Register("__ListId",
    //    typeof(string), typeof(clsCreateVLW));
    //__ListItemProperty = DependencyProperty.Register("__ListItem",
    //    typeof(int), typeof(clsCreateVLW));
}
Public clsCreateVLW()
{
}
```

We next declare the property that allows the specification of the Web administrator who will be assigned to the site being created by the activity. (Remember that some principal must have full control over any securable SharePoint object at all times.) This information is important later in the code when we begin to explore SharePoint security objects like principals (an *SPUser* object).

```
[Browsable(true)]
[DesignerSerializationVisibilityAttribute
    (DesignerSerializationVisibility.Visible)]
[ValidationOption(ValidationOption.Required)]
public string vlwWebAdministrator
{
    get { return ((string) GetValue(vlwWebAdministratorProperty)); }
    set { SetValue(vlwWebAdministratorProperty, value); }
}
```

Next the code defines member properties, such as one for the value of the parent Web string that will be created when using this workflow and the property for the VLW Web string.

```
[DesignerSerializationVisibility(DesignerSerializationVisibility.Visible),
    ValidationOption(ValidationOption.Required), Browsable(true)]
public string VLWParentWeb
{
    get { return vlwParentWeb; }
    set { vlwParentWeb = value; }
}
[DesignerSerializationVisibility(DesignerSerializationVisibility.Visible),
    ValidationOption(ValidationOption.Required), Browsable(true)]
public string VLWSite
{
    get { return vlwSite; }
    set { vlwSite = value; }
}
```

Then the code defines a member property that declares which template should be used when creating this VLW. This template is usually just an orthodox team site; however, you can acquire a reference to a custom template (one that is not a site definition, but instead saved and provisioned through the use of an .STP file using *GetCustomWebTemplates*) or a site definition (an orthodox SharePoint site using *GetWebTemplates*) in the template collection. Regardless of which method is used, it returns an *SPWebTemplateCollection* object to build a site.

```
[DesignerSerializationVisibility(DesignerSerializationVisibility.Visible),
    ValidationOption(ValidationOption.Required), Browsable(true)]
public string VLWTemplateId
{
    get { return vlwTemplateID; }
    set { vlwTemplateID = value; }
}
```

Other properties declared include those for the title of the VLW, the URL for the VLW, and the VLW's description.

The code overrides the *Execute* method, which also occurs in the delete VLW workflow activity. (You will see more details later in the chapter.) We also ensure that the arguments passed to the method are not null references (in this case the execution context, which represents the state of the object along with the relevant parameters of the object in its instance). This execution context, also known as the Activity Execution Context (AEC), is triggered when the *Start* method of the activity is called. The benefit of the AEC is that it lets you spawn or destroy child activities as they occur or, if the parent activity is finished with its relevant work, the parent activity can close itself, assuming that the child activities have all completed their work so that the integrity of the activities is maintained.

```
protected override ActivityExecutionStatus Execute(ActivityExecutionContext
    executionContext)
{
    if (executionContext == null)
        throw new ArgumentNullException("executionContext");
    SPSecurity.CodeToRunElevated elevatedCode = new
    SPSecurity.CodeToRunElevated(elevatedSubCode);
    SPSecurity.RunWithElevatedPrivileges(elevatedCode);
    return ActivityExecutionStatus.Closed;
}
```

The *Execute* method is an overridden method that is dispatched by the CLR. I'll describe the *Execute* method in more detail later in the chapter when we look at the Delete VLW activity. The activity is expected to perform any cleanup work that is required prior to its transition to the *Closed* state. If your cleanup work is short, you can do it and return the *ActivityExecution-Status.Closed* state (assuming that there is no spawning of related child activities). If the cleanup work is more extensive, return *ActivityExecutionStatus.Faulting* and wait for the required callbacks (such as exceptions as they are thrown within the current instance) before ultimately returning *Closed*, as shown in the following code.

```
protected override ActivityExecutionStatus
    HandleFault(ActivityExecutionContext executionContext,
    Exception exception)
{
    if (executionContext == null)
        throw new ArgumentNullException("executionContext");
    if (exception == null)
        throw new ArgumentNullException("exception");

    ISharePointService oInstance =
        ((ISharePointService) executionContext.GetService(typeof
            (ISharePointService)));
    If (oInstance != null)
        oInstance.LogToHistoryList(WorkflowInstanceId,
            SPWorkflowHistoryEventType.WorkflowComment, 0,
            TimeSpan.MinValue, string.Empty,
            string.Format("Failed to create the VLW
            web in the SharePoint instance. {0}",
            exception.Message), string.Empty);

    return ActivityExecutionStatus.Closed;
}
```

Note   You could optionally implement the *FaultHandlersActivity* directly from the Visual Studio Toolbox. If you have multiple child activities in the overall workflow, you can use the *FaultHandlers* activity within the aggregate workflow. An important item to note regarding the use of the *FaultHandlers* activity is that although you can have more than one *FaultHandler*, they cannot have the same *FaultType*.

We use the *SPWebTemplate* object to obtain a site definition or a site template (in our case, the VLW site definition). This custom method, named *HarvestWebTemplate*, is used to retrieve the relevant site definition and then instantiate a new VLW. This is an advanced approach for getting a template—using an intelligent loop. When broken down, the approach is similar to the following code, although slightly more extended. Although this code retrieves an *SPWeb-Template* object, it does not provide the type of granular result that we require for the custom activity to function—it demonstrates well a proof of concept for the targeted result.

```
SPWebTemplateCollection myTemplateCollection =
    site.[GetCustomWebTemplates]or [GetWebTemplates]([language ID](1033 for
    English));
SPWebTemplate webTemplate = myTemplateCollection[strTemplateName];
```

The code for the *HarvestWebTemplate* method is shown in Listing 4-1. The method is declared a static method because we are offering instances of the *HarvestWebTemplate* method and are invoking only the one concrete definition of *HarvestWebTemplate*.

Listing 4-1   The *HarvestWebTemplate* method.

```
private static SPWebTemplate HarvestWebTemplate(SPSite site, uint language,
    string templateId)
{
    if (site == null)
        throw new ArgumentNullException("site");
    if (templateId == null)
        throw new ArgumentNullException("templateId");

    SPWebTemplate curWebTemplate = ((SPWebTemplate) null);

    SPWebTemplateCollection curTemplateCollection =
        site.GetWebTemplates(language);

    if (curTemplateCollection != null)
        foreach (SPWebTemplate iterateTemplate in ((IEnumerable)
            curTemplateCollection))
        {
            if (iterateTemplate != null)

                if (iterateTemplate.Name == templateId)
                {
                    curWebTemplate = iterateTemplate;
                    break;
                }
        }
```

```
        if (curWebTemplate == null)
        {
            curTemplateCollection = site.GetCustomWebTemplates(language);
            if (curTemplateCollection != null)

                foreach (SPWebTemplate customTemplate in ((IEnumerable)
                    curTemplateCollection))
                {
                    if (customTemplate != null)

                        if (customTemplate.Name == templateId)
                        {
                            curWebTemplate = customTemplate;
                            break;
                        }
                }
        }

        return curWebTemplate;
}
```

The last section of code in clsCreateVLW.cs shows some of the programming related to the Windows SharePoint Services security model and the site provisioning methods. The code includes references to a number of the SharePoint security objects, including *SPRoleAssignment* and *SPRoleDefinition*. The code performs some preliminary operations (see the next section for additional details) and then checks whether the administrator property for the site is null or empty—we must be sure that we have this value so that a principal is assured to have control over a securable SharePoint object at all times.

```
if (string.IsNullOrEmpty(vlwWebAdministrator))
{
    if (web.Webs != null)
    using (web.Webs.Add(virtualLearningURL, virtualLearningTitle,
    virtualLearningDescription, web.Language, vlwTemplate, false, false))
    {
      return;
    }
}
```

We then set up a new *using* statement for the *Webs.Add* method with the relevant arguments, set the *webadminstrator* property to a string, and check whether the value of this property is null. If it is, we exit the loop.

```
using (SPWeb vlwWeb = web.Webs.Add(virtualLearningURL, virtualLearningTitle,
    virtualLearningDescription, web.Language, vlwTemplate, true, false))
{
    string admin = vlwWebAdministrator;
    if (admin != null)
    {
```

We need to also set the principal information. The *SPPrincipalInfo* object is an important concept in SharePoint because it allows you to get all sorts of information about a user within your SharePoint environment. You can even combine it with nongeneric collections through the use of the *IList* interface so that you can build indexing functions that allow you to search through the relevant principals. You can further refine functionality such as this by using *SPrincipal* enumerations that allow you to define what you want to search for in more detail, executing against a specific type such as whether the return value you want is a SharePoint user (*SPPrincipalType.User*) or SharePoint group (*SPPrincipalType.SharePointGroup*), to name a few. You can also define the source for where the search is targeted by using the *SPPrincipal-Source* enumeration. This lets you define a particular source, such as a Windows source (*SPPrincipalSource.Windows*), or search everything (*SPPrincipalSource.All*). To make use of these enumerations as an example, you can use the following code:

```
IList<SPPrincipalInfo> PrincipalInfo = SPUtility.SearchPrincipals();
```

> **Tip**   Don't discount the *SPUtility* class. You will find that it includes several helpful methods that otherwise would have to be manually coded (and you may have manually already created!), such as transferring to a branded SharePoint error or success page (very useful when you want to transfer a user in a manner that is similar to how Windows SharePoint Services handles operations), sending simple e-mail messages, sending access requests, and others.

Here we are using the *ResolveWindowsPrincipal* method from the *SPUtility* class to resolve the principal identity. This method takes the relevant Web application, an input string value (in this case the site administrator), the principal type (see the previous paragraph for a more detailed explanation), and an indication of whether you are supplying the input as an e-mail string only (which is uncommon but is included as an option and is needed to fill all the arguments for the method). You can see that we are defining the source using the type enumeration by defining the *All* type. However, you could modify this if you want to resolve the identity more narrowly, such as *DistributionList*, *None*, *SecurityGroup*, *SharePointGroup*, or *User*.

```
SPPrincipalInfo PrincipalInfo =
    SPUtility.ResolveWindowsPrincipal(((SPWebApplication) null),
        admin,SPPrincipalType.All, false);
if (PrincipalInfo != null)
{
```

We then create an *SPRoleAssignment* object to define the role assignments for the administrator. We pass in parameters during this process, such as the name, display name, and the e-mail address of the administrator, which are gathered from the *SPPrincipal* object information that was previously resolved. This information is available through the various properties that are exposed through this object. (We are passing in *string. Empty* in the last parameter because this is reserved for inserting notes about the user, which you may or may not populate at your organization.) We also ensure that we have role definitions that we can bind the new role assignment to and use the *GetByType* method (using a specified type from the *SPRoleType* enumeration to return the result from an *SPRoleDefinitionCollection*), passing in the *SPRole-Type.Administrator*, to build a reference to the administrator role definition. We define a new *SPRoleDefinitionBindingCollection* object using the collection of role definition bindings for the principal role assignment, ensure that the role definition is not null (as a guard clause), and then use the *SPRoleDefinitionBindingCollection.Add* method to add the specified role definition to the binding collection object.

```
SPRoleAssignment PrincipalRoleAssignment = New
    SPRoleAssignment(PrincipalInfo.LoginName, PrincipalInfo.Email,
    PrincipalInfo.DisplayName, string.Empty);

if (vlwWeb.RoleDefinitions != null)
{
    SPRoleDefinition adminRoleDefinition = vlwWeb.RoleDefinitions.GetByType
        (SPRoleType.Administrator);

    SPRoleDefinitionBindingCollection bindingCollection =
        PrincipalRoleAssignment.RoleDefinitionBindings;

    if (adminRoleDefinition != null)
        bindingCollection.Add(adminRoleDefinition);
}

if (vlwWeb.RoleAssignments != null)
```

At the end, we use *web.RoleAssignments.Add(roleAssignment)* to add the role assignment to the role collection and update all the changes that we have made using the *SPWeb.Update* method. Calling *Update* commits the changes to the database and ensures that the interface instance that is being passed in is not null. Then we use the *LogToHistoryList* method from the *ISharePointService* interface in the *Microsoft.SharePoint.Workflow* namespace to commit the changes that this activity has made. Because execution of the activity can be considered successful, we can log this success to the history list using the *ISharePointService.LogToHistoryList* method so that the SharePoint administrator is aware that the operation was completed successfully. If any exceptions have occurred during this process, we have to negate the Web creation and back out of the operation, delete the possibly partially created Web, and log our failure to create the necessary *SPWeb* object using the *ISharePointService.LogToHistoryList* method. Logging this result to the history list allows a level of auditing so that the administrator is consistently aware of the successes and failures that have occurred in this activity and the current state of the activity within a custom workflow.

```
                vlwWeb.RoleAssignments.Add(PrincipalRoleAssignment);
            }
        }
        vlwWeb.Update();
    }
}

    oInstance.LogToHistoryList(base.WorkflowInstanceId,
        SPWorkflowHistoryEventType.WorkflowComment, 0, TimeSpan.MinValue,
        string.Empty,
```

```
            string.Format("A New VLW Was created at: {0}", virtualLearningURL),
            string.Empty);
    }
  }
}

catch (Exception exception)
{
    if (virtualLearningURL.Length > 0)
    {
        using (SPSite site = new SPSite(vlwParentWeb))
        {
            using (SPWeb web = site.OpenWeb())
            {
                if (web.Webs != null)
                    web.Webs.Delete(virtualLearningURL);
            }
        }
    }
    if (oInstance != null)
        oInstance.LogToHistoryList(base.WorkflowInstanceId,
            SPWorkflowHistoryEventType.WorkflowComment, 0,
            TimeSpan.MinValue, string.Empty,
            string.Format("Failed to create the new VLW. {0}", exception.Message),
            string.Empty);
    }
  }
  }
}
```

A Look at clsDeleteVLW.cs

Much of the code for the delete VLW activity is the same or similar to the VLW site creation activity in terms of required objects. The main method calls, however, are reversed because we are removing an *SPWeb* object as opposed to adding a new *SPWeb* object. The override of the *Execute* method, which represents the entry point to the custom activity and is necessary for the workflow engine to know what to execute when the activity runs, is also of interest here. It contains a reference call to the *CodeToRunElevated* delegate, with a constructor call that adheres to the method name that is defined later in the class file. You could perform this operation within an inline delegate method wrap without extracting any methods and run the code with the necessary permissions, but following the architecture I've outlined provides a higher degree of readability, which makes it easier to extend the code later because code clutter is reduced.

We also run the activity code with Full Control rights by using *RunWithElevatedPrivileges*, which will default to using the SharePoint\System account regardless of the execution rights of the user to which this activity workflow instance is bound. I've taken this approach to resolve any security problems that might arise. It allows the application's feature receiver to be executed by any user because the subset of code that will be called will not have to adhere to stringent security criteria. After the subset is called, we also have to call *ActivityExecution-*

Status.Closed, which specifies that the activity is finished with its custom code execution and the next activity can be called in the workflow execution chain—or the workflow can exit out.

```
protected override ActivityExecutionStatus Execute(ActivityExecutionContext
    ExecutionContext)
    {
    if (ExecutionContext == null)
    throw new ArgumentNullException("ExecutionContext");

    ExecContext = ExecutionContext;

    SPSecurity.CodeToRunElevated elevatedCode = new
        SPSecurity.CodeToRunElevated(ElevatedSubCode);

    SPSecurity.RunWithElevatedPrivileges(elevatedCode);

    return ActivityExecutionStatus.Closed;
    }
```

Listing 4-2 shows the *ElevatedSubCode* method. This method contains the code that runs with elevated privileges. The method gets a reference to both the site and Web objects with *using* statements so that we ensure that we are using objects that can be disposed of. We use a character array to construct parameters that will be used when building the URL for the site to be deleted. This approach makes the most sense because we are using Unicode characters to construct the URL.

We then construct the URL of the Web object that is going to be deleted with the *Delete* method and format a *string out* to do this. The output of this operation will be consumed later, so it is best to put this portion in a console application to check whether the output that is constructed is well formed. You could also write this line in a fashion similar to the following if you wanted to build some of the code lines together as opposed to splitting the declarations:

```
string constructedUrl = (web.ServerRelativeUrl.TrimEnd(new char[] { '/' }) + "/" +
    this.webToDeleteUrl).Trim(new char[] { '/' });
```

We then start to build out the site scheduled for deletion in a string that consumes our character arrays, taking in the property arguments as we've declared them. We ensure that the *AllWebs* property is available and is doing what it is supposed to be doing, which allows us access to the collection of all Web sites that are contained within the site collection and required for the VLW site teardown to occur. We then make sure that the URL that we are passing into the *Delete* method is there; otherwise, we should retrace our steps and exit out. The *Delete* method simply takes the URL that should be deleted as a parameter. We also check whether the instance is not null. If this instance is not null, we should write something to the workflow history list. In this message, we should include some of the basic information about what the workflow has achieved and pass in a little string that informs the user of what action has taken effect, along with the relevant time values that relate to the context of this workflow.

Listing 4-2   The *ElevatedSubCode* method in clsDeleteVLW.cs.

```
private void ElevatedSubCode()
{
    ISharePointService oInstance = ((ISharePointService)
        ExecContext.GetService(typeof (ISharePointService)));

    using (SPSite site = new SPSite(strVlwDeleteUrl))
    {
        using (SPWeb web = site.OpenWeb())
        {
            char[] achPrefixSlash = new char[] {'/'};
            char[] achSuffixSlash = new char[] {'/'};

            if (web.ServerRelativeUrl != null)
            {
                string strConstructedUrl = (string.Format("{0}/{1}",
                    web.ServerRelativeUrl.TrimEnd(achPrefixSlash),
                    strVlwDeleteUrl)).Trim(achSuffixSlash);

                if (strConstructedUrl != null)
                    site.AllWebs.Delete(strConstructedUrl);
            oInstance.LogToHistoryList(base.WorkflowInstanceId,
                SPWorkflowHistoryEventType.WorkflowComment, 0,
                TimeSpan.MinValue, string.Empty, string.Format
                ("The VLW at: \'{0}\' was removed from the VLW
                deletion activity.", strConstructedUrl), string.Empty);
            }
        }
    }
}
```

Now that you have automated the site creation and deletion actions by using the activities within a custom workflow of your own design, you can report on and audit the creation and destruction of *SPWeb* objects by building a simple tree view control in a stand-alone application such as a WinForm or in a Web Part that displays a representation of your current site structure, showing each current site title property as a *TreeNode* object. The code would look like this with a WinForm:

```
private static void GetSitesForTreeView(TreeNode ParentTreeNode, string url)
    {
        SPWebCollection webCollection = new SPSite(url).OpenWeb().Webs;
        try
        {
            foreach (SPWeb web in  webCollection)
            {
                TreeNode node  = new TreeNode();
                node.Text = web.Title;
                ParentTreeNode.Nodes.Add(node);
```

```
              if (web.Webs.Count != 0)
              {
                  node.Nodes.Add("");
              }
          }
      }
      catch (Exception exception)
      {
        // Add Corporate Exception Handling Logic
      }
  }
```

We will see how to extend this TreeView further in the next section to query security properties, such as whether the current site objects inherit permissions.

Set Permission Classification Workflow

The way that the create and delete VLW activities function is different from the way that the classify permissions workflow is designed. The classify permissions workflow operates in a simpler fashion, whereby the code behind it is placed directly within the workflow code files. I've used this approach because we are not going to use the classification code actions in more than one workflow instance, and although the properties of the workflow could be ported to custom activity properties, they are globally defined, so wrapping the code with a generic wrapper is not warranted. The workflow does not require any sort of interaction by the user; it simply needs to be deployed and instantiated.

Managing permissions for a specific document library and related Windows SharePoint Services securable objects can be difficult and quickly become unmanageable, particularly if you have an approach that you want to implement consistently across a specific instance of Windows SharePoint Services. You can, however, use well-defined metadata within the document library, coupled with a custom workflow, to build a classification scheme for permissions that applies permissions with minimal end-user intervention. (You often define a column such as this within a custom content type by declaring the relevant *<field ref>* attribute, which is a method used later within the VLW solution.) This approach provides for automatic assignment of permissions regardless of whether the user has any experience managing securable objects within Windows SharePoint Services. It requires instead that the user specify only some familiar metadata that can be used to relate and then assign the permissions. (If you want, you can set this metadata as a required field within the SharePoint site's user interface to ensure that permissions are maintained and consistently assigned.) For a student-based system in which users might not be interested in investing time to understand the technology behind permissions assignment, it makes sense to create a workflow for the SharePoint site that can be associated with the assignment library and looks at metadata for permission classification and assignment. The field that harnesses the required metadata is placed within a custom content type, which, as you will see shortly, is used when the custom feature receiver creates the relevant site repository.

The set permission classification workflow demonstrates several programmatic Windows SharePoint Services tasks that are performed when working with securable objects within the Windows SharePoint Services framework. When using the classification permission workflow, the developer requires some static variables for declaration by the workflow to execute correctly, as they are read-only constants that should not be mutable because they are globally true. For example, we are directly specifying a permissions list through the use of the global *permsList* field, a classification column through the use of the *classificationColumn* field, and the column that holds the group values through the *groupsColumn* field. The remaining public fields used by this workflow are fairly standard for custom workflows. We need to declare a new workflow ID for the workflow engine run time to assign to this workflow instance when it is instantiated, for example.

The code does most of its work in the *SPSecurity.CodeToRunElevated* method, which simply represents the subset of code that runs under privileges different from the current user's. This allows us to not have to specify a custom impersonation class to be consumed by this piece. Instead, it can directly assimilate the privileges and permissions of the SharePoint\System account so that when a new workflow instance is initiated, it runs with heightened privileges to avoid any permissions problems associated while referencing the necessary lists.

We first set up our activation method to run the elevated subset of code. The code makes a reference to the SharePoint site collection (*SPSite*) within a *using* statement—again to adhere to proper object disposal—and uses the same approach when establishing a reference to the Windows SharePoint Services Web (*SPWeb* object). Before proceeding, we ensure that the *permList* read-only field is not null. (We are making this field read-only because it will consistently take the same string value, so it does not make sense to make it mutable.) If the field is null, we should exit out of the method because the field is required by the workflow. (Because the field is declared within the workflow, it should never be null. However, if you are making your field selection dynamic, you should use a null-checking guard clause to ensure that the column reference can be harnessed by the code so that all objects are properly created.) We then create a new *SPList* object to represent the permission list that plays an intrinsic role in this workflow. We also create an *SPListItem* object that holds the item that this workflow is instantiating. The code uses a *foreach* loop to iterate through the list items in the permission list to match permissions in relation to the permissions classification. We also build in a conditional test to see whether the permission item in the classification column is equivalent to the item classification.

We create an *SPGroup* object that will use the declarative group items that are placed within the relevant site columns and check whether the group previously declared, which will be passed in, is null.

Then we create an *SPRoleAssignment* object to define the role assignment (which is the same as a permission level), taking the group as a parameter. We check whether the permission column is equivalent to Allow-Edit, and if the column is, we define a single role definition with the *SPRoleDefinition* object. We can qualify role definitions by using a *GetByType* method and the *SPRoleType* enumeration to define a Contributor because this role has the right to edit a specific securable object within a SharePoint site.

We then use the *Add* method for *RoleDefinitionBindings*, which provides a collection of the available role definition bindings that we can add the role assignment to. The code checks whether the permission column is equivalent to Read-Only, and if it is, we define a single role definition with the *SPRoleDefinition* object. Again, we can qualify role definitions by using a *GetByType* method and using the *SPRoleType* enumeration to define a Reader. The code also checks whether the assignment has unique role assignments (whether it is currently inheriting from its parent object). If it is, we break the inheritance so that we can apply our role changes. By passing in *true* to *BreakRoleInheritance*, we are saying to stamp the current permissions. If we set this to *false*, it would wipe all the permissions and essentially require us to start from scratch.

Checking Inheritance State

The Windows SharePoint Services object model includes several support constructs to check the inheritance state. If you aren't sure whether a SharePoint securable object has unique role assignments, you can test your environment in small reporting applications that populate a label control using the *HasUniqueRoleAssignments* Boolean property, which tells you whether the object, such as a site, has unique inheritance. We can supplement this by using the *FirstUniqueAncestorWeb* property to get the first site that has unique permissions. By coupling a label control with the *TreeView* control described earlier for site auditing, you can quickly build inheritance auditing using code such as the following:

```
private Label lblDisplayInherited;
private bool SecurityForWebIsUnique;
if (SelectedWeb.HasUniqueRoleAssignments)
        {
            lblDisplayInherited.Text = string.Format("Security is not inherited
                For Web {0}", SelectedWeb.Title);
            SecurityForWebIsUnique = true;
        }
        else
        {
            lblDisplayInherited.Text = string.Format("Security for web: {0} is
                inherited from: {1}", SelectedWeb.Title,
                SelectedWeb.FirstUniqueAncestorWeb.Title);
            SecurityForWebIsUnique = false;
        }
```

Finally, we add the role to the *RoleDefinitionBindings*, which essentially is a collection of role definitions for a specific role assignment. Listing 4-3 shows the method.

Listing 4-3   The *CodeToRunElevated* method from the classify permissions workflow.

```
private void onWorkflowActivated_Invoked(object sender,
ExternalDataEventArgs e)
{
    SPSecurity.RunWithElevatedPrivileges(CodeToRunElevated);
}


private void CodeToRunElevated()
{
    SPSite sites = new SPSite(spSite);

    SPWeb web = sites.OpenWeb();

    SPList permList = web.Lists[permsList];
    SPListItem newItem = workflowProperties.Item;

    string itemClassification = newItem[classificationColumn].ToString();

    foreach (SPListItem permListItem in permList.Items)
    {
        if (permListItem[classificationColumn].ToString() ==
            itemClassification)
        {
            string groupName = permListItem[groupsColumn].ToString();
            SPGroup group =
                web.Groups[groupName.Substring(groupName.IndexOf("#") + 1,
                groupName.Length - (groupName.IndexOf("#") + 1))];
            SPRoleAssignment role = new SPRoleAssignment(group);

            if (permListItem[permsColumn].ToString() == "Allow Edit")
            {
                SPRoleDefinition roleDef =
                    web.RoleDefinitions.GetByType(SPRoleType.Contributor);
                role.RoleDefinitionBindings.Add(roleDef);
            }

            if (permListItem[permsColumn].ToString() == "Read Only")
            {
                SPRoleDefinition roleDef =
                    web.RoleDefinitions.GetByType(SPRoleType.Reader);
                role.RoleDefinitionBindings.Add(roleDef);
            }
            if (!newItem.HasUniqueRoleAssignments)
            {
                newItem.BreakRoleInheritance(true);
            }
            newItem.RoleAssignments.Add(role);
        }
    }
}
```

Appending Data with an Event Receiver

The VLW application's event receiver is designed to append a piece of metadata to the *Name* property of submitted assignments (an *SPFile* object) when the assignment is added to the library or associated metadata is updated. This metadata provides the site administrator with vital information about a student's assignment and increases administrative insight into the condition of a final assignment that would otherwise not be available through metadata already available in the Submitted Assignments library. By making use of the custom content type defined for the VLW solution (which contains a *<FieldRef>* element for a Date-Time Published field defined in a *<Field>* element declaration), it makes good sense to append this necessary information to the document so that when the assignment is submitted (through the use of the Windows SharePoint Services Application Page and accompanying feature file described later in the chapter), the relevant submitted date information is brought along with the document by modifying the *SPFile* object's *Name* property.

The event receiver captures two actions: when an item object is added to the library and when an item object's metadata is updated. However, because a document when submitted is considered to have been added to the SharePoint document library (it is stored before metadata capture occurs and is applied), we have to override only the *ItemUpdated* event, an asynchronous event that occurs after the relevant change activity has occurred on the uploaded *SPFile* object. The construction of this event receiver also shows some of the programmatic concepts involved in architecting and extending an enterprise content management (ECM) system when using Windows SharePoint Services as a document repository. Because we need to account for granular information about *SPFile* objects, queries must be made for whether the *SPFile* object is checked out by a principal (*SPUser*). If the file object is checked out, we need to check in the file object with a version type declaration (using the *SPCheckinType* enumeration to specify either a major or minor check-in type), along with the version comment indicating that the document was checked in using an intuitive string value parameter. These steps are necessary to ensure that the event receiver does not make changes to an *SPFile* object while the object is checked out by a principal. If this condition is met, you can branch behavior by testing whether the *SPFile.CheckOutStatus* property is not equal to anything other than *SPCheckOutStatus.None* (therefore compensating for both short-term and long-term checkout types). This test is required to account for document libraries that require that *SPFile* objects be checked out before making any changes to them, a common file-control mechanism and setting enabled in SharePoint document libraries.

The event receiver has some minor code notations that demonstrate that other DateTime formatting options are possible when you decide how to adjust the *SPFile* object's name. Zulu time, because it represents Coordinated Universal Time (UTC/GMT), is presented in the receiver code; however, other formats could be used depending on how a developer wants to tailor it. (Zulu time is written in 24-hour format. It uses four digits and is followed by the letter Z—0616Z, for example.) I chose Zulu time because it is a fairly universally accepted time standard. If you want additional, more advanced formatting, you can use the *DateTimeFormatInfo* class patterns (DTFI) in the *System.Globalization* namespace, which could take many forms depending on requirements. As a straightforward example of how to use this class to extend the appending options, you could use the *CultureInfo* class to provide culture-specific information regarding date conventions by passing in the culture name string, and include some additional formatting options by specifying properties of the DTFI object, such as separators that should be used for the date as well as the time.

```
System.Globalization.CultureInfo info = new CultureInfo("CultuereNameString");
DateTimeFormatInfo datetime = info.DateTimeFormat;
datetime.DateSeparator = "\";
dtf.TimeSeparator = "\\";
datetime.FullDateTimePattern = "yyyyddMM hh:mm:ss";
```

The *AppendDate* event trap inherits from the *SPItemEventReceiver* base class so that the code can access the appropriate item event method that it will override. (A list-level event that is triggered, for example, when a field is updated, would instead inherit from the *SPListEventReceiver* base class.) Because the event receiver is designed to append a piece of mutable information (the data that it is appended is located within a definable SharePoint list column, making it a piece of metadata that the user can define), after update events can solely be overridden because the item will first be added to the document library and later the required metadata will be gathered from the principal. The event trap overrides the *ItemUpdated* method to compensate for this, handling both when a user uploads a new document to the SharePoint library as well as when a user adjusts the date of an *SPFile* object that was previously uploaded to the SharePoint library—specifically when they change the date of the assignment, which is held in another piece of metadata. In this circumstance, the previously defined date is dropped in both the metadata and from the *Name* property of the *SPFile* object, and a new date is appended based on the column values as specified by the student.

Event receivers are deployed as a simple compiled assembly (and like feature receiver files, they require GAC deployment) and are activated through a Windows SharePoint Services feature that you can target at a specific list type or a content type. (The latter requires developing a custom Feature Receiver to associate the receiver to a content type by harvesting available content types for your *SPWeb* object through the *AvailableContentTypes* property.) In this case, we could target the custom content type that is defined in the solution because we will append the date to assignments that are submitted to that document library.

The code also indicates to run this event receiver with privileges that the user might not normally have and then sets up appropriate site and Web references as well as the list item to which this event is bound. We allow *GET* requests on the Web by setting *AllowUnsafeUpdates* to true to allow the possibility of updates to the database through the use of the requests (subtracting several authentication requirements), and then get a reference to the parent list, which is nothing more than a helper object used later for data massaging. Next we set up references to the *SPFile* objects that we need. These represent the assignments stored in the assignment library that are going to be adjusted. The references to these objects will be heavily consumed later in the code file. The code also defines some helper strings for output later in the code. The casting that you see in this section of the code is not necessary, but some developers might find the redundancy helpful for clarity.

The code also performs some simple guard-type matching to see whether the associated metadata column is actually a *DateTime* field. This test can be considered superfluous because this value should be set as this type (the field declaration of the assignment content type specifies the type as *DateTime* field), but if the list does ever change or if the event receiver is deployed to other locations, some sort of check should be in place to determine what type of field we are going to pull from to manipulate the name of the *SPFile* object.

The code puts in a placeholder for further date/time formatting options and then parses the date so that it can be converted in the next line. We can convert the time to the string that is required by the other assets within the environment. This could be converted to whatever friendly time format you want to use. Again, I've used Zulu time because it appends clearly and is a commonly used date/time formatting option.

The code includes a test of whether the current statement contains an underscore, which means it has been converted before (separating the name of the *SPFile* object from the appended date/time data that subsequently occurs in the event receiver). If it does, we set a new title with the legacy date stripped out and return only the filename using a substring. Next we set the *itemsDisplay* string to the new item's display name if this is true. We also set the name column to a different value. The *itemDisplayName* value will eventually be passed in for the *Name* property for the *SPFile* object.

We have to make a new *SPFile* object because we have modified its properties since it was originally created; otherwise, we'll receive an error when accessing the previous *SPFile* object. As a result of the name change, the URL is no longer considered to be a valid property because the *Name* property plays a part in constructing where the *SPFile* object is located. We then check in the file with the comments that we have made the property reference swap so that a user who is auditing the document library for versions is aware of the title changes to the checked-in assignments.

 Note The solution file for the event receiver is a standard class library template; no extensions are required. However, because the inheritance is of a Windows SharePoint Services type, you need to have the relevant SharePoint assemblies available to use IntelliSense and build the project.

Listing 4-4 shows the event receiver code.

Listing 4-4 The *AppendDate* event receiver.

```
using System;
using System.Collections.Generic;
using System.ComponentModel;
using System.Text;
```

```csharp
using System.Web.UI;
using Microsoft.SharePoint;
using System.Web.UI.WebControls.WebParts;
using System.Globalization;

namespace oba.Book.Receivers
{
    public class AppendDate : SPItemEventReceiver
    {
        public readonly static string publishedSpColumn = "Date-Time Published";


        public override void ItemUpdated(SPItemEventProperties properties)
        {
            base.ItemUpdated(properties);
            if (properties != null)
                appendDate(properties);
        }

        private static void appendDate(SPItemEventProperties properties)
        {
            if (properties == null)
                throw new ArgumentNullException("properties");

            SPSecurity.RunWithElevatedPrivileges(delegate()
            {
                using (SPSite site = new SPSite(properties.SiteId))
                {
                    using (SPWeb web = site.OpenWeb(properties.RelativeWebUrl))
                    {
                        SPListItem listItem = properties.ListItem;

                        listItem.Web.AllowUnsafeUpdates = true;

                        SPList parentList = properties.ListItem.ParentList;

                        SPFile grabFile = listItem.File;
                        if (grabFile != null)
                        {
                            SPFile queryFile = web.GetFile(grabFile.Url);

                            string itemDisplayName = listItem.DisplayName;
                            string listDisplayName = parentList.Title;

                            if (queryFile.CheckOutStatus !=
                              SPFile.SPCheckOutStatus.None)
                            {
                                queryFile.CheckIn(string.Format("{1} automatically
                                    checked In For Property Reference Integrity From
                                    Web: {0}, List: {1}, Item: {2}", web,
                                    itemDisplayName, listDisplayName),
                                    SPCheckinType.MinorCheckIn);
                            }
```

```
                                        queryFile.CheckOut();

                                        if (publishedSpColumn != null)
                                            if (queryFile.Item[publishedSpColumn].GetType() ==
                                                typeof(DateTime))
                                            {
                                                DateTimeFormatInfo dtfi = new
                                                    DateTimeFormatInfo();

                                                DateTime publishedDate = DateTime.Parse
                                                    (listItem[publishedSpColumn].ToString(),
                                                    dtfi);

                                                string zuluTimeString =
                                                    publishedDate.ToUniversalTime().ToString
                                                    ("yyyyMMddHHmm");

                                                if (itemDisplayName.Contains("_"))
                                                {
                                                    string newItemDisplayName =
                                                        itemDisplayName.Substring
                                                        (0, itemDisplayName.LastIndexOf('_') +
                                                        0);

                                                    itemDisplayName = newItemDisplayName;
                                                }

                                                queryFile.Item["Name"] =
                                                    string.Format("{0}_{1}", itemDisplayName,
                                                    zuluTimeString);
                                            }


                                        queryFile.Item.Update();

                                        SPFile newQueryFile = queryFile.Item.File;
                                        string newQueryFileName = queryFile.Name;

                                        newQueryFile.CheckIn(string.Format("{2} property
                                            references adjusted From Web: {0}, List: {1}, Item:
                                            {2}", web, listDisplayName, newQueryFileName),
                                            SPCheckinType.MinorCheckIn);
                                    }
                                }
                            }
                        }
                    )
                }
            }
        }
```

Provisioning Site and Security Objects Through a Feature Receiver

The main VLW feature receiver is meant to set up the assets on the site that are not created by the workflow and associated activities. When you activate the VLW feature, it creates a document library associated with a content type (defined in the XML files described later in the chapter) and a standard document library and ensures the creation of two SharePoint groups (VLW administrators and VLW students) and custom permission levels (role definitions) associated with those groups that specify granular permission levels for group association. By provisioning the site with these resources, we can create all the required SharePoint ECM and security materials so that some of the site provisioning efforts are offloaded from the administrator through easily activated functions. To do this, we override the *FeatureActivated* function so that we can specify a certain set of subcode to be run within this override that will execute when a user clicks the activation button on the SharePoint site. Providing this functionality allows an administrator (or the administrator as specified in the *vlwadministrator* property in activities) to use a single feature-activation button within the SharePoint site settings to provide the site and security assets necessary to create a fully functional VLW—without having to do any programming. It also allows an administrator to create generic VLWs by keeping this feature inactive, which allows the use of the custom site provisioning activities for other organizational site-creation tasks.

Several security concepts and programmatic tasks related to the Windows SharePoint Services object model are introduced in this feature receiver. You use the *SPRoleDefinition* object to define custom permission levels by using the *SPBasePermissions* class to define the permissions that link to the *SPRoleDefinition* object, making it the representation of a permission level that you can see in a SharePoint site's user interface. Two role definitions (which, again, represent permission levels) are presented in the solution, one for the VLW administrators and another targeted to students.

After the new role definitions are defined, a loop checks whether the new site contains the appropriate groups (the VLW administrators group and the VLW students group) or whether they need to be created. If the loop fails to find that these groups have been defined at the Web level, they are created. If they are found, we don't need to create them, so we simply return out of the method. To complete the routine, the permission levels will be associated with the groups so that an *SPUser* object in an *SPGroup* object will acquire the groups' roles from the custom *RoleDefinitions* held in the *RoleDefinitionBindings* property (which represents a collection of the *RoleDefinitions*).

Here is the first portion of the code. It sets up the reference to the *SPWeb* object to create an object with a Web reference against which the feature will be activated. It also specifies some string values such as library names, student and administrator groups, and various descriptions (which could be declared within the method's scope, but declaring them as method-level strings lets you change the values easily).

```
{
    public class VLWFeatureReciever : SPFeatureReceiver
    {
        public override void FeatureActivated(SPFeatureReceiverProperties
            properties)
        {
            using (SPWeb site = (SPWeb) properties.Feature.Parent)
            {
                string strAssignmentLib = site.Title + "Assignment Library";
                    string strSubmittedLib = site.Title + "Submitted
                        Assignments";
                string strStudentGroup = site.Title + "VLW Team Members";
                string strAdminGroupName = site.Title + "VLW Team
                  Administrators";
                string strStuGroupDesc = "The" + site.Title + "member group that
                  uses the VLW for collaboration";
                string strAdminGrouDesc = "The" + site.Title + "team
                  administrator group that manages the VLW";
```

Next the code sets up the field that holds the author (or owner) value, using an *SPUser* object to represent a user by getting the site author (which should be the value from the create VLW activity's *vlwadministrator* property because this sets up the administrator of the site), and makes references to the ancestral document as well as custom content types since we will be creating both. Because we are using a custom content type for the working assignments, we have to remove the document content type and then associate the custom content type with the assignment library that we will create. Since we are going to be creating a standard document library for the assignments that have been submitted, we are also going to spawn an *SPContentType* object that makes a reference to the standard document content type.

```
SPUser lvwOwner = site.Author;
SPContentType documentContentType = site.ContentTypes["Document"];
SPContentType assignmentContentType = site.ContentTypes
    ["Assignment Content Type"];
SPDocumentLibrary docLib;
SPListCollection lists = site.Lists;
SPListTemplate listTemplate = site.ListTemplates["Document Library"];
Guid guid = lists.Add(strAssignmentLib, "Provides Storage For VLW Assignments",
    ListTemplate);
docLib = lists[guid] as SPDocumentLibrary;
```

The code then makes reference to the method that we can use to test whether the document library that is a concern during provisioning has already been created on the site. We don't want to override the creation by spawning a new document library if this feature has been previously activated and deactivated. The code executes only if the library doesn't already exist. If it does exist, there really is no point in continuing the execution.

```
bool doesAssignLibExists = DoesLibExist(site, strAssignmentLib);

            if (doesAssignLibExists)
            {
                if (docLib != null)
```

```
            {
                if (documentContentType != null)
                    docLib.ContentTypes.Delete(documentContentType.Id);
                if (assignmentContentType != null)
                    docLib.ContentTypes.Add(assignmentContentType);
                docLib.OnQuickLaunch = false;
                docLib.ForceCheckout = true;
                docLib.RequestAccessEnabled = true;
                docLib.ContentTypesEnabled = true;
                docLib.Update();
            }
}


bool doesSubmittedLibExists = DoesLibExist(site, strSubmittedLib);

            if (!doesSubmittedLibExists)
            {
                lists.Add(strSubmittedLib, "Provides Storage For Submitted
                    Assignments", listTemplate);
            }
```

Now we have to set up the role definition on the site. If you need to reference a *RoleDefinition* by type, you can do so within a *RoleDefinition* collection in the following manner, which is helpful when constructing an arbitrary Windows SharePoint Services application that is going to tap into the security framework (we have seen this before in previous sections with the custom activity code):

```
SPRoleDefinitionCollection lvwRoleCollection = site.RoleDefinitions;
SPRoleDefinition myRoles = lvwRoleCollection.GetByType(SPRoleType.Administrator);
```

We next define the site administrator permission level (role definition) and provide a friendly name and description. We give administrators full rights using *SPBasePermissions.FullMask* and then gradually strip away the rights that we don't want them to have so that we can maintain some control over the site. For example, we wouldn't want them to be able to use remote API calls, and we would like to limit their interaction as much as possible.

After we have defined the permissions, we add the *BasePermissions* property to the *RoleDefinitions* and then define the student permission level, again providing a friendly name and description. We give the students all the rights that would normally be granted to the contributor level but take away the rights for the student to delete items from the site (to maintain the integrity of assignments that are submitted).

```
            if (!site.HasUniqueRoleDefinitions)
            {
                site.RoleDefinitions.BreakInheritance(true, true);
            }

            site.AllowUnsafeUpdates = true;
            SPRoleDefinition roleDefinitionAdmins = new SPRoleDefinition();
            roleDefinitionAdmins.Name = "VLW Administrator Permissions";
```

```
roleDefinitionAdmins.Description = "The Site Administrators Role
    Definition Has Full Rights Besides Applying Style Sheet and
    Creating New SharePoint Groups";
roleDefinitionAdmins.BasePermissions =
    SPBasePermissions.FullMask ^
            SPBasePermissions.ApplyStyleSheets |
            SPBasePermissions.CreateGroups |
            SPBasePermissions.UseRemoteAPIs |
            SPBasePermissions.CreateSSCSite;

site.RoleDefinitions.Add(roleDefinitionAdmins);

SPRoleDefinition roleDefinitionStudents = new
    SPRoleDefinition();
roleDefinitionStudents.Name = "VLW Contributor Permissions";
roleDefinitionStudents.Description =
    "The Student Has All The Rights Of A Contributor, However
        Can Not Delete ListItems (Enforcing Assignment Integrity
        Post-Submission)";
roleDefinitionStudents.BasePermissions =
    SPBasePermissions.ViewListItems |
    SPBasePermissions.AddListItems |
    SPBasePermissions.EditListItems |
    SPBasePermissions.OpenItems |
    SPBasePermissions.ViewVersions |
    SPBasePermissions.ManagePersonalViews |
    SPBasePermissions.ViewFormPages |
    SPBasePermissions.Open |
    SPBasePermissions.ViewPages |
    SPBasePermissions.CreateSSCSite |
    SPBasePermissions.BrowseDirectories |
    SPBasePermissions.BrowseUserInfo |
    SPBasePermissions.AddDelPrivateWebParts |
    SPBasePermissions.UpdatePersonalWebParts |
    SPBasePermissions.UseClientIntegration |
    SPBasePermissions.UseRemoteAPIs |
    SPBasePermissions.CreateAlerts |
    SPBasePermissions.EditMyUserInfo;

site.RoleDefinitions.Add(roleDefinitionStudents);
```

In the next section of the code, we add the necessary SharePoint groups. If you wanted to add members to these groups, you could use an extracted method call or place the code post condition. The code would look like this:

```
site.SiteGroups[strStudentGroup].AddUser(userLogin, userEmail, commonName,
    miscNotes);
```

We create a new *SPRoleDefinitionCollection* object to reference the role definitions that are available on the site for which the feature is being activated. We also create a new *SPRoleAssignmentCollection* object to reference the role assignments that are available. Because an *SPMember* object can represent either an *SPUser* object or an *SPGroup* object, we can use the

SPMember object to get access to our custom groups that were created earlier in the feature receiver code.

We then get a reference to the student site group and a reference to the administrator site group. We use an *SPPrincipal* object to represent the groups that were created previously to relate the permissions to the groups. We also use an *SPRoleAssignment* object to assign the principal object to the role assignment (in other words, assign the site group to the *RoleAssignment*). After we create the new *RoleAssignment* objects, we instantiate a new *SPRoleDefinition-BindingCollection* object to work with the role assignments that are bound to a role assignment and add the custom role definitions to the objects that we want to maintain securely. We then add the assignment to the collection.

```
if (!vlwGroupExists(site, strStudentGroup))
{
site.SiteGroups.Add(strStudentGroup, lvwOwner, lvwOwner, strStuGroupDesc);
}

if (!vlwGroupExists(site, strStudentGroup))
{
site.SiteGroups.Add(strAdminGroupName, lvwOwner, lvwOwner, strAdminGrouDesc);
}

SPRoleDefinitionCollection curDefinitions = site.RoleDefinitions;

SPRoleAssignmentCollection curAssignments = site.RoleAssignments;

SPMember studentCrossSiteGroup = site.SiteGroups[strStudentGroup];

SPMember adminCrossSiteGroup = site.SiteGroups[strAdminGroupName];

SPPrincipal studentSp = (SPPrincipal) studentCrossSiteGroup;
SPPrincipal adminSp = (SPPrincipal) adminCrossSiteGroup;

SPRoleAssignment roleStudentAssign = new SPRoleAssignment(studentSp);
SPRoleAssignment roleAdminAssign = new SPRoleAssignment(adminSp);

SPRoleDefinitionBindingCollection roleDefBindingsStu =
  roleStudentAssign.RoleDefinitionBindings;
SPRoleDefinitionBindingCollection roleDefBindingsAdmin =
  roleAdminAssign.RoleDefinitionBindings;
roleDefBindingsStu.Add(oCurDefinitions[roleDefinitionAdmins.ToString()]);
              roleDefBindingsAdmin.Add(curDefinitions[roleDefinitionStudents.ToString()]);

 curAssignments.Add(roleStudentAssign);
 curAssignments.Add(roleAdminAssign);
 site.Update();
```

At the end of the receiver, you can see some brief helper methods procuring test conditions for whether certain SharePoint assets exist. The first of these methods tests whether a certain group exists, returning a Boolean flag. We start a *foreach* loop to iterate through all the site groups that are available on the site and test whether the group name that is being passed into the method as an argument returns out of the operator comparison. We use the *String.ToLower* method to handle case sensitivity. If the loop doesn't return a positive string match, we return false and don't execute the subcode that depends on this operator comparison output. We also include flags that are used to determine whether the document library and assignment library already exist at the site that the event receiver is being run against because we need to take caution to not create things twice. We use the *SPWeb.GetList* method to see whether the libraries exist, setting the flag appropriately to true or false depending on what we find.

```
public bool vlwGroupExists(SPWeb site, string lvwGroup)
{
    foreach (SPGroup grouplist in site.SiteGroups)
    {
        if (grouplist.ToString().ToLower() == lvwGroup.ToLower())

            return true;
    }
    return false;
}

private static bool DoesLibExist(SPWeb site, string lib)
{
    bool doesLibExist;
    try
    {
        site.GetList(string.Format("/Lists/{0}", lib));
        doesLibExist = true;
    }

    catch
    {
        doesLibExist = false;
    }
    return doesLibExist;
}
```

Viewing and Changing Active Directory Information Through a SharePoint Web Part

The files that define the application's Web Part do not require any sort of project template and can be opened in any Visual Studio environment. Because the Active Directory Web Part references and manipulates Active Directory objects, you do need a reference to the *System. DirectoryServices* assembly, which provides an abstracted API that allows access and options for working with objects that are present within your specific corporate LDAP directory instance.

The VLW solution also demonstrates how to build a Web Part that can integrate directory services functionality into a portion of a SharePoint site, which is beneficial because Active Directory is a common method for authentication and user storage within an enterprise environment.

This first portion of the Active Directory Web Part is designed to read into Active Directory through an Active Directory search object, retrieve Active Directory information about the current user, and then render the information in the Web Part's display. This display could show an arbitrary number of Active Directory properties, depending on your needs. As you can see in Figure 4-2, the Web Part shows several pieces of information regarding the current user's Active Directory information (provided that the search finds the user within Active Directory). An implementation such as this could lead to more elegant applications if you want. For example, this approach could form a simple basis from which to incorporate an Active Directory management application in SharePoint. By exposing this information in a Web Part, the user can be informed of her Active Directory information. If custom fields exist that are particular to an academic environment, such as a user's major area of study, these fields can be exposed to the user in a friendly display format.

OBA Display User	▾
University Username:	**Robert Lyon**
University Email:	**someone@example.com**
Campus Phone:	**850-555-0100**
Department:	**Computer Sciences Major, Mathematics Minor**

Figure 4-2   Using a Web Part to display a user's information from Active Directory.

In the second part of this section, where we enhance the Active Directory Web Part, we will look at how we can incorporate some Active Directory functionality by building a password self-service application so that we can easily implement a password rotation policy that offloads some administrative effort on the user. This is an important security concept for reasons I will explain shortly.

The first portion we are going to examine allows you to construct output from Active Directory properties and display it to the user. You will notice in the code that we establish the relevant *using* statements to the directory services portion so that we can use managed code to access the Active Directory resources that we want to display in the Web Part. The Web Part class has several elements of inheritance that are necessary for the Web Part to operate correctly. It inherits from the Web Part base class, which can use either the orthodox ASP.NET 2.0 base class for Web Parts or a custom Web Part base class that your organization developed. (You might use this approach to maintain practices such as standard corporate exception handling across all Web Parts; for example, if you are building an exception collection as errors occur within your Web Part.) The last step is to implement the *IDesignProviderHtml* interface so that if the page that is implementing this Web Part is opened within SharePoint Designer, it will render out a small message to the user that the Web Part can only be displayed in a Web browser.

We use the *DirectorySearcher* object throughout this code to perform a query on the current user and his or her relevant business information. Subsequently, we need to use the *Filter* method to siphon the returned information from the *DirectorySearcher* object. To get the current user, we use the *GetCurrent* method in the *WindowsIdentity* class and then use the *name* property, which will return the full user's domain name. We can then massage out strictly the user name by doing a simple *SubString* against the full name. The *Filter* method consumes the *curUser* argument that identifies the Windows user that we are looping against. This should equate to the SAM account name of the user, and therefore should be an appropriate means of returning the relevant user information.

To build the results of the query that have been returned from the instance, we use a *SearchResultCollection* that holds the *SearchResult* instances from the *FindAll* method. This method is used to populate the collection with the specified filtered results. We then check the collection count to see whether it returned any values. If it did, we can cast the return to a string and render the contents of the return into an HTML stream that will render out in the Web Part. (We will use these same objects, *DirectoryEntry* and *DirectorySearcher*, when we enhance the Web Part to handle password changes.)

The protected method *CreateChildControls* is called by the ASP.NET page framework to notify server controls that use composition-based implementation to create any child controls they contain in preparation for posting back or rendering. *RenderContents* renders the contents of the control to the specified writer. This method is used primarily by Web Part developers, carried over from composite (server) control development. Listing 4-5 shows the Web Part code.

Listing 4-5   Code from DisplayUserWebPart.cs.

```
using System;
using System.DirectoryServices;
using System.Web.UI;
using System.Security.Principal;
using Microsoft.SharePoint.Utilities;
using Microsoft.SharePoint.WebControls.WebParts;using Microsoft.Sharepoint.WebPartPages;

namespace oba.Book.WebParts
{
    public class DisplayADUserWebPart : WebPart, IDesignTimeHtmlProvider
    {
        private string curUser;
        private string curDomUser;
        private string userLoginName;
        private string userMailAddy;
        private string userDepartment;
        private string userTelephone;

        public DisplayADUserWebPart()
        {
            this.getCurUser();
            this.curUserParams();
        }
```

```csharp
public string GetDesignTimeHtml()
{
    return SPEncode.HtmlEncode("This WebPart Will Not Render In SharePoint
        Designer. Please Open In A Web Browser.");
}

private void getCurUser()
{
    this.curDomUser = WindowsIdentity.GetCurrent().Name;
    this.curUser =
        this.curDomUser.Substring(((int)(this.curDomUser.LastIndexOf("\\") +
        1)));
}

private void curUserParams()
{
    using (DirectorySearcher searcher = new DirectorySearcher())
    {
        searcher.Filter =
            string.Format("(&(samaccountname={0})(objectClass=user))",
            this.curUser);
        try
        {
            using (SearchResultCollection userResults = searcher.FindAll())
            {
                if (userResults.Count > 0)
                {
                    try
                    {
                        this.userLoginName =
                            userResults[0].GetDirectoryEntry().
                            Properties["displayName"].Value.ToString();
                    }

                    catch (Exception exception)
                    {
// Add Corporate exception handling logic
                    }

                    try
                    {
                        this.userDepartment =
                            userResults[0].GetDirectoryEntry().
                            Properties["department"].Value.ToString();
                    }

                    catch (Exception exception)
                    {
// Add Corporate exception handling logic
                    }

                    try
                    {
                        this.userTelephone =
                            userResults[0].GetDirectoryEntry().
```

```
                                      Properties["telephoneNumber"].Value.ToString();
                    }
                    catch (Exception exception)
                    {
// Add Corporate exception handling logic
                    }

                    try
                    {
                        this.userMailAddy =
                            userResults[0].GetDirectoryEntry().
                            Properties["mail"].Value.ToString();
                    }
                    catch (Exception exception)
                    {
// Add Corporate exception handling logic
                    }
                }
            }
        }
        catch (Exception exception)
        {
// Add Corporate exception handling logic

        }
    }
}

protected override void RenderContents(HtmlTextWriter output)
{
    this.EnsureChildControls();
    string stream = "";
    try
    {
        stream = string.Format("{0} <table width=100%>", stream);
        stream = string.Format("{0} <tr><td colspan=3>", stream);

        if ((this.userLoginName != null) && (this.userLoginName.Length > 0))
        {
            {
                stream = string.Format("{0}
                    </td></tr><tr><td> </td><td>", stream);
                stream = string.Format("{0} University Username:</td><td><b>
                    {1} </b>", stream, this.userLoginName);
            }

            if ((this.userMailAddy != null) && (this.userMailAddy.Length >
                0))
            {
                stream = string.Format("{0}
                    </td></tr><tr><td> </td><td>", stream);
                stream = string.Format("{0} University
                    Email:</td><td><b>{1}</b>", stream, this.userMailAddy);
            }
```

```
                    if ((this.userTelephone != null) && (this.userTelephone.Length >
                        0))
                    {
                        stream = string.Format("{0}
                            </td></tr><tr><td> </td><td>", stream);
                        stream = string.Format("{0} Campus
                            Phone:</td><td><b>{1}</b>", stream, this.userTelephone);
                    }
                    if ((this.userDepartment != null) && (this.userDepartment.Length
                        > 0))
                    {
                        stream = string.Format("{0}
                            </td></tr><tr><td> </td><td>", stream);
                        stream = string.Format("{0} Department:</td><td><b>{1}</b>",
                            stream, this.userDepartment);
                    }
                }
                else
                {
                    stream = string.Format("{0} </td></tr><tr><td> </td><td
                        colspan=2>", stream);
                    stream = string.Format("{0} <b>Unable To Locate The User In
                        Active Directory</b>", stream);
                }
                stream = string.Format("{0} </td></tr>", stream);
                stream = string.Format("{0} </table>", stream);
            }


            catch (Exception exception)
            {
                stream = (string.Format("{0} <BR>An Exception Occurred: {1}",
                    stream, exception.StackTrace));
            }

            output.Write(stream);
        }
    }
}
```

Now that you have seen how to display information from Active Directory in Windows Share-Point Services, how can you go about implementing controls to manipulate the information within the LDAP store? One of the most common requests for altering this information is a password self-service option that lets users change their passwords so that a policy for password rotation can be implemented. This is an important concept to take into consideration when securing your Windows SharePoint Services environment because password rotation will allow an extraordinarily simple mechanism against brute-force and random human password guessing. The results of such an implementation are shown in Figure 4-3.

```
OBA Display User                                              ▾
    University Username:    Robert Lyon
    University Email:       someone@example.com
    Campus Phone:           850-555-0100
    Department:             Computer Sciences Major, Mathematics Minor
Old Password:
[                         ]

New Password:
[                         ]

[ Change Password ]
```

Figure 4-3 Adding functionality to the Web Part lets us manipulate information in the Active Directory store—in this case, enabling a user to change his or her password.

Before developing the actual method that is going to be used to change the user's current password, we have to adjust the code shown in Listing 4-5 to allow the invocation of the method and to define new fields that will allow the user to input string values. To do this, we are going to declare a new *HtmlInputButton* control to place within the Web Part and then associate the *OnClick* event for the control with an event handler. Furthermore, we have to define three new HTML input fields: one to take the old Active Directory password, another to take the new password string, and a field that will allow confirmation and verification of the new password. We will eventually extract the values from the *HtmlInputText* controls by using the *Value* property and casting that result to a string using *ToString*.

```
private Label lblOldPwd;
private Label lblNewPwd;
private Label lblConfPwd;
private HtmlInputText hitConfPwd;
private HtmlInputText hitOldPwd;
private HtmlInputText hitNewPwd;
private HtmlInputButton butChangePassword;
private Literal breakTag;
```

To compare the new Active Directory password with the confirmation field, we can use a simple *if* statement that will compare the values from the *HtmlInputText* controls. This is just a simple string comparison using the *String.Equals* method that will determine whether the two values returned are equivalent. If the statement returns *true*, we can run the change password method.

```
if (this.hitConfPwd.Value.ToString().Equals(this.hitNewPwd.Value.ToString()))
        {
        }
```

Within the overridden *CreateChildControls* method in the Web Part, we wire the event handler and can also specify attributes for the buttons and fields.

```
protected override void CreateChildControls()
{
    this.butChangePassword = new HtmlInputButton ();
    this. butChangePassword.Value = "Change Password";
    this.butChangePassword.ServerClick += new EventHandler(this.changePwd_click);
```

```
this.Controls.Add(this.butChangePassword);
this. hitOldPwd = new HtmlInputText("password");
this. hitOldPwd.MaxLength = 30;
...
```

}

To avoid repetitive break calls to separate the controls, you can just use a small method to add a *Literal* control with the text specified as "</br>". Then add the declaration to the controls collection so that you could call *LiteralBreak*.

```
private Literal breakTag;
    private void LiteralBreak()
    {
        this.breakTag = new Literal();
        this.breakTag.Text = "</br>";
        this.Controls.Add(breakTag);
    }
```

Following this step, we have to implement the actual password change method that is the workhorse of the modifications. In this method we harness some of the previously defined objects, notably the current user's domain name and the current user's SharePoint user name. The *ChangeADPassword* method takes two parameters—the old password and the new password—which are required to perform some operations. However, the comparison of the new password and the confirmation that the values are the same are both handled within the *if* statement shown earlier. To do this, we create a new *DirectorySearcher* object within a *using* statement, looping through and looking for the user account information with the *DirectorySearcher.FindOne* method, which returns the *SearchResult* object that will specify whether the user exists. If this object is not null, we create a *DirectoryEntry* object to represent a user object in the LDAP source and then use the *Invoke* method of the *DirectoryEntry* object to call the *ChangePassword* method. Last, we have to call *DirectoryEntry.CommitChanges* to update the underlying LDAP store with the changes that we have made.

```
internal string ChangeADPassword(string oldPassword, string newPassword)
    {
        string feedback = "Password Change Completed";

        try
        {
            SearchResult result;
            using (DirectorySearcher searcher = new
                DirectorySearcher("(sAMAccountName=" + this.curUser + ")", new
                string[] {"sAMAccountName", "cn"}))
            {
                searcher.SearchRoot.Username = this.curDomUser;
                searcher.SearchRoot.Password = oldPassword;
                result = searcher.FindOne();
            }
            if (result == null)
            {
                return "The SharePoint User Does Not Appear to Have An Active
                    Directory Account.";
```

```
        }
        using (DirectoryEntry entry = new DirectoryEntry(result.Path,
            this.curDomUser, oldPassword))
        {
            entry.RefreshCache();
            object changePassword = entry.Invoke("ChangePassword", new
                object[] { oldPassword, newPassword });
            entry.CommitChanges();
        }
    }
    catch (Exception exception)
    {
        // Add Corporate exception handling logic
    }

    return feedback;
}
```

By using *DirectoryEntry.Invoke* and calling ADSI interface methods, you can develop all types of Active Directory Web Parts. You could, for example, create a Web Part that uses the *Groups* method to return a user's groups within a Web Part display.

Defining a Content Type and Feature

The primary content types used in the VLW solution are the custom assignment content type and the built-in document content type for generic submitted assignments. The custom content type, although derived from the base document content type (and thereby specified by the 0x0101 ancestral content type identifier), includes the relevant fields for storing associated metadata when assignments are submitted to the VLW. This metadata is decorated in the content type XML by *<field ref>* elements that will be added as *<Field>* elements to represent columns in a SharePoint list. In the Windows SharePoint Services object model, however, these elements are represented by *SPFieldLink* objects held within a *SPFieldLinkCollection*. For example, if you want to query all the *SPFieldLink* objects in the *SPFieldLinkCollection*, you could use the *FieldLinks* property of the *SPContentType* object to query the predefined fields, as demonstrated here:

```
SPContentType ContentType = web.AvailableContentTypes["Assignments"];
SPFieldLinkCollection Links = ContentType.FieldLinks;
for (int i = 0; i < Links.Count; i++)
{
}
```

 The assignment content type is wrapped within a SharePoint feature file for deployment, which also allows for binding functionality such as event receivers that can be associated with the feature. The one uniform receiver can be packaged in the same solution file. It can also be tied to the deployment of the site and the security feature receiver by specifying the receiver assembly and class within a single SharePoint feature field. The content type is inherently tied to the feature receiver because the feature receiver uses this content type to provision the new document library.

Features can contain a number of elements of site functionality. You can turn features on or off–activate them, in other words–at different scopes, either from the Stadms.exe command line or through the Feature activation commands in SharePoint. The scope of a feature can be for a site, a site collection, a Web application, or a farm.

The content type is defined in two distinct XML files. The first, shown in Listing 4-6, describes the content type and its reference to its various fields through the *field ref* declarations, which bind the content type to its sister file that describes those fields. The content type inherits from the base document library content type because we will create an assignment library based on that content type.

Listing 4-6   The content type definition.

```xml
<?xml version="1.0" encoding="utf-8" ?>
<Elements xmlns="http://schemas.microsoft.com/sharepoint/">
<!-- Inherit from the document library ancestral type 0x0101 because the VLW
  assignments will be submitted as documents, so it makes sense to use this as the
  base content type. We should also specify the attributes about the content type,
  like the name, group, description, and version of the content type
-->
<ContentType ID="0x0101005681071F88374fe0BFD45E7C0340C529" Name="VLWAssignmentLib"
  Group="VLW Assignment Content Type" Description="Provided The Necessary Data
  Blueprint in Order To build Assignment Document Libraries In A VLW" Version="0">
<FieldRefs>
<!-- Assignment ID, Set This Field As Required In The Content Type, To Appear In
  The Assignment ID Column
  -->
<FieldRef ID="{02D17F85-11E6-4244-8B96-88FF22E38F02}" Name="AssignmentID"
  Required="TRUE" ShowInNewForm="TRUE" ShowInEditForm="TRUE" />
<!--  The Formal Name Of the Assignment To Appear In The Name Column
  -->
<FieldRef ID="{6973068E-4A88-4899-96E3-FD7ED4AD2983}" Name="AssignmentName"
  Required="TRUE" ShowInNewForm="TRUE" ShowInEditForm="TRUE" />
<!-- The Boolean Value To Indicate Whether The Assignment Has Been Submitted, To
  Appear In the Assignment Published Column
  -->
<FieldRef ID="{ADBAC5E8-C13B-4643-9321-ECD35A6E48EB}" Name="PermissionApplication"
  Required="TRUE" ShowInNewForm="TRUE" ShowInEditForm="TRUE" />
<FieldRef ID="{3B15C581-C39D-486d-A2A8-D40B2A508DF8}" Name="AssignmentPublished"
  Required="TRUE" ShowInNewForm="TRUE" ShowInEditForm="TRUE" />
<!-- The Date-Time Published Of The Assignment, Consumed In An Event Trap, In
  Order To Append To The Name Metadata, To Appear In the Date Time Published Column
  -->
<FieldRef ID="{A7231A7F-5432-49bd-BB1D-D7DDB851B3E8}"
  Name="AssignmentPublishedDate" Required="TRUE" ShowInNewForm="TRUE"
  ShowInEditForm="TRUE" />
</FieldRefs>
<XmlDocuments>
```

```
-  <XmlDocument
     NamespaceURI="http://schemas.microsoft.com/sharepoint/v3/contenttype/forms">
-  <FormTemplates
     xmlns="http://schemas.microsoft.com/sharepoint/v3/contenttype/forms">
   <Display>DocumentLibraryForm</Display>
   <Edit>DocumentLibraryForm</Edit>
   <New>DocumentLibraryForm</New>
   </FormTemplates>
   </XmlDocument>
   </XmlDocuments>
   </ContentType>
   </Elements>
```

The field types that are introduced are Text, DateTime, and Boolean types because we are looking to build a simple document library that contains only the necessary metadata for a student to submit assignments and keep track of those submissions. We need to know the assignment name, the date and time that the assignment was submitted (which will trigger the append date event receiver and subsequently append this data to the *Name* property of the target *SPFile* object), and an option for the user to inform the remaining students who are involved in the project of whether the assignment has been submitted.

Listing 4-7 shows the second file, which defines the content type list.

Listing 4-7 The definition of the custom content type list.

```
<?xml version="1.0" encoding="utf-8"?>
<Elements xmlns="http://schemas.microsoft.com/sharepoint/">
  <!-- Assignment Field Types, Used To Build The Assignment List Definition -->

  <!-- Assignment ID Field, Used To Uniquely Define This Assignment -->
  <Field ID="{02D17F85-11E6-4244-8B96-88FF22E38F02}"
      Name="AssignmentID"
      SourceID="http://schemas.microsoft.com/sharepoint/v3"
      StaticName="AssignmentID"
      Group="Assignment Management Columns"
      Type="Number"
      Sealed="FALSE"
      ReadOnly="FALSE"
      Hidden="FALSE"
      DisplayName="Assignment ID"
      ColName="AssignmentID">
  </Field>

  <!-- Assignment Name Field, Used To Describe This Document, This Is Altered With
    Event handlers eventually with the time published -->
  <Field ID="{6973068E-4A88-4899-96E3-FD7ED4AD2983}"
      Name="AssignmentName"
      SourceID="http://schemas.microsoft.com/sharepoint/v3"
      StaticName="AssignmentName"
      Group="Assignment Management Columns"
      Type="Text"
```

```xml
      Sealed="FALSE"
      ReadOnly="FALSE"
      Hidden="FALSE"
      DisplayName="Assignment Name"
      ColName="AssignmentName">
  </Field>
  <!--Permission Application Field, Used By The Permission Classification Workflow
    That Was Developed earlier In this chapter-->
  <Field ID="{ADBAC5E8-C13B-4643-9321-ECD35A6E48EB}"
      Name="PermissionApplication"
      SourceID="http://schemas.microsoft.com/sharepoint/v3"
      StaticName=" PermissionApplication"
      Group="Assignment Management Columns"
      Type="Text"
      Sealed="FALSE"
      ReadOnly="FALSE"
      Hidden="FALSE"
      DisplayName="Permission Application"
      ColName=" PermissionApplication ">
  </Field>

  <!-- Whether the assignment was published. Used In Some Workflows, and Assignment
    Submission Module. Will update this specific field-->
  <Field ID="{3B15C581-C39D-486d-A2A8-D40B2A508DF8}"
    Name="AssignmentPublished"
    SourceID="http://schemas.microsoft.com/sharepoint/v3"
    StaticName="AssignmenPublished"
    Group="Assignment Management Columns"
    Type="Boolean"
    Sealed="FALSE"
    ReadOnly="FALSE"
    Hidden="FALSE"
    DisplayName="Assignment Published"
    ColName="AssignmentPublished">
  </Field>
</Elements>

  <!-- Date and Time Published Field, I Used By The Event receiver in order to
  alter the title of the submitted assignment -->
  <Field ID="{A7231A7F-5432-49bd-BB1D-D7DDB851B3E8}"
    Name="AssignmentPublishedDate"
    SourceID="http://schemas.microsoft.com/sharepoint/v3"
    StaticName="AssignmentPublishedDate"
    Group="Assignment Management Columns"
    Type="Date and Time"
    Sealed="FALSE"
    ReadOnly="FALSE"
    Hidden="FALSE"
    DisplayName="Assignment Published Date-Time"
    ColName="AssignmentPublishedDate">
  </Field>
```

Submitting Assignments: The VLW Solution's Application Page

Application pages have a greater ease of use in Windows SharePoint Services 3.0. They enable, for example, the creation of custom interface and application components. They can be deployed on a server basis (because the page will be run from a virtual reference, and pages that exist in the _layouts directory of a particular SharePoint instance are not available for editing in SharePoint Designer) and require that the page be deployed into the _layouts directory on the server, which lends itself well to building custom interface components such as a custom SharePoint ECB (Edit Control Block) targeting *SPList* objects to invoke the page. Because application pages remain in the _layouts directory, you can establish a tokenized reference to the application.master page so that the page appears similar to the remaining application pages that exist in the SharePoint instance. As you will see shortly, custom application pages inherit from the *LayoutsPageBase* class that provides all the constructs required to create and run a page that exists in the _layouts directory.

All the code that is included in the application page for the VLW solution is contained within the page's load event, the *Page_Load* event handler. (Application pages, as opposed to site pages, can contain inline code, which is a large benefit for development purposes, although you can also deploy the code behind into a private assembly.) The code runs when the user invokes the page from the Edit Control Block, moving an assignment from the working assignment library to the submitted assignment library for administrator approval. The application page functionality is deployed and made available through the use of a SharePoint feature that allows it to target a specific list type, such as document libraries. When the feature is activated, it appends the Submit To menu item to the Edit Control Block in the document library. This set of operations is helpful for students who do not want to have multiple versions of an assignment (the working assignment and the submitted assignment) within the document library. Without this functionality, they would need to do one of the following:

- Use the built-in move functionality, which could prove problematic in that it would allow the source file to remain and requires the URL of the destination to be input.

- Copy and paste using WebDAV (Windows Explorer view). If the portal is an extranet, this feature might be disabled if integration with the 2007 Office system is disabled. The login tokens can't pass from the Web application to a 2007 Office system client.

- Use FrontPage RPCs (Remote Procedure Calls) to program a set of logic to move the document.

- Download a new copy of the assignment and upload it again to the assignment library.

Because the submitted document library might be locked down for access only by the administrator, the application page allows the context to be adjusted so that the move function can occur under an impersonated context that allows the user to submit the assignment without elevated account credentials. The approach shown in the VLW solution requires just one click for students to submit an assignment to the administrator for approval. In addition to the obvious functionality improvements, it is easy for the student from a user interface standpoint because it allows him or her to simply use a drop-down menu to submit the relevant assignment. The menu option is shown in Figure 4-4.

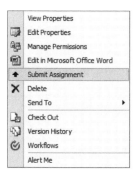

Figure 4-4   The custom menu item used to submit assignments.

You will notice that this code contains a lot of static content because the submission is to one place and one place only—only one submitted library for assignments exists for the same *SPWeb*. Because the name of the submission library is always the same (created with a constant name string when the feature receiver is run), we can hard-code the path to the submission document library and compensate differences between URLs for various sites with some simple string manipulation to assimilate the correct URL. However, if you want this portion of a solution to be dynamic, you can load the relevant places for publication into a selectable menu item. You can build a menu of places to which to publish a document by using a *Portal-SiteMapProvider* object to harness an arbitrary number of *SiteMapNodes* objects from a *SiteMapNodeCollection* that could represent the various available locations. JavaScript could then be used to populate a text box, and your publish button could read the *controlID* of the text box control to collect the publishing location for the *SPFile.CopyTo* or *SPFile.MoveTo* methods. This would require minimal code that would look something like the following:

```
curSiteUrl = SPControl.GetContextSite(Context).Url.ToLower();
 string folderURL = SPFolder.ServerRelativeUrl;
string builder = curSiteUrl + folderURL;
 output.AddAttribute(HtmlTextWriterAttribute.Href, "javascript:Select('" + _builder
    + "', '" + _textBoxClientId + "')"
output.RenderBeginTag(HtmlTextWriterTag.A);
 output.Write(" Select Destination");
output.RenderEndTag();
```

The associated JavaScript would follow this example:

```
    function Select(myUrl, myControl)
    {
        var anotherVar = document.getElementById(myControl);
        anotherVar.value = myUrl;
    }
```

This portion of the VLW solution is important because it shows the manipulation of the inherent interface for the *ListFormWebPart* object (which is responsible for the CRUD functionality of SharePoint lists—create, read, update, delete) through the use of features. It also shows how to bind through query strings functionality within the ECB reference that can be passed into an application page so that the application page is aware of arguments that can be consumed within the page's methods.

Application pages must be run from the _layouts directory of a SharePoint installation because they make dynamic, tokenized references to SharePoint objects, such as the site reference from which the page is being run and the master page that is responsible for the design of the application page. Therefore, if you open the pages in SharePoint Designer, you'll get a message that the master page reference has thrown an error. It is best to open the pages in Notepad or a similar text editor that will allow you to not bind another object to the page; however, if you want to use IntelliSense when writing your inline C# code, you can open the page in Visual Studio.

Alternative Ways to Move Items and Submit Assignments

Moving an *SPListItem* object and an *SPFile* object is a large function in Windows SharePoint Services. Within the VLW solution particularly, moving *SPFile* objects that represent documents is crucial. The *MoveTo* and *CopyTo* methods that natively exist in Windows SharePoint Services do not compensate for cross-site moves; they only allow for moving or copying *SPFile*, *SPListItem*, and *SPFolder* (representing a subfolder in a document library) objects within the same *SPWeb* instance. As you will see shortly, you can use custom code to extend the option to move objects across various site instances.

To support an extended environment, you may want to first offer both a *SPFile.MoveTo* and *SPFile.CopyTo* option by building an enumeration that holds the relevant values and then running the conditions within an *if* statement so that the user can select either method. A simple enumeration for the native Windows SharePoint Services move and copy to functions would look something like the following:

```
public enum PublishingMethod
{
    Assignment_CopyTo,
    Assignment_MoveTo
}
```

Because these native functions won't perform cross-site transfers of objects, you could extend this with the option to do binary stream copies by defining remaining members of the enumeration, whose method we will see shortly.

```
public enum PublishingMethod
{
    Assignment_CopyTo,
    Assignment_MoveTo,
    Assignment_BinaryCopy,
    Assignment_BinaryMove
}
```

To look at named constants within the enumeration that references the appropriate method to use through an *SPListItem* metadata reference (which would provide a user with a choice of methods through something like a choice field), you could define a simple *if* condition by simply referencing the appropriate column and comparing the string value.

```
private string submissionTypeColumn = "Submission Type";
SPList list = privLvwSite.Lists[new Guid(ListId)];
SPListItem assignListItem = list.Items.GetItemById(Convert.ToInt32(ItemId));
if (assignListItem[submissionTypeColumn].ToString() == "Assignment_CopyTo")
{
}
```

If you wanted the submission to occur based on a dynamic selection, here's some of the code you might use:

```
if ((this.PublishingMethod ==
PublishingMethod.Assignment_CopyTo) || (this.PublishingMethod
== PublishingMethod.Assignment_MoveTo))
{
if (this.PublishingMethod ==
PublishingMethod.Assignment_CopyTo)
{
moveFile.CopyTo(privLvwSite.Url.ToString() +
"/Submitted Assignments" + relativeMoveFile.ToString(),
true);
}
else
{
moveFile.MoveTo(privLvwSite.Url.ToString() + "/Submitted Assignments" +
    relativeMoveFile.ToString(), true);
 }
}
```

If you wanted to instead do a cross-site move, you would have to use something besides the native SharePoint *MoveTo* and *CopyTo* methods by using the *OpenBinary* method, the *SPFolder.Files* property, and the *Add* method that is provided through the *SPFileCollection*. You have to use the *SPFile.OpenBinary* method to open the *SPFile* object in a binary format returning a byte array, assuming the *SPFile* object contains more than 0 bytes because we can then stream the contents to another document library in a separate *SPWeb* object.

```
SPFile myFile = null;
if ((this.PublishingMethod == PublishingMethod.Assignment_BinaryCopy) ||
    (this.PublishingMethod == PublishingMethod.Assignment_BinaryMove))
{
myFile = [destination].Files.Add([url of file], [Your File].OpenBinary(), true);
```

You could place the relevant submission code within the page load method so that the assignment is moved immediately when the user clicks the feature file, which is a way to avoid requiring user interaction to move an assignment—it is controlled from the feature reference that builds the relevant Edit Control Block within the document library that targets the assignment content type.

The *Page_Load* event code appears in Listing 4-8. After getting the context of the HTTP request for the current site and Web using *SPContext*, the code requests the *ListID* from the query string to get the list that contains the item that is going to be moved. We also request the *ItemID* from the query string to get the item that is going to be copied because this will provide the unique reference by passing in the GUID of the item to avoid any conflicts in reference. We use the *RunWithElevatedPrivileges* method with a delegate to run the code because the user might not have access to perform this operation. (However, this code instead takes the form of the code that runs the custom activity, where the reference is not inline.)

We get a reference to the site collection by passing in the site collection ID and a reference to the relevant item Web by passing in the relevant Web ID. We also allow unsafe updates to the database as a result of a *GET* request by setting the *AllowUnsafeUpdates* property to *true*. If this is not present, the code will return an error when it is executed because we are making updates to the SharePoint database without validating a security principal. Because the Feature Receiver contains the code to create a new Submitted column, we can update that metadata so that the assignment is considered submitted and so that the other users that use the site are aware of the current state of the specific assignment. We can also check whether the item contains the title field, which it should. If it does contain this field, we append a string saying the item was submitted with the current date and time appended.

We use the *SPWeb.GetFile* method to get the assignment that is going to be moved. This method takes the URL of the item as a parameter to return an *SPFile* object that represents the assignment that is going to be moved. We check whether the *SPFile* object is checked out using the *SPCheckOutStatus* enumeration. If it is checked out, we check in a major version and place in the comment field an indication that the assignment was checked in so that the assignment submission could occur. We put this *SPFile* object in a temporary string so that it can be massaged with some truncation functions and so that it can be formatted into the eventual *SPFile.MoveTo* method parameter correctly. As you will see, you have to use this temporary file to build the relative paths so that nested folder pieces are maintained and the site is consistently synchronized.

To handle errors that occur within the application page, you can use the *SPUtility* class, which contains two helpful methods, *SPUtility.TransferToErrorPage* and *SPUtility.TransferToSuccessPage*, which allow us to pass a simple message in the form of a string parameter that will take the style and associated application page attributes of normal SharePoint errors and successes so that the aggregate application appears uniform. This approach is often better when developing application pages than writing errors, or in a combination of both, to separate sources such as *System.Diagnostics.TextWriterTraceListener* or *System.Diagonistics.EventLog* objects because it provides the user with direct feedback about what the problem is, which can then be reported to the SharePoint administrator.

Listing 4-8   The *page_load* event code.

```
<script runat="server">

protected void Page_Load(object sender, EventArgs e)
    {
    SPSite lvwSiteCollection = SPContext.Current.Site;

    SPWeb lvwSite = SPContext.Current.Web;

    string ListId = Request.QueryString["ListId"];

    string ItemId = Request.QueryString["ItemId"];

    SPSecurity.RunWithElevatedPrivileges(delegate(){

    using (SPSite privLvwSiteCollection = new SPSite(lvwSiteCollection.ID))
    {
        using (SPWeb privLvwSite = privLvwSiteCollection.OpenWeb(lvwSite.ID))
        {
            privLvwSite.AllowUnsafeUpdates = true;

            SPList list = privLvwSite.Lists[new Guid(ListId)];

            SPListItem item = list.Items.GetItemById(Convert.ToInt32(ItemId));
            foreach (SPField field in item.Fields)
            {
                try
                {
                    if (fields.ContainsField("Submitted"))
                    {
                        item["Submitted"] = "Yes";
                        item.Update();

                    }
                    continue;
                }
                catch
                {
                    continue;
                }
            }

            if (item.ParentList.EnableModeration)
            {
                try
                {
                    SPModerationInformation moderationInformation =
                        item.ModerationInformation;
                    if (moderationInformation.Status !=
                        SPModerationStatusType.Pending)
                    {
                        moderationInformation.Status =
                            SPModerationStatusType.Pending;
```

```
                             item.Update();
                    }
               }
               catch (Exception exception)
               {
               // Add Corporate Exception Handling Logic
               // Or
               SPUtility.TransferToErrorPage("An error occured when
                    changing the moderation status" + exception.Message);
               }
          }

          SPFile moveFile = privLvwSite.GetFile(item.Url.ToString());

          if (moveFile.CheckOutStatus != SPFile.SPCheckOutStatus.None)
          {
               moveFile.CheckIn(string.Format("Checked In For Assignment
                    Submission", lvwSite.Name.ToString()),
                    SPCheckinType.MajorCheckIn);
          }

          string tempFile = moveFile.Url.ToString();

          int i = tempFile.IndexOf("/");

          string relativeMoveFile = tempFile.Substring(i, tempFile.Length
             - i);


          try
          {
               moveFile.MoveTo(privLvwSite.Url.ToString() + "/Submitted
                    Assignments" + relativeMoveFile.ToString(), true);
          }

          catch
          {
          // Add Corporate Exception Handling Logic
          // Or

               SPUtility.TransferToErrorPage("An error occured when
                    submitting the assignment" + exception.Message);// Add
          }
     }
   }
  }
 }
</script>
```

Listing 4-9 shows the feature file for the assignment submission functionality, which is fairly standard. Since the ECB declaration is held within the element file for the feature, the Feature.xml file simply references the elements file, thereby playing the main role of providing the facilities for activation.

Listing 4-9   The feature file for the assignment submission functionality.

```xml
<?xml version="1.0" encoding="utf-8" ?>
- <Feature Id="5944AE65-3EB1-47fa-91A6-37B5E766DBA2" Title="Assignment Submission
  Module" Description="Provides an ECB That Allows The Student To Submit Their
  Assignment From The Assignment Content Type Based Document Library To The
  Submitted Document Library" ImageUrl="CALVIEW.GIF" Version="1.0.0.0" Scope="Site"
  xmlns="http://schemas.microsoft.com/sharepoint/">
- <ElementManifests>
  <ElementManifest Location="elements.xml" />
  </ElementManifests>
  </Feature>
```

The custom action is defined in the file elements.xml, shown in Listing 4-10. The first important thing to note about this particular element file is the dynamic, tokenized site reference through the use of the ~*site* declaration so that the site attribute is replaced at run time by the true value of the site. We also use dynamic tokens that reference the *SPList* and *SPListItem* GUIDs, which will be required by the application page during the *Request.QueryString* method to retrieve the value of these variables in the HTTP query string and know exactly which *SPFile* object to submit. Finally, the *Location* attribute is being specified within the *EditControlBlock* value, which specifies the target location for the custom action.

Listing 4-10   Elements.xml for the VLW custom action.

```xml
<?xml version="1.0" encoding="utf-8" ?>
- <Elements xmlns="http://schemas.microsoft.com/sharepoint/">
- <CustomAction Id="obaFeaturesSubmitAssignment.ECBItemMenu"
  RegistrationType="ContentType" RegistrationId="101"
  ImageUrl="/_layouts/images/ARRUPA.GIF" Location="EditControlBlock" Sequence="300"
  Title="Submit This Assignment">
  <UrlAction
  Url="~site/_layouts/SubmitAssignment.aspx?ItemId={ItemId}&ListId={ListId}" />
  </CustomAction>
  </Elements>
```

VLW Solution Utility

A utility also included with the VLW solution (in a console application) allows the user to show the association data for a specific workflow by passing in the string name of the workflow along with the name of the site that she wants to run the tool against. This utility is helpful because the XML that forms the association data affiliated with a workflow can be difficult to dissect and is often not available on the association page. In addition, looping through the lists in a site collection or a similar large-scale object can take an exorbitant amount of clicking by a user. This utility demonstrates work you can do with the workflow manager object and workflow associations and provides insights into a running workflow instance.

Summary

The Office Business Application described in this chapter demonstrates one way to integrate Windows SharePoint Services and Office SharePoint 2007 Server platforms with the 2007 Office system. It also demonstrates how to package site provisioning and the implementation of a relevant security model in a Windows SharePoint Services feature.

Workflow activities—the building blocks of custom workflows—are an important component of developing with the Windows SharePoint Services object model. Workflows can encapsulate the logic of business and organizational processes and be associated with standard events to ensure that information is collected and operations are performed uniformly. Making the logic of workflows available to users of a SharePoint site through simple-to-use menu commands ensures both a positive user experience and that the data an organization requires can be easily collected and managed.

Chapter 5
Creating a Statement of Work with Open XML Formats

—John Holliday, Microsoft SharePoint MVP

Large documents often have different workflow and collaboration requirements for different sections of the document. Consider a consulting company, for example, that needs to produce detailed statements of work for its clients. Although a statement of work (SOW) is delivered as a single document, each section might be composed by a separate team, each contributing specialized knowledge required for that section. A typical statement of work might involve sales, business development, project management, and technical teams, for example. The sales team interacts with the client to establish a project's requirements. The business development team establishes the budget and revenue targets. The project management team establishes the timelines and work schedules based on estimates and assessments provided by the technical team.

As a result, each section of a statement of work document might require a different set of tools and resources to enable the team responsible for that section to work efficiently and complete its work. Each team needs to work independently of the others but in a coordinated fashion to produce a statement of work that reflects the aggregation of their individual contributions. Each team needs to work independently to maximize efficiency—avoiding time wasted focusing on content that is outside the scope of their business function—but their efforts must be coordinated so that the other teams have the information they need to supply their content in a timely manner.

The Office Business Application (OBA) solution described in this chapter shows how you can use Open XML to generate a statement of work document in a variety of formats. We'll first explore the details of an XML schema (XSD) for a statement of work that defines project information and the business relationships between the parties involved in the project. From there, I'll describe a C# application programming interface (API) I developed to generate a statement of work document based on the schema. The document can be created as a Microsoft Office Word 2007 document, a Microsoft Office PowerPoint 2007 presentation, or a Microsoft Office Excel 2007 spreadsheet. For demonstration purposes and to show one way that users can make use of the schema and collect the information needed for the final statement of work, I also created a Microsoft Office InfoPath 2007 form template that can serve as a vehicle for entering data and then generating the statement of work in the format you need. The statement of work API can easily be implemented in other types of user interfaces—a custom task pane, for example—or incorporated into the operations and properties of a Windows SharePoint Services site. At the end of the chapter you'll see how to call the API from a custom feature in Windows SharePoint Services.

Figure 5-1 shows the overall architecture of the statement of work solution. The following list briefly describes the solution's components and their operations:

- The statement of work XSD defines abstract data model.

- The XSD is then used to generate a wrapper class in C#. The wrapper class is extended to implement document-generation interfaces.

- Document templates are created in Office Word 2007, Office Excel 2007, and Office PowerPoint 2007 using elements required by the SOW API. The document templates are included as embedded resources in the API assembly.

- The statement of work XSD is loaded into Office InfoPath 2007 to create a custom form template using Microsoft Visual Studio Tools for Office (VSTO).

- The InfoPath form calls the statement of work API to generate finished documents on the client. (For demonstration purposes, I've used a console application to generate documents from the command line.)

- The InfoPath form is registered as an administrator form on Office SharePoint Server 2007.

- Form data is stored in a SharePoint form library.

- The form library includes an event receiver that calls the statement of work API to generate documents on the server.

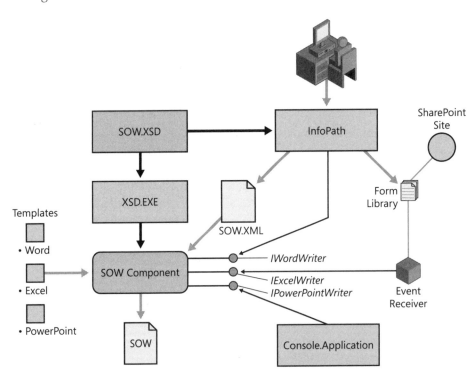

Figure 5-1 The architecture of the statement of work solution.

Software Requirements

The statement of work console application and other projects were created using the beta 1 version of Microsoft Visual Studio 2008. Because the beta 1 release did not support an Office InfoPath 2007 project, I developed the InfoPath form template for this solution using Visual Studio 2005. I also used the Microsoft SDK for Open XML Formats when developing this solution. This SDK is built on top of the *System.IO.Packaging* API and provides strongly typed part classes to manipulate Open XML documents. Microsoft .NET Framework 3.0 is required to use the SDK.

Building the Statement of Work Schema, Input Form, and Document Templates

The statement of work schema defines the overall structure of the statement of work document. It includes a high-level description of each document section and additional metadata that is used to generate physical or virtual representations of the document. It could also include information that would be used with Windows SharePoint Services to construct a document workspace or generate one or more workflows that manage the document's life cycle. The schema serves both as an external data source for an Office InfoPath 2007 form that can be used to gather the requirements for a particular statement of work and, as I'll describe later in the chapter, as input to an XSD conversion tool to generate C# wrapper classes.

The schema, which I built manually, is fairly comprehensive and is defined in the file StatementOfWork.xsd. Figure 5-2 shows the major sections.

The high-level elements in the schema are *CompanyInfo*, *ClientInfo*, and *ProjectInfo*. The *CompanyInfo* element defines information such as the name of the presenter, the name of the individual who signs the statement of work, and that individual's title. The *ClientInfo* element defines a list of contacts and other standard information such as the client's address. Each contact can be described through attributes that indicate whether the contact is the primary contact for that client and whether the contact has signing authority.

The *ProjectInfo* element contains generally more complex and interesting elements that together define the business arrangements entailed in the statement of work, including details such as a project title's as well as elements such as assumptions, policies, schedules, and members of the project team. The following portion of the schema defines the overall *ProjectInfo* type. The list that follows summarizes and shows examples of several of the key elements in the *ProjectInfo* section.

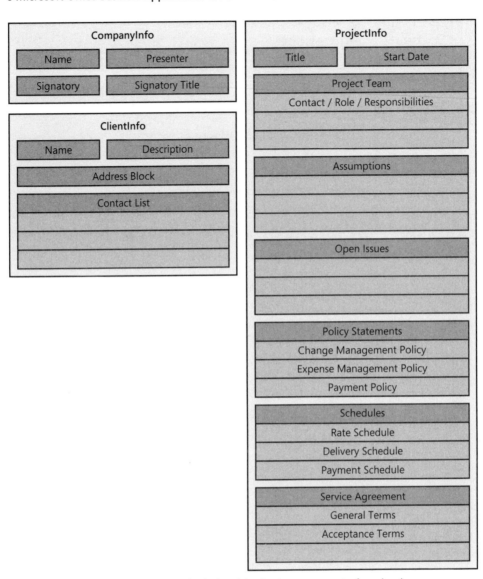

Figure 5-2 The major sections and relationships in the statement of work schema.

```
<xs:complexType name="ProjectInfo">
  <xs:sequence>
    <xs:element name="Title" type="xs:string" minOccurs="1"
      maxOccurs="1"/>
    <xs:element name="StartingDate" type="xs:date" minOccurs="1"
      maxOccurs="1"/>
    <xs:element name="Team" type="Team" minOccurs="1" maxOccurs="1"/>
    <xs:element name="Assumptions" type="Assumptions" minOccurs="1"
      maxOccurs="1"/>
     <xs:element name="Policies" type="Policies" minOccurs="1"
      maxOccurs="1" />
```

```
    <xs:element name="Schedules" type="Schedules" minOccurs="1"
      maxOccurs="1"/>
    <xs:element name="Agreement" type="Agreement" minOccurs="1"
      maxOccurs="1"/>
  </xs:sequence>
</xs:complexType>
```

- **Assumptions**   The *Assumptions* element is defined by a category and a title. The categories into which an assumption can fall are enumerated toward the end of the schema and include project phases such as Requirements, Design, and Architecture; administrative areas such as Legal and Insurance; and project details such as Delivery, Scheduling, and so on.

- **Policies**   *Policies* are used to describe the behavior of a related group of content elements and to control how they are generated. For instance, separate policies can be defined for the following three areas: *ChangeInScope* (or *ChangePolicy*), *Expenses*, or *Payments*.

  - **ChangePolicy**   This type provides for a general statement of the change-management policy and a description of the methodology that will be applied. This element's attributes are *Allowed*, which takes a Boolean value and specifies whether changes to the statement of work are allowed, and *PaidBy*, which designates the party responsible for paying for changes of this type. If changes are not allowed, the content generation logic I developed can substitute appropriate boilerplate.

  - **ExpensePolicy**   This type is defined by a policy statement and a list of *ExpenseItems*, an element that is further defined by the attributes *ExpenseCategory*, *ResponsibleParty*, and *Limit*, which can be used to designate a limit on the amount a client might be required to pay for travel or meals.

  - **PaymentPolicy**   This type again provides for a policy statement as well as payment terms.

- **Schedules**   The *Schedules* type defines three kinds of schedules: *RateSchedule*, *DeliverySchedule*, and *PaymentSchedule*.

  - **RateSchedule**   This schedule is made up of one or more *RateItems*. A *RateItem* is described by a type, a unit price, and a unit—for example, consulting at $200 per hour. The types that can be used are enumerated as *SalesItems* in the enumeration section of the schema and include items such as Design, Mentoring, Development, Programming, and Project Management.

  - **DeliverySchedule**   This schedule consists of one or more *Deliverables*, which are defined by a name, type, start and due dates, estimated units, and the unit being used. The *SalesItem* type, which is used in generating the rate schedule, is used again in this element to generate the list of deliverables. For example, let's say we have a rate schedule that describes the different types of services that we will provide, such as consulting, training, and so on. Each type of service is described by a *SalesItem* entity, which includes the amount charged for that service. The delivery schedule itemizes the actual deliverables and relates back to the sales item being delivered. For example, there could be two training deliverables (SharePoint Developer Training and Windows 2003 Administration Training), which are of type *Training*, and one or more consulting deliverables (SharePoint Consulting, Web Design Consulting) of type *Consulting*. To calculate the total amount due, the content generation logic refers back to the rate schedule to get the rate for each deliverable.

❑ **PaymentSchedule** This schedule consists of *Payables* and describes a phased payment approach. *Payables* are defined by type, amount, and a due date. Amounts of each phase can be designated by percentage and the particular amount calculated from the total amount.

The following section of the schema defines the details of the three schedules and shows their relationship. In the statement of work document, the schedules are represented in tables, which, as you'll see later in the chapter, requires some particular handling in the data substitution mechanisms I've used.

```
<!-- Schedules -->
<xs:complexType name="Schedules">
    <xs:sequence>
      <xs:element name="RateSchedule" type="RateSchedule" minOccurs="1"
        maxOccurs="1"/>
      <xs:element name="DeliverySchedule" type="DeliverySchedule"
        minOccurs="1" maxOccurs="1" />
      <xs:element name="PaymentSchedule" type="PaymentSchedule"
        minOccurs="1" maxOccurs="1" />
    </xs:sequence>
</xs:complexType>
<xs:complexType name="RateSchedule">
    <xs:sequence>
      <xs:element name="RateItem" type="RateItem" minOccurs="0"
        maxOccurs="unbounded"/>
    </xs:sequence>
    <xs:attribute name="DefaultDailyRate" type="xs:double" use="required"/>
</xs:complexType>
<xs:complexType name="RateItem">
    <xs:simpleContent>
      <xs:extension base="xs:string">
        <xs:attribute name="Type" use="required" type="SalesItem"/>
        <xs:attribute name="UnitPrice" use="required"
          type="xs:double"/>
        <xs:attribute name="Unit" use="required" type="Unit"/>
      </xs:extension>
    </xs:simpleContent>
</xs:complexType>
<xs:complexType name="DeliverySchedule">
    <xs:sequence>
      <xs:element name="Deliverable" type="Deliverable" minOccurs="0"
        maxOccurs="unbounded"/>
```

```
      </xs:sequence>
  </xs:complexType>
  <xs:complexType name="Deliverable">
      <xs:simpleContent>
        <xs:extension base="xs:string">
          <xs:attribute name="Name" type="xs:string" use="required"/>
          <xs:attribute name="Type" use="required" type="SalesItem"/>
          <xs:attribute name="StartDate" type="xs:date" use="required"/>
          <xs:attribute name="DueDate" type="xs:date" use="required"/>
          <xs:attribute name="EstimatedUnits" type="xs:double"
            use="required"/>
          <xs:attribute name="Unit" use="required" type="Unit"/>
        </xs:extension>
      </xs:simpleContent>
  </xs:complexType>
  <xs:complexType name="PaymentSchedule">
      <xs:sequence>
        <xs:element name="Payable" type="Payable" minOccurs="0"
          maxOccurs="unbounded"/>
      </xs:sequence>
      <xs:attribute name="TotalAmount" type="xs:double" use="optional"/>
  </xs:complexType>
  <xs:complexType name="Payable">
      <xs:simpleContent>
        <xs:extension base="xs:string">
          <xs:attribute name="Type" type="PaymentType" use="required"/>
          <xs:attribute name="Amount" type="xs:double" use="required"/>
          <xs:attribute name="DueBy" type="xs:date" use="required"/>
        </xs:extension>
      </xs:simpleContent>
  </xs:complexType>
```

■ **Team**   Rather than using a list of specific individuals, the *Team* type is defined by associating team members with roles. Each type of role can be further defined by a list of its responsibilities. The *Team* type is an example of how the statement of work data definition does not always map gracefully into the structure of the document that is generated. It is more natural, for instance, for someone entering data to think in terms of the team and the roles each team member plays. When generating documents, however, certain roles might be more important than others for a given document. Thus, the content generation logic you use needs to determine how best to render the data for a given content placeholder.

The statement of work schema continues in a similar vein to describe agreement and acceptance terms, boilerplate elements, and various enumerations that complement the types defined earlier. Figure 5-3 shows a portion of a sample XML file based on the schema that is populated with data that defines a specific statement of work. You can examine the file sample.xml to see how the schema is fully implemented.

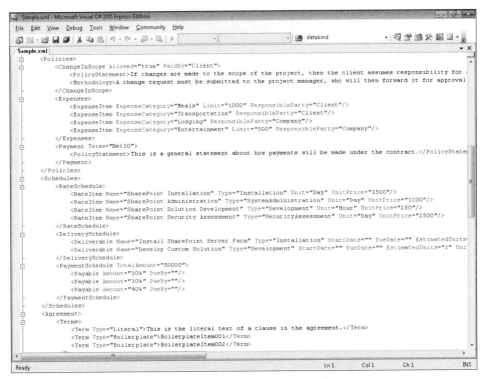

```
Sample.xml - Microsoft Visual C# 2005 Express Edition

File  Edit  View  Debug  Tools  Window  Community  Help

                                                              databind

Sample.xml
    <Policies>
        <ChangeInScope Allowed="true" PaidBy="Client">
            <PolicyStatement>If changes are made to the scope of the project, then the client assumes responsibility for
            <Methodology>A change request must be submitted to the project manager, who will then forward it for approval
        </ChangeInScope>
        <Expenses>
            <ExpenseItem ExpenseCategory="Meals" Limit="1000" ResponsibleParty="Client"/>
            <ExpenseItem ExpenseCategory="Transportation" ResponsibleParty="Client"/>
            <ExpenseItem ExpenseCategory="Lodging" ResponsibleParty="Company"/>
            <ExpenseItem ExpenseCategory="Entertainment" Limit="500" ResponsibleParty="Company"/>
        </Expenses>
        <Payment Terms="Net30">
            <PolicyStatement>This is a general statement about how payments will be made under the contract.</PolicyState
        </Payment>
    </Policies>
    <Schedules>
        <RateSchedule>
            <RateItem Name="SharePoint Installation" Type="Installation" Unit="Day" UnitPrice="1500"/>
            <RateItem Name="SharePoint Administration" Type="SystemAdministration" Unit="Day" UnitPrice="1200"/>
            <RateItem Name="SharePoint Solution Development" Type="Development" Unit="Hour" UnitPrice="250"/>
            <RateItem Name="SharePoint Security Assessment" Type="SecurityAssessment" Unit="Day" UnitPrice="2500"/>
        </RateSchedule>
        <DeliverySchedule>
            <Deliverable Name="Install SharePoint Server Farm" Type="Installation" StartDate="" DueDate="" EstimatedUnits
            <Deliverable Name="Develop Custom Solution" Type="Development" StartDate="" DueDate="" EstimatedUnits="3" Uni
        </DeliverySchedule>
        <PaymentSchedule TotalAmount="50000">
            <Payable Amount="30%" DueBy=""/>
            <Payable Amount="30%" DueBy=""/>
            <Payable Amount="40%" DueBy=""/>
        </PaymentSchedule>
    </Schedules>
    <Agreement>
        <Terms>
            <Term Type="Literal">This is the literal text of a clause in the agreement.</Term>
            <Term Type="Boilerplate">BoilerplateItem001</Term>
            <Term Type="Boilerplate">BoilerplateItem002</Term>

Ready                                            Ln 1        Col 1       Ch 1                INS
```

Figure 5-3   A sample XML file based on the statement of work schema.

Creating an InfoPath 2007 Form for Data Input

Now that we have a schema that defines a statement of work, we need a tool of some sort with which to collect the data required to create a specific instance. One approach to take to provide this capability is an Office InfoPath 2007 form, which could be deployed to a Windows SharePoint Services document library; wrapped in workflows that initiate data collection, review, and approval; and tied to event handlers that would trigger the creation of the statement of work in various file formats. With the advent of Microsoft Office Forms Server 2007, the use of an Office InfoPath 2007 form can be extended to users working only in a Web browser rather than with a client instance of Office InfoPath 2007 itself.

> **More Info**   A full description of Office Forms Server 2007 is beyond the scope of this chapter. You can find more information at *http://office.microsoft.com/en-us/formsserver/ HA100393371033.aspx.*

Creating an InfoPath 2007 form template from an existing schema is actually easier than creating one from scratch. Because the schema is locked, it is relatively straightforward to use layout tables in InfoPath 2007 to arrange the controls on the form's surface. Be sure that you take account of required fields that might be hidden in the form. If any required field values are missing or invalid, the statement of work API will refuse to serialize the form. You might need to take extra steps (beyond standard XML schema validation) to validate the data before it is submitted. In some but not in all cases, Office InfoPath 2007 will alert you.

 After building the form shown in Figure 5-4, I added some buttons that call the statement of work API to generate each of the document types. Another approach would be to create a custom task pane with buttons that hook back into the form to call the API. You could implement a task pane in Office Word 2007 or Office Excel 2007, for example. A custom task pane would also provide a way to add more descriptive text around the buttons.

> **More Info**   For examples of custom task panes and the capabilities that they provide, see the Office Business Application solutions described in Chapter 2, "Managing and Automating the Budget Approval Process," and Chapter 3, "Managing Sales Forecasting with an Office Business Application."

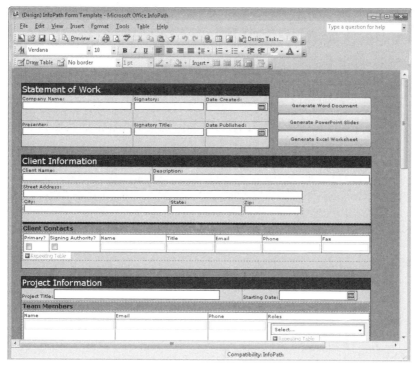

Figure 5-4   An Office InfoPath 2007 form based on the statement of work schema.

The following method (from the file formcode.cs) is called when a user clicks the button to generate the statement of work in Office Word 2007. The statements in the method will become familiar as you learn more about the statement of work API. For example, the *IWord-Writer* interface is a custom interface that I defined as an extension to the basic *StatementOf-Work* class that is generated from the schema. You'll see how this interface is implemented later in the chapter.

```
public void btn_GenerateWordDocument_Clicked(object sender, ClickedEventArgs
    e)
{
    // prompt the user for the destination file
    SaveFileDialog dlg = new SaveFileDialog();
    dlg.Filter = "Word Documents (*.docx)|*.docx";
    dlg.Title = "Generate Statement of Work";
    if (DialogResult.OK == dlg.ShowDialog())
    {
        XPathNavigator nav = MainDataSource.CreateNavigator();
        StatementOfWork sow = StatementOfWork.LoadXml(nav.OuterXml);
        IWordWriter writer = sow as IWordWriter;
        writer.Save(dlg.FileName, true);
    }
}
```

Creating the Statement of Work Office Word 2007 Template

The statement of work document is generated in Office Word 2007 based on a template that has most of the finished formatting in place. The question that you need to address in producing the Office Word 2007 version of the statement of work document, however, is how best to merge the data fields from the XML file into the template when creating the finished document.

One problem when working with WordProcessingML, especially in versions of Microsoft Word prior to the 2007 Office system, is that the XML created by Word is defined at a low level. By that I mean that a document's content is not stored as "sentences" and "words," but as "ranges" that can be broken up arbitrarily during the editing process. Broken ranges present a problem for any text-substitution strategy that relies on tokens entered into the document's text.

For example, if you want to embed a placeholder into the text for your client's name, you might use a token such as "$$CLIENT_NAME$$" and then enter this text at various places in the document. When the document template is saved, however, it is possible—depending on the sequence of edits and other factors—that the token will be broken up into multiple ranges, as in the following example:

```
<w:p w:rsidR="00143B45" w:rsidRDefault="006B0D6F" w:rsidP="00932C37">
    <w:pPr>
        <w:pStyle w:val="Header2"/>
    </w:pPr>
    <w:r>
        <w:t xml:space="preserve">$$CLIENT_N </w:t>
```

```
    </w:r>
    <w:r w:rsidR="00ED016B">
        <w:t>A</w:t>
    </w:r>
    <w:r>
        <w:t>ME$$</w:t>
    </w:r>
</w:p>
```

In a case such as this, the single token has been broken into three ranges. If you tried to perform a simple text substitution, the substitution would fail and the result would be an incorrect document.

One way around this problem in Office Word 2007 is to use *content controls* to act as atomic placeholders for the data you want to merge. Content controls are defined by the Open XML format specification as individual controls that you can add and customize for use in templates, forms, and documents. For example, many online forms are designed with a drop-down list control that provides a restricted set of choices for the user of the form. Content controls can provide instructional text for users, and you can set controls to disappear when users enter their own text.

> **More Info**   You can find more information about content controls, including the types of controls that Office Word 2007 supports, at *http://office.microsoft.com/en-us/word/ HA100307501033.aspx.*

Although you could go further and bind content controls directly to custom XML document parts, that approach is not the best for document generation because it is unlikely that you'll have a one-to-one mapping between schema elements and the generated content. In most cases, additional logic is required to resolve the data references and transform them into the appropriate text.

Using content controls ensures that the replacement token is never broken into separate ranges in the XML, but it also means you have to do a bit more work to accomplish the actual merging of data. A content control appears in the XML document as follows:

```
<w:sdt>
    <w:sdtPr>
        <w:alias w:val="Client Name"/>
        <w:tag w:val="ClientName"/>
        <w:id w:val="109942697"/>
        <w:placeholder>
            <w:docPart w:val="CD22455AF74842B2B07D4456EFB0EE54"/>
        </w:placeholder>
        <w:showingPlcHdr/>
    </w:sdtPr>
    <w:sdtContent>
```

```
    <w:tc>
        <w:tcPr>
            <w:tcW w:w="6315" w:type="dxa"/>
        </w:tcPr>
        <w:p w:rsidR="003B41B9" w:rsidRPr="00932C37" w:rsidRDefault="004274A8"
          w:rsidP="004274A8">
            <w:pPr>
                <w:pStyle w:val="TableEntry"/>
            </w:pPr>
            <w:r w:rsidRPr="006A77D5">
                <w:rPr>
                    <w:rStyle w:val="PlaceholderText"/>
                    <w:rFonts w:eastAsia="Times"/>
                </w:rPr>
                <w:t>Click here to enter text.</w:t>
            </w:r>
        </w:p>
    </w:tc>
    </w:sdtContent>
</w:sdt>
```

Be sure to note that each control appears as a first-class element of the XML document, which means that you can use XPath expressions to locate them. Each control consists of a properties section and a content section. We can navigate to the content section and replace the paragraph text with the matching data from the input data stream.

You can place content controls throughout a document—in a header or a footer, for example—and use the same tag name in multiple places. You'll see how the strategy of using content control carries over to the statement of work API later in the chapter. In a nutshell, you'll see that the tag name I assigned to each content control in the template matches an item in an enumeration I declare named *FieldType*. When the statement of work document is generated, the code matches field types with placeholders in the template as part of the mechanism for data substitution.

Figure 5-5 shows some of the content controls placed in the Office Word 2007 template.

Creating the Statement of Work Presentation Template

In a fashion similar to the Office Word 2007 document template, I created a template for statement of work presentations in Office PowerPoint 2007. As mentioned in the previous section, for Office Word 2007 documents I used embedded content controls to act as placeholders for substituted field values taken from the XML data file. The main advantage of using content controls is that they are easy to find and we can guarantee that Office Word 2007 will not split a token across multiple character ranges. Unfortunately, Office PowerPoint 2007 does not support embedded content controls, which means that the only way to perform field substitution is to use specially formatted text tokens in the body of the slides of the presentation template.

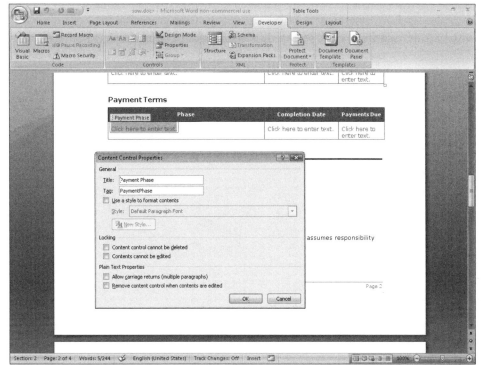

Figure 5-5   The statement of work Word 2007 template is built from content controls.

Depending on the content of a given token, however, it might span ranges, which makes reliably finding the token nearly impossible. Using a token such as "_Version_", for example, would not span ranges because "Version" is a recognized word. But if you enable the spelling checker, using a token such as "_DatePublished_" would cause the token to be split into three separate ranges because the string of characters *DatePublished* is assumed to be a misspelling, and Office PowerPoint 2007 inserts an error object between the enclosing quotation mark characters and what it thinks is a misspelled word.

To avoid this problem, you can use all uppercase characters in the embedded token—for example, "_DATEPUBLISHED_". This token is unlikely to be split, but using this approach means that you cannot use the *Enum.Parse* method (which converts the string representation of the name or numeric value of one or more enumerated constants to an equivalent enumerated object) when matching tokens to field types in the *StatementOfWork* class that is generated for the API.

Figure 5-6 shows an example of a slide from the Office PowerPoint 2007 template.

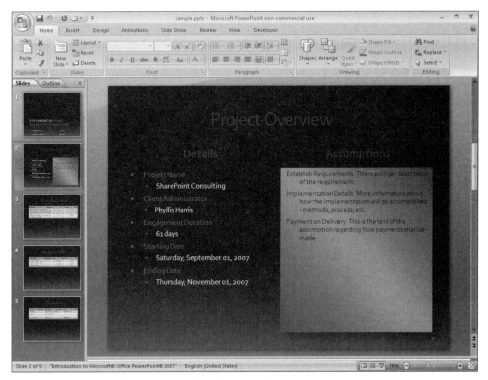

Figure 5-6   In the Office PowerPoint 2007 template, specially formatted tokens are used as placeholders.

Using the Statement of Work API

The API for the statement of work solution is made up of several classes that perform the work necessary to substitute data from an XML document into content placeholders (of various types) and produce a statement of work in various 2007 Office system formats, including Office Word 2007, Office PowerPoint 2007, and Office Excel 2007.

A Quick View of the Test Console Application

To verify that the API works properly, I created a console application that simply loads an XML file and calls the API that I created to generate each of the three document types— Office Word 2007, Office PowerPoint 2007, and Office Excel 2007. The console application is defined in the file program.cs.

In program.cs, you'll see a call to a *StatementOfWork* object, which is created by using an XSD class-generator tool. The custom tool I used is a modified version of the XSD Schema Generator developed originally by Chris Sells. The modified version has been updated for use with Visual Studio 2008. Program.cs also makes reference to three custom interfaces—*IWordWriter, IPowerPointWriter,* and *IExcelWriter*—that relate to the 2007

Office system file formats in which the statement of work is generated. The following code is from program.cs. You can use code such as this in a variety of situations, not just in a console application. Converting a *StatementOfWork* object to (for example) a *WordWriter* or one of the other interface types and then calling the *Save* method makes it easy to generate statement of work documents from different contexts, such as an Office InfoPath 2007 form or an event receiver associated with an Office SharePoint Server 2007 site.

```
// Deserialize the SOW model into an object.
StatementOfWork sow = StatementOfWork.ReadFrom(filePath);
Console.WriteLine("Processing: {0}", sow.ProjectInfo.Title);

// Construct the base output filename.  The extension will be determined
// when the file is actually generated.
string outputFileName = Path.GetFileNameWithoutExtension(filePath);

...

void GenerateDocument(StatementOfWork sow, string fileName)
{
Console.WriteLine("Generating MSWord Document");
IWordWriter writer = sow as IWordWriter;
writer.Save(fileName, true);
}

void GenerateWorksheet(StatementOfWork sow, string fileName)
{
Console.WriteLine("Generating MSExcel Worksheet");
IExcelWriter writer = sow as IExcelWriter;
writer.Save(fileName, true);
}

void GeneratePresentation(StatementOfWork sow, string fileName)
{
Console.WriteLine("Generating MSPowerPoint Presentation");
IPowerPointWriter writer = sow as IPowerPointWriter;
writer.Save(fileName, true);
}
```

We'll take a look at the *StatementOfWork* class and the various interfaces in more detail in later sections of the chapter.

The statement of work API itself is based on a C# object model that is generated as a partial class using an XSD class-generator tool. If you want to review the structure of the partial class, take a look at the file StatementOfWork.cs. You'll see the correspondence between members of the *StatementOfWork* class and the types and elements defined in the statement of work XML schema.

Extending the *StatementOfWork* Class

In this section I'll focus on extensions that I created to the *StatementOfWork* class. You'll find the extensions to the *StatementOfWork* class in the file StatementOfWorkEx.cs, which includes custom properties and methods for constructing 2007 Office system documents from the serialized XML data stream, using reflection to define substitution fields and tables within the templates. These extensions allow us to define everything we need to produce our statements of work, giving us control over the schema as well as the API.

In the following code, you'll notice that the extended class includes three custom interfaces, which are used to create specific types of documents as well as several methods. The solution needs interfaces such as these—*IWordWriter*, *IExcelWriter*, and *IPowerPointWriter*—to support saving the model to the various OpenXML file formats and because each format has different requirements. We'll look at the definition and implementation of the *IWordWriter* interface as an example later in the chapter.

```
public partial class StatementOfWork : IWordWriter, IExcelWriter, IPowerPointWriter
    {
        private string m_theme = string.Empty;
        private string m_templatePath = string.Empty;
        private List<FieldHandler> m_fieldHandlers = null;
        private List<TableHandler> m_tableHandlers = null;
        private Dictionary<string,string> m_boilerplateText = null;
```

The enumeration that follows the extended class declaration is related to the use of content controls in the Office Word 2007 template. Recall that the template is set up to use content controls because the controls help solve the problem of splitting references across ranges. This enumeration defines all the recognized field types that can be used as placeholders within the document template. Each content control in the template includes a tag property—for example, the control shown earlier in Figure 5-5—that matches one of the enumerated fields in the following code:

```
public enum FieldType
{
    CompanyName,
    Version,
    DatePublished,
    Presenter,
    ClientName,
    ClientAdministrator,
    ProjectName,
    EngagementDuration,
    BeginDate,
    EndDate,
    Assumptions,
    ChangePolicy,
    ExpensePolicy,
    ServiceAgreement,
```

```
        Acceptance,
        ClientSignatureName,
        CompanySignatureName,
        ServiceItemName,
        ServiceItemDescription,
        ServiceItemDeliveryDays,
        ServiceItemCostEstimate,
        PaymentPhase,
        PaymentPhaseDueDate,
        PaymentPhaseAmountDue,
        MemberName,
        MemberRoles,
        MemberContact,
        Null
}
```

Field Handlers

To work with the enumerated fields, which are matched programmatically to tag names in the content controls that serve as placeholders in the Office Word 2007 template, the code defines two custom attribute classes, *FieldHandler* and *TableHandler*. Because dealing with content controls in tables requires more and specialized work, I'll cover that topic in detail in the section "The Trouble with Tables" later in the chapter. Figure 5-7 illustrates the mechanism that I implemented for handling placeholders in the body of the document–a "pull" model in which the API first locates the placeholders and then finds a matching field handler to retrieve its content.

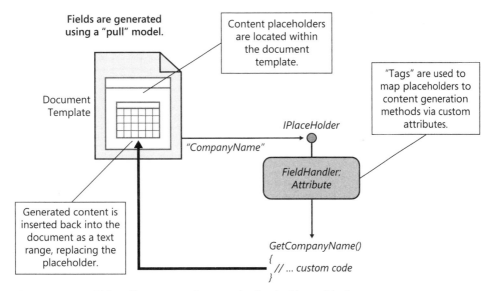

Figure 5-7   Field handlers are used to match placeholders with data.

The following code defines the *FieldHandler* class, which we use to associate a given property or method with a field in the statement of work template:

```
[ AttributeUsage(AttributeTargets.Method) ]
public class FieldHandler : Attribute
    {
        MethodInfo m_methodInfo = null;
        FieldType m_fieldType = FieldType.Null;
        public FieldHandler(FieldType fieldType) { m_fieldType = fieldType; }
        public FieldType Type { get { return m_fieldType; } }
        public MethodInfo Method { get { return m_methodInfo; } set {
          m_methodInfo = value; } }
        public object GetValue(object obj) { return Method.Invoke(obj, null); }
    }
```

This class, which can be applied only to methods, is used in a series of calls that are involved in the creation of the statement of work. (The reason I've restricted the attribute usage to methods is that some of the properties are defined in the schema wrapper, which is automatically generated.) It is important to keep in mind that the API uses methods and not just lookups to resolve placeholders to the actual content. As you can see in the following examples, the logic for the methods can be arbitrarily complex. The following code, for example, is for the *GetStartDate* and the *GetEndDate* methods. The starting date is explicitly stated in the statement of work schema; however, a project's end date is calculated on the basis of values defined in the delivery schedule.

```
[ FieldHandler(FieldType.BeginDate) ]
    public string GetStartDate()
    {
        return this.StartingDate.ToLongDateString();
    }
    private DateTime StartingDate
    {
        get
        {
            return this.ProjectInfo.StartingDate;
        }
    }

[ FieldHandler(FieldType.EndDate) ]
    public string GetEndDate()
    {
        return this.EndingDate.ToLongDateString();
    }
    private DateTime EndingDate
    {
        get
        {
            DateTime dt = this.ProjectInfo.StartingDate;
            foreach (Deliverable deliverable in
              this.ProjectInfo.Schedules.DeliverySchedule)
            {
                if (deliverable.DueDate.CompareTo(dt) >= 0)
```

```
                    dt = deliverable.DueDate;
            }
        return dt;
    }
}
```

The methods in this portion of the extended *StatementOfWork* class move through information provided about a project in the XML document and perform appropriate work—such as string conversion—to serialize and prepare it for use in the statement of work document. In addition to the fairly straightforward examples of the *GetStartDate* and *GetEndDate* methods, I developed methods such as *GetChangeManagementPolicy,* which constructs the change management policy that applies to a statement of work. The change management policy is calculated by searching for a *ChangeInScope* policy and then determining whether changes are allowed and who must pay for them. If a policy statement and methodology are included, they are also appended to the resulting text block. Here is the *GetChangeManagementPolicy* method's definition:

```
[ FieldHandler(FieldType.ChangePolicy) ]
public string GetChangeManagementPolicy()
{
    StringBuilder sb = new StringBuilder();
    if (this.ProjectInfo.Policies.ChangeInScope.Allowed)
    {
        // Add a sentence stating who shall be responsible for paying for
        // the changes.
        sb.Append(string.Format("Any additional expense incurred by changes
          to this statement of work shall be paid for by the {0}.",
            this.ProjectInfo.Policies.ChangeInScope.PaidBy.ToString().ToLower()));
        // Add the policy statement, if provided.
        string statement =
          this.ProjectInfo.Policies.ChangeInScope.PolicyStatement.Value;
        if (!string.IsNullOrEmpty(statement))
            sb.Append(" " + statement);
        // Add the change methodology, if provided.
        string methodology =
          this.ProjectInfo.Policies.ChangeInScope.Methodology.Value;
        if (!string.IsNullOrEmpty(methodology))
            sb.Append(" " + methodology);
    }
    else
    {
            sb.Append("Changes to this statement work are not allowed after execution of
              the agreement.");
    }
    return sb.ToString();
}
```

You'll see shortly how field handlers are used to generate the statement of work document. Essentially, we gather a list of placeholders in the template and then get the field handlers for the fields that match the placeholders. For each match, we perform data binding, and after saving the XML data stream for a particular part of a document, the statement of work document is populated.

Examining *IWordWriter*

As mentioned earlier in the chapter, as part of generating the statement of work document, the *StatementOfWork* object is converted to a type related to the particular document format we want, types that are defined in three custom interfaces whose implementation involves saving a file in a particular format—Office Word 2007, Office PowerPoint 2007, or Office Excel 2007. Listing 5-1 shows the definition of the *IWordWriter* interface.

Listing 5-1   The *IWordWriter* interface.

```
using System;
using System.Collections.Generic;
using System.Linq;
using System.Text;

namespace JohnHolliday.OBA.StatementOfWork
{
    public interface IWordWriter
    {
        /// <summary>
        /// Saves the statement of work as a Microsoft Word document.
        /// </summary>
        /// <param name="fileName"></param>
        /// <param name="bOverwrite"></param>
        void Save(string fileName, bool bOverwrite);
    }
}
```

The following code shows the implementation of the *IWordWriter* interface, specifically the *Save* method. (See the file StatementOfWorkEx.cs.) The interface generates an Office Word 2007 document for the statement of work using the *System.IO.Packaging* API and the SDK for Open XML Formats. The document that is generated is based on the template described earlier in the chapter that contains the content placeholders. The *Save* method adjusts the file extension to the .docx format if necessary, creates an Office Word 2007 document (an *SOWDocument* object), and then calls a routine named *Build*, which we will examine in the next section. The *TemplatePath* method simply retrieves the fully qualified path to the template file that we want to use.

```
void IWordWriter.Save(string fileName, bool bOverwrite)
{
    if (!fileName.ToLower().Contains(".docx"))
      fileName += ".docx";
    using (SOWDocument doc = new SOWDocument(fileName))
      doc.Build(this);
}

string IWordWriter.TemplatePath
{
    get
    {
```

```
        return m_templatePath;
    }
    set
    {
        m_templatePath = value;
    }
}
```

The Trouble with Tables

It is unfortunate that the current implementation of content controls does not support data binding for repeating elements, such as in tables. This requirement is so common that it is likely to find its way into future versions of Microsoft Office and Microsoft Word. For now, however, we have to come up with another strategy for handling data we want to place in tables.

The approach I've taken, which is outlined in Figure 5-8, is to insert a table into the document template and lay out the table so that it contains the number of columns the data requires but only one row. This row serves as the template row for the actual rows that ultimately appear in the table in the generated document.

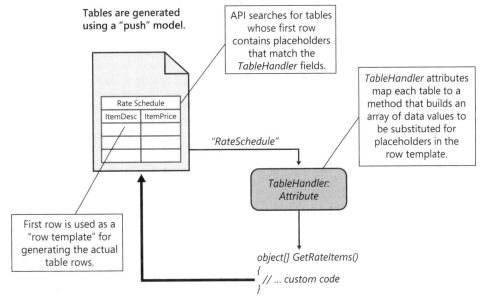

Figure 5-8   Tables are handled with a "push" mechanism.

Essentially, you can insert a specially tagged content control into each cell of the template row and then replace it with the actual data that you want to appear in that column for each row that is generated. By replacing the entire content control with the merged data in each column, you end up with a properly formatted table with the correct number of rows as determined by the number of items specified in the data source.

In contrast to the *FieldHandler* attribute, which is applied using a "pull" model in which the API first locates the placeholders and then finds a matching field handler to retrieve its content, the *TableHandler* attribute is applied using a "push" model. In the push model, the API first locates the *TableHandler* methods and then searches through the document looking for tables that match the signature. When this class is applied to a method, it specifies the field types associated with each table row. The calling routine uses this information to locate the related content placeholders along with the enclosing table definition in the main document.

The class includes a constructor that is used when a method is marked as a table handler. The parameter named *TableType* indicates the type of table a particular handler refers to. The parameter named *fields* specifies the list of field types associated with this table. Field types are declared in left to right order and define the columns of the generated table.

The *Method* property returns a *MethodInfo* structure that describes the actual method used to generate the table data, and the *GetRelatedPlaceholders* method (described in more detail in the next section) filters a list of content placeholders to include only those placeholders that are related to the table handler we're working with. The parameter *placeholders* specifies the list of placeholders to be filtered. The method returns a new list containing only the related placeholders.

```
public class TableHandler : Attribute
{
    MethodInfo m_methodInfo = null;
    TableType m_tableType = TableType.Null;
    List<FieldType> m_fields = new List<FieldType>();

    public TableHandler(TableType tableType, params FieldType[] fields)
    {
        m_tableType = tableType;
        foreach (FieldType fieldType in fields)
        m_fields.Add(fieldType);
    }
    public MethodInfo Method {
        get { return m_methodInfo; }
        set { m_methodInfo = value; }
    }

    public List<IPlaceholder> GetRelatedPlaceholders(List<IPlaceholder>
        placeholders)
    {
        List<IPlaceholder> relatedPlaceholders = new List<IPlaceholder>();
        foreach (IPlaceholder placeholder in placeholders)
            try
            {
                foreach (FieldType ft in m_fields)
                    if (ft.ToString().Equals(placeholder.Tag,
                        StringComparison.InvariantCultureIgnoreCase))
                    {
                        relatedPlaceholders.Add(placeholder);
                        break;
                    }
            }
```

```
        }
        catch { }
        // return the filtered list
        return relatedPlaceholders;
    }
}
```

In the table-handling code, the *FindSourceNode* method is then called to locate the enclosing table node within an XML document. The enclosing table is the nearest table that fully encloses all the placeholders that match the fields associated with the table. For example, consider a table handler declared as follows:

```
[TableHandler(TableType.RateSchedule,
    FieldType.ServiceItemDescription
    Fieldtype.ServiceItemPrice)]
```

An Office Word 2007 document template might then contain a table that matches the following XML:

```
<w:tbl>
    <w:tblPr>...</>
    <w:tblGrid>...</>
    <w:tr>
        <w:trPr>...</>
        <w:sdt>
            <w:sdtPr>
                <w:tag w:val="ServiceItemDescription"/>
```

The purpose of this method is to locate the *<w:tbl>* node that contains all the placeholders associated with fields specified by the table handler. If any of the required fields are missing, the return value is null. This example is specific to Office Word 2007, but different placeholder implementations can support different document types.

In the *FindSourceNode* method, the *placeholders* parameter refers to the list of content placeholders to be used for matching fields. The *nsManager* parameter is the namespace manager for the XML document. The method returns the enclosing table node in the XML document.

```
public XmlNode FindSourceNode(List<IPlaceholder> placeholders, XmlNamespaceManager
   nsManager)
{
    XmlNode sourceNode = null;
    foreach (IPlaceholder relatedControl in placeholders)
    {
        XmlNode tableNode = relatedControl.FindNearestTableNode(nsManager);
        if (tableNode == null) return null;
        if (sourceNode == null) sourceNode = tableNode;
        if (sourceNode != tableNode) return null;
    }
    // return the node
    return sourceNode;
}
```

The *CreateTableNode* method creates a new table node based on the data contained in the statement of work and the content placeholders that are related to the table handler. This method works by extracting the first table row and then using it as a template for the actual table rows. Finally, the underlying table handler method (the one marked by the *TableHandler* attribute) is called to get the raw substitution data as a simple object array. Pre-existing table rows are removed.

> **Note**   This method assumes that the table has a header row.

The *CreateTableNode* method takes several parameters:

- *Sow*, the object containing the data to be merged
- *Placeholders*, the list of related placeholders
- *oldTableNode*, the table node to use as a template
- *nsManager,* the namespace manager for the XML document

The method returns a new XML node that defines the table in Office Word 2007.

```
public XmlNode CreateTableNode(StatementOfWork sow, List<IPlaceholder>
    placeholders,XmlNode oldTableNode, XmlNamespaceManager nsManager)
```

We must have at least one placeholder. Otherwise, we return null. Assuming we have a place-holder, we use the first placeholder as a class-factory proxy because we don't know what kind of underlying placeholder object we are dealing with. Next, we clone the existing table, locate the table rows (assuming a header row is included), and get the raw data that will be merged. After determining the number of rows to be added to the table, we add the rows using the data and the content placeholders.

```
{
    if (placeholders.Count == 0) return null;
    IPlaceholder placeholderProxy = placeholders[0];

    XmlNode newTableNode = oldTableNode.Clone();

    XmlNodeList existingRows =
        newTableNode.SelectNodes(placeholderProxy.TableRowElementTag, nsManager);
    if (existingRows.Count < 2) return null; // must have a template row and a
                                             //header row
    object[] data = (object[])Method.Invoke(sow, null);
    int nRows = data.Length;
    int dataIndex = 0;
    for (int row = 0; row < nRows; row++)
```

Now we clone the template row, skipping the header row, and get a new collection of content placeholders for the row, binding each placeholder to the raw data.

```
{
XmlNode newRow = existingRows[1].Clone();
List<IPlaceholder> rowPlaceholders = placeholderProxy.FindPlaceholders(newRow,
    nsManager);
if (rowPlaceholders.Count != m_fields.Count)
{
    throw new ApplicationException(
        string.Format("Field count for table '{0}' does not match content
            placeholders found in the document template.",
            m_tableType.ToString()));
}

int columnIndex = 0;
object[] dataRow = (object[])data[row];

foreach (IPlaceholder placeholder in rowPlaceholders)
```

The code then assigns a unique ID to the placeholder and binds the placeholder to the raw data. Assigning a unique identifier allows a user to continue to work with the content control normally within the finished document. We then add the row to the table just above the template row.

```
{
    placeholder.SetId(row * nRows + dataIndex + 1);
    placeholder.DataBind(dataRow[ columnIndex++ ]);
    dataIndex++;
}
newTableNode.InsertBefore(newRow, existingRows[1]);
```

We then remove all previous rows from the table and return the resulting table node.

```
for (int i = 1; i < existingRows.Count; i++)
  newTableNode.RemoveChild(existingRows[i]);

return newTableNode;
```

The *DataBind* method performs the data binding operation for a table handler as defined by the *SOW* object. Its parameters are an *SOW* object, the list of content placeholders, and the namespace manager.

```
public void DataBind(StatementOfWork sow, List<IPlaceholder> placeholders,
  XmlNamespaceManager nsManager)
{
    // get the list of related placeholders
    List<IPlaceholder> relatedPlaceholders = GetRelatedPlaceholders(placeholders);
    if (relatedPlaceholders.Count > 0)
    {
        // get the node to be replaced
        XmlNode tableNode = FindSourceNode(relatedPlaceholders, nsManager);
        if (tableNode != null)
        {
        // get the parent node of the table node
        XmlNode parentNode = tableNode.ParentNode;
```

```
if (parentNode != null)
{
    // create the new table node
    XmlNode newNode = CreateTableNode(sow, relatedPlaceholders, tableNode,
        nsManager);
    if (newNode != null)
    {
        // insert the new table node
        parentNode.InsertBefore(newNode, tableNode);
        // remove the old table node
        parentNode.RemoveChild(tableNode);
    }
}
}
}
}
```

One advantage of using this approach for dealing with tables is that it relieves the designer of the Office Word 2007 template from having to conform to the way the API operates. The same paradigm for data substitution holds whether the designer is defining a table or an individual placeholder with the document. You can simply insert placeholders where you want the data to appear.

Building the Statement of Work Office Word 2007 Document

In this section, I'll describe more of the mechanisms that perform the data substitution required to generate the statement of work document. First I'll describe another custom interface that I created, *IPlaceHolder*, and its role in data substitution. Then I'll turn to the code that defines an *SOWDocument* object, a class used to generate the Office Word 2007 version of the statement of work.

Examining *IPlaceHolder*

As I mentioned earlier, because of the varying nature of content placeholders, I needed an approach that could apply equally to the different formats. The *IPlaceHolder* interface defines an abstraction for a data value that can be substituted for content within a document. In the interface definition, we declare a placeholder identifier, the placeholder title, and the tag that is used to match substitution fields as well as the text value to be substituted.

The interface definition also defines members for getting the element tag for nodes containing table rows and for locating the nearest table that encloses a particular placeholder. You can see how these members are used in the code described in the section "The Trouble with Tables" earlier in the chapter.

In its *FindPlaceholders* method, the interface provides for a means of retrieving the list of content placeholders found within a node. The *DataBind* method resolves data references from a *FieldHandler* instance to the corresponding data in a *StatementOfWork* object. The data values are retrieved from the *FieldHandler* and are then bound to the placeholder for final substitution in the finished document. Listing 5-2 shows the definition for *IPlaceHolder*.

Listing 5-2   The *IPlaceHolder* interface.

```
using System;
using System.Collections.Generic;
using System.Linq;
using System.Text;
using System.Xml;

namespace JohnHolliday.OBA.StatementOfWork
{
    public interface IPlaceholder
    {
        string Id { get; set; }
        string Title { get; set; }
        string Tag { get; set; }
        string Text { get; set; }
        XmlNamespaceManager NamespaceManager { get; }

        string TableRowElementTag { get; }
        void SetId(int newId);
        XmlNode FindNearestTableNode(XmlNamespaceManager nsManager);
        XmlNode FindNearestEnclosingNode(XmlNamespaceManager nsManager, string
          path);

        List<IPlaceholder> FindPlaceholders(XmlNode node, XmlNamespaceManager
          nsManager);

        void DataBind(StatementOfWork sow, StatementOfWork.FieldHandler
          fieldHandler);
        void DataBind(object data);
    }
}
```

The *SOWDocument* Class

The meat of the conversion for an Office Word 2007 document occurs in the *SOWDocument* class, which is defined in the file SOWDocument.cs. The code creates a *WordprocessingDocument* wrapper class for building statements of work and then creates and initializes an *XmlDocument* for a given package part. We then load the document from the stream and set up the Office Word 2007 namespace for navigating the XML. Next the code constructs a new statement of work document from the template, and then content substitution begins on the document part. You'll also see references to the *IPlaceHolder* interface and its *FindPlaceholders* method, which here loads the placeholders gathered from the template.

> **Note**   As with all XML schemas, namespaces are used here to ensure that each element is
> unambiguous. For example, a paragraph is generally represented using the *<p>* XML
> element tag. Because this tag could refer to an Office Word 2007 paragraph or to an Office
> PowerPoint 2007 paragraph, namespaces are used to disambiguate them. For an Office Word
> 2007 document, the paragraph tag is *<w:p>*, and for Office PowerPoint 2007, the tag is
> *<a:p>*. When working with XML documents, you often need to intermingle tags from multiple
> namespaces; to avoid having to deal with each namespace individually, you can use an
> object called a *namespace manager* to keep track of them.

Content substitution, which involves locating content controls placed in the document and
then modifying the XML based on each control, takes place largely in two methods: *Process-
ContentFields* and *ProcessTableFields*. Individual controls might require different processing
depending on where the control is placed (such as within a table cell), its name (such as a
known section, which requires special handling) or its attributes (such as a special style).

As you learned in the previous section, tables are handled by placing content controls in the
first row within the document template and then replacing the entire enclosing table with a
generated XML snippet that contains the actual row data. The embedded content controls are
used to specify the type and location of data for each table column. You'll see that for field
handlers we use a "pull" model in which we first locate the placeholders and then search for
field handlers to bind them to. For table handlers, in the "push" model, we first get the list of
table handlers as defined by the statement of work and then process each against the list of
placeholders, searching for tables that match the table handler signature.

Both *ProcessContentFields* and *ProcessTableFields* are called from a routine named *Build*, which
moves through each part defined for a document (the main document, tables in the main
document, headers, footer, notes, and comments) calling the appropriate method. After
checking that the part is available, we get the XML document for the document part and
perform a data binding operation for all placeholders associated with a particular field
handler. At this point, the XML document contains updated data as determined by the
content controls and the data binding operation. We store the data back into the document
and replace the existing document content. Listing 5-3 shows the *SOWDocument* class.

Listing 5-3   The *SOWDocument* class.

```
using System;
using System.Collections;
using System.Collections.Generic;
using System.Diagnostics;
using System.Linq;
using System.Text;
using System.IO;
using System.IO.Packaging;
using System.Reflection;
using System.Xml;
using System.Xml.Serialization;
using System.Web;
```

```csharp
using Microsoft.Office.DocumentFormat.OpenXml.Packaging;

namespace JohnHolliday.OBA.StatementOfWork.Parts.Word
{
    public class SOWDocument : IDisposable
    {
        WordprocessingDocument m_doc = null;
        MainDocumentPart m_mainPart = null;

        private XmlDocument OpenXmlDocumentPart(OpenXmlPart part,
          XmlNamespaceManager nsManager)
        {
            XmlDocument xd = new XmlDocument();
            using (Stream stream = part.GetStream())
            {
                xd.Load(stream);

                string wordNamespace = xd.DocumentElement.NamespaceURI;
                nsManager.AddNamespace("w", wordNamespace);
            }
            return xd;
        }

        public SOWDocument(string fileName)
        {
            m_doc = WordprocessingDocument.Open(
                Helpers.CopyResourceTemplate(fileName,
                    "JohnHolliday.OBA.StatementOfWork.Templates.sow.docx"),
                        true);
            m_mainPart = m_doc.MainDocumentPart;
        }

        private void ProcessContentFields(StatementOfWork sow, OpenXmlPart part)
        {
            if (part == null) return;

            XmlNamespaceManager nsManager = new XmlNamespaceManager(new
              NameTable());
            XmlDocument xd = OpenXmlDocumentPart(part, nsManager);

            // load the placeholders
            List<IPlaceholder> placeholders =
              WordPlaceholder.FindPlaceholders(xd,nsManager);

            foreach (IPlaceholder placeholder in placeholders)
            {
                StatementOfWork.FieldHandler fieldHandler =
                  sow.GetFieldHandler(placeholder);
                if (fieldHandler != null) placeholder.DataBind(sow, fieldHandler);
            }

            using (Stream outputStream = part.GetStream(FileMode.Create,
              FileAccess.Write))
            {
                xd.Save(outputStream);
```

```
                    outputStream.Close();
            }
    }

    private void ProcessTableFields(StatementOfWork sow, OpenXmlPart part)
    {
        // part must be available
        if (part == null) return;

        // get the xml document for the document part
        XmlNamespaceManager nsManager = new XmlNamespaceManager(new
          NameTable());
        XmlDocument xd = OpenXmlDocumentPart(part, nsManager);

        // load the placeholders
        List<IPlaceholder> placeholders = WordPlaceholder.FindPlaceholders(xd,
          nsManager);

        // locate the tables as defined by the sow
        List<StatementOfWork.TableHandler> tableHandlers = sow.TableHandlers;

        // allow each table handler to locate the controls it needs and
        // then use them to generate the replacement table
        foreach (StatementOfWork.TableHandler tableHandler in tableHandlers)
            tableHandler.DataBind(sow, placeholders, nsManager);

        // store the xml document back into the part
        using (Stream outputStream = part.GetStream(FileMode.Create,
          FileAccess.Write))
        {
            xd.Save(outputStream);
            outputStream.Close();
        }
    }

    public void Build(StatementOfWork sow)
    {
        try
        {
            // process the fields in the main document
            ProcessContentFields(sow, MainPart);

            // process the tables in the main document
            ProcessTableFields(sow, MainPart);

            // process the headers
            foreach (OpenXmlPart header in MainPart.HeaderParts)
                ProcessContentFields(sow, header);

            // process the footers
            foreach (OpenXmlPart footer in MainPart.FooterParts)
                ProcessContentFields(sow, footer);

            // process the other special parts
            ProcessContentFields(sow, MainPart.EndnotesPart);
```

```
                ProcessContentFields(sow, MainPart.FootnotesPart);
                ProcessContentFields(sow, MainPart.CommentsPart);
        }
        catch (Exception x)
        {
            Debug.Fail("Failed to assemble document.",x.ToString());
        }
    }


    /// <summary>
    /// Retrieves the main part of the document.
    /// </summary>
    public MainDocumentPart MainPart
    {
        get
        {
            return m_mainPart;
        }
    }


    #region IDisposable Members

    /// <summary>
    /// Handles the closing of the document when this object is disposed.
    /// </summary>
    public void Dispose()
    {
        if (m_doc != null)
        {
            m_doc.Dispose();
        }
    }

    #endregion
}
```

Integrating the Statement of Work API with a SharePoint Form Library

As I mentioned earlier in the chapter, you can use the statement of work API in contexts such as the Office InfoPath 2007 form template, a custom task pane, or, as you'll see in this section, as part of a Windows SharePoint Services feature that is implemented for a form library on a SharePoint site. The steps I describe include loading the Office InfoPath 2007 form template into a form library and creating a feature that adds a set of custom commands to the drop-down menu of each instance of data in the library. I've used separate commands, shown in Figure 5-9, to generate each of the document types (Office Word 2007 and Office Power-Point 2007 in this example) from the data associated with the Office InfoPath 2007 form.

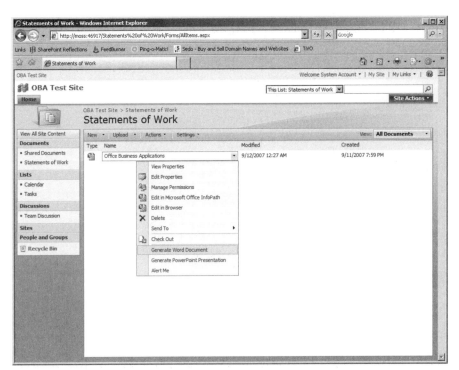

Figure 5-9   Custom commands in a SharePoint form library make use of the statement of work API.

The first step is to prepare the Office InfoPath 2007 form for publishing to the SharePoint site. For the statement of work API to accept the submitted data, we have to ensure that the values for required fields are set to reasonable defaults. To do that, open the form template in Office InfoPath 2007 and then select the Data Source view. For every required field (shown with a red asterisk), select a default value from the choices presented by Office InfoPath 2007. For the enumerated types, you can select a value from the drop-down list. For other types, such as date types, you can specify a function such as *today()*. When you have finished, save the template.

The next step is to publish the template to a network share. In this case, I want to enable users to fill out the form in their browser, so I set the form compatibility option to allow browser-based forms. Then I select To A Network Location in the Publishing Wizard and save the form as a fully trusted form. As an optional step, you can promote various properties so that they appear as columns in the SharePoint form library. I promoted the project title, client name, and starting date.

After publishing the form, you upload it to Office SharePoint Server 2007, a step that you perform from the Application Management page on the SharePoint Central Administration site. In the InfoPath Forms Services section, choose Upload Form Template and then browse to the location of the published form. On the Manage Form Templates page, select Activate To A Site Collection from the drop-down menu for the template. This step creates a new Statement of Work content type that can be associated with a form library.

The final step is to create a form library on a site and then modify the settings so that it uses the statement of work template. I created a form library called Statements of Work. I then opened the list settings page, chose Advanced Settings, and set the Allow Management Of Content Types option to Yes. I also set the Opening Browser-Enabled Documents option to Display As A Web Page, and I disabled the New Folder command on the New menu. Finally, in the Content Types section, I chose the Add From Existing Site Content Types link and selected Statement Of Work from the available site content types list. This content type is the one that was created when I uploaded the statement of work template. To avoid confusing users of the form, I removed the default Form content type from the settings page. The resulting form library has a single command under the New menu, shown in Figure 5-10, that opens a new statement of work form in the browser.

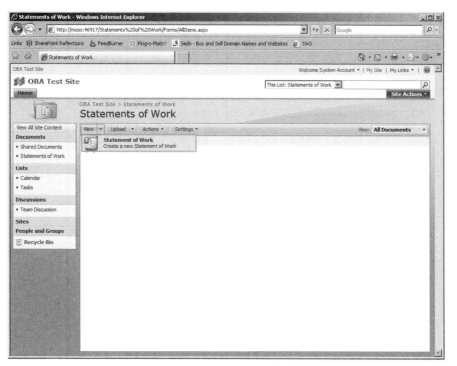

Figure 5-10   Users can generate a new statement of work based on a content type.

Next, we want to add a custom command to any list associated with the new content type. To do that, I created a SharePoint solution project that installs a statement of work feature. The feature defines two custom actions, shown in Listing 5-4 and Listing 5-5.

Listing 5-4   The Feature.xml file for the statement of work SharePoint feature.

```
/* feature.xml */
<Feature  Id="1EE85E89-6884-4eb8-995F-AD21FD1EC8EF"
    Title="Statement of Work Document Generation"
    Description="Provides tools for generating statement of work documents"
    Version="1.0.0.0"
    Scope="Web"
  DefaultResourceFile="ipfscore"
  xmlns="http://schemas.microsoft.com/sharepoint/">
  <ElementManifests>
    <ElementManifest Location="Elements.xml"/>
  </ElementManifests>
  <Properties>
  </Properties>
</Feature>
```

Listing 5-5   The Elements.xml file for the statement of work SharePoint feature.

```
/* elements.xml */
<Elements xmlns="http://schemas.microsoft.com/sharepoint/">
  <CustomAction
    Id="JohnHolliday.OBA.SOW.Word"
    RegistrationId="0x01010100E7EEDDF8F1A82E4AA49D355C331D7ACE"
    RegistrationType="ContentType"
    Location="EditControlBlock"
    Sequence="1001"
    Title="Generate Word Document"
    >
    <UrlAction Url="/_layouts/DocumentGenerator.aspx?Format=Word&amp;Site=
        {SiteUrl}&amp;List={ListId}&amp;ID={ItemId}&amp;Item={ItemUrl}"/>
  </CustomAction>
  <CustomAction
    Id="JohnHolliday.OBA.SOW.PowerPoint"
    RegistrationId="0x01010100E7EEDDF8F1A82E4AA49D355C331D7ACE"
    RegistrationType="ContentType"
    Location="EditControlBlock"
    Sequence="1002"
    Title="Generate PowerPoint Presentation"
    >
    <UrlAction Url="/_layouts/DocumentGenerator.aspx?Format=
        PowerPoint&amp;Site={SiteUrl}&amp;List={ListId}&amp;
        ID={ItemId}&amp;Item={ItemUrl}"/>
  </CustomAction>
</Elements>
```

For each custom action defined in the Elements.xml file shown in Listing 5-5, I set the registration type to "ContentType." To associate the custom action with the correct content type, I navigated to the content type settings page for the Statement of Work content type and copied the GUID from the browser's address bar.

After you have built and deployed the feature, the custom action now appears in the edit control block of the statement of work item in the form library. When the command is executed, the *UrlAction* field specifies a custom .aspx page that contains the logic used to generate the document. (See the file DocumentGenerator.cs.) For simplicity, I used a single page to handle all file formats, passing the desired format as a request parameter. I also pass the site, list, and item ID parameters to make it easier to code the page. Within the page's code, I retrieve the request parameters and then call the SharePoint API to obtain the referenced list item. After I have the item, I can get the raw XML data and convert it to an instance of the *StatementOfWork* class by using the following code:

```
using (StreamReader reader = new StreamReader(m_listItem.File.OpenBinaryStream()))
{
   string xmlData = reader.ReadToEnd();
   StatementOfWork sow = StatementOfWork.LoadXml(xmlData);
   // ...
}
```

Now that I have a *StatementOfWork* instance, I can use the custom API to generate the statement of work into a memory stream as follows:

```
MemoryStream stream = new MemoryStream();
((IWordWriter)sow).Save(stream);
```

Finally, I can return the document directly in the ASP.NET *Response* object.

```
Response.ClearHeaders();
Response.AddHeader("content-disposition", string.Format("attachment;
    filename={0}.docx",sow.Name));
Response.ClearContent();
Response.ContentEncoding = System.Text.Encoding.UTF8;
Response.ContentType = DocumentMIMEType;
BinaryWriter writer = new BinaryWriter(Response.OutputStream);
writer.Write(data);
writer.Close();
Response.Flush();
Response.Close();
```

To get the document to open properly, you have to set the correct MIME type into the *Response* object. The following routine shows the MIME types to use for the 2007 Office system documents:

```
private string DocumentMIMEType
{
  get {
  switch (m_docType)
  {
  case DocumentType.Word:
    return "application/vnd.openxmlformats-
     officedocument.wordprocessingml.document";
  case DocumentType.Excel:
    return "application/vnd.openxmlformats-officedocument.spreadsheetml.sheet";
```

```
case DocumentType.PowerPoint:
    return "application/vnd.openxmlformats-
    officedocument.presentationml.presentation";
}
return "text/plain";
    }
}
```

Summary

As mentioned at the outset of this chapter, many types of documents contain information that is assembled from different teams and sometimes different data sources. With Open XML, you can create and modify documents of this type from data collected in XML format, which speeds document assembly, access to the data that the documents contain, and the reuse of the content.

After the development or implementation of an API such as the statement of work API I've described in this chapter, users can employ its functionality from a number of locations, including user interface elements in their client applications or from customizations you make to an Office SharePoint Server 2007 site.

Chapter 6
Sales Force Automation

—Bhushan Nene, Microsoft Corporation

Sales force automation (SFA) is one of the principal functional areas of customer relationship management (CRM) applications. SFA functionality includes customer and account management, opportunity management, sales forecasting, and order management. Many popular CRM solutions from independent software vendors (ISVs) such as Microsoft, Oracle, SalesForce.com, and SAP are Web-based applications. These solutions all provide tools for customizing their user interfaces, defining business rules and workflows, and analyzing transactional and historical data. They have the potential to provide organizations with an appropriate return on investment by increasing customer satisfaction and revenue, but their success is directly related to the level at which users adopt them, the quality of the data they contain, and their ability to support collaboration. In these areas, however, traditional solutions fall short: their Web-based user interfaces require connectivity and often require users to navigate through many screens to complete a task. In addition, their workflows are too structured and formal to model human collaboration, which is generally more ad hoc and often involves exceptions and delegation. This shortfall is part of the classic "results gap" that separates line-of-business applications and information workers. In this chapter, I will show you an Office Business Application (OBA) for sales force automation that bridges this gap. It provides salespeople with access to customer and sales data in Microsoft Office Outlook 2007 so that they can refer to it at any time. The solution uses Microsoft Office Word 2007 to create sales quotes and a Windows SharePoint Services workflow to facilitate team collaboration.

In the following sections, I'll describe the business process that the SFA solution addresses, the operations and functionality of the SFA solution, the solution's architecture, and some of the details of how I developed and implemented the solution.

Business Process and Solution Background

The Office Business Application for sales force automation (OBA for SFA) is designed to support the opportunity-to-order business process for a sales force. In general, a salesperson tracks customers, leads, and opportunities in a CRM application. The salesperson's interaction with customers typically takes place in personal meetings, in conference calls, through a Live Meeting session, and through the exchange of e-mail messages. The salesperson captures important aspects of these interactions by copying meeting notes and e-mail messages to the CRM application.

Based on the outcome of a sales interaction, a salesperson updates information in the CRM application. For example, a salesperson might record the probability of a product upgrade or the potential for an opportunity. When necessary, a salesperson prepares a sales quote in the CRM system, generates a quote document, and sends it to the customer for approval. After the customer approves the quote, the salesperson submits the order to the CRM system, and this order eventually flows into an enterprise resource planning (ERP) application that provides order fulfillment functionality. This business process is shown in Figure 6-1.

Figure 6-1   A summary of sales interaction.

The OBA for SFA transforms this process by using three main components: an Office Outlook 2007 add-in, an Office Word 2007 add-in, and a Windows SharePoint Services workflow. Figure 6-2 shows the opportunity-to-order process as it is carried out in the OBA for SFA. In the following sections, I'll describe the operations of each component in more detail.

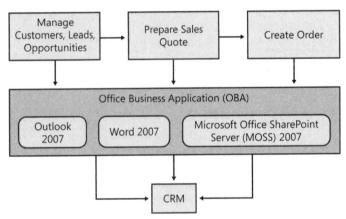

Figure 6-2   The OBA for SFA changes the opportunity-to-order process for sales interactions.

Working with Customer and Opportunity Data in Outlook

Many salespeople spend a lot of time away from the office visiting customers in the field. While they are away from their offices, they need access to customer and opportunity information, which is often a subset of information instead of all the data managed by a CRM application. Although mobile carriers have upgraded their data networks over the past few years, this type of access is not always possible or practical from a customer's site or during travel.

The OBA for SFA uses Office Outlook 2007 as the primary user interface for interacting with customer and opportunity information. An example of the Office Outlook 2007 customizations is shown in Figure 6-3. Office Outlook 2007 provides a familiar environment because salespeople use the application frequently, communicating with customers through e-mail and managing their meetings and contacts. Office Outlook 2007 provides a better user experience than a CRM system's user interface because of this familiarity. In addition, some data is cached locally to address offline scenarios.

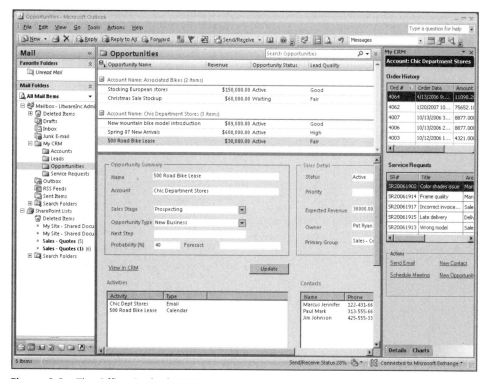

Figure 6-3   The Office Outlook 2007 user interface for the OBA for SFA.

In the OBA for SFA, information in Office Outlook 2007 is organized under a folder named My CRM. Detailed information is organized in subfolders of the My CRM folder for opportunities, accounts, and leads. Users can organize the content of each folder using native Office Outlook 2007 features such as custom views, sorting, and filtering.

Each CRM entity is displayed using a custom form region in Office Outlook 2007. The form region provides Create, Update, and Delete functionality and includes appropriate data validation. Because data is cached locally, a salesperson has access to this information when she is working offline. The information is synchronized with the CRM application when a network connection is established.

For a salesperson, it is important to have a thorough view of the data about a customer. When specific data is displayed in the Office Outlook 2007 form region, additional data is provided through a custom task pane, which is used to provide context for the current entity. For example, while a salesperson views account or opportunity information in a form region, he might find it helpful to glance at the customer's order history or view outstanding service requests for that customer in the task pane.

A salesperson has many interactions with customers through meetings and e-mail messages. Many of these interactions are important for historical reasons and need to be captured in a CRM application. Because salespeople use Office Outlook 2007 to manage e-mail and meetings, they traditionally have to copy and paste this information into the CRM application. This task becomes a chore, and important data is often not captured. The OBA for SFA extends the built-in message and meeting forms in Office Outlook 2007 to provide a user interface with which to associate and link e-mail messages and meetings to a specific CRM opportunity or account. By providing this functionality within Office Outlook 2007, a salesperson can more easily establish these associations. Links are also provided in the custom task pane to send e-mail or schedule a meeting while a salesperson is looking at an opportunity or account. These links launch appropriate Office Outlook 2007 forms and populate the e-mail recipient list or meeting invitee list with contacts and information related to the account, customer, or opportunity, automatically linking the meeting or message to the account or opportunity within the CRM system. Features such as these improve the probability that a salesperson will capture important customer interactions, which leads to higher-quality data in the CRM system itself. Figure 6-4 shows an example of a dialog box used to link an e-mail message with an opportunity and an account.

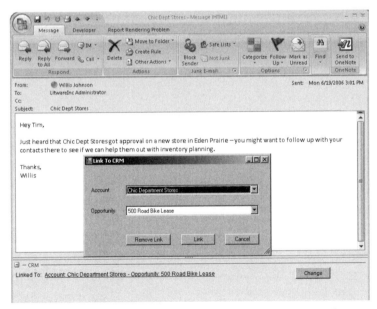

Figure 6-4   Linking an opportunity and an account to an e-mail message.

Creating a Sales Quote in Office Word 2007

In a traditional CRM system, salespeople create sales quotes by entering product information, terms and conditions, and contact information in the CRM application and then generating a sales quote document in Word or PDF format to send to their customers. The OBA for SFA provides a more natural way of creating the quote directly in Office Word 2007 and updating the CRM system later with data in the Office Word 2007 document. The solution uses an Office Word 2007 template that is stored in a SharePoint document library. A salesperson can create a quote by going to the SharePoint document library, but the solution also provides a way to create the quote from Office Outlook 2007 within the context of the sales opportunity. In Office Outlook 2007, while the salesperson is viewing the opportunity, she can use a custom Ribbon to create the quote. The functionality provided on the Ribbon instantiates a new Office Word 2007 document from the sales quote template in the SharePoint library and passes the context about the opportunity from Office Outlook 2007 to the document. Based on the context, data elements such as customer contact names and address are populated in the document.

The solution also retrieves product catalog information using a custom task pane in Office Word 2007. A salesperson can browse products by category or search the catalog. The custom task pane also displays product details, including an image of the product. A salesperson can select the product and add it to the product items table in the quote. A salesperson can also modify the quantity and discount and update the total. An example is shown in Figure 6-5.

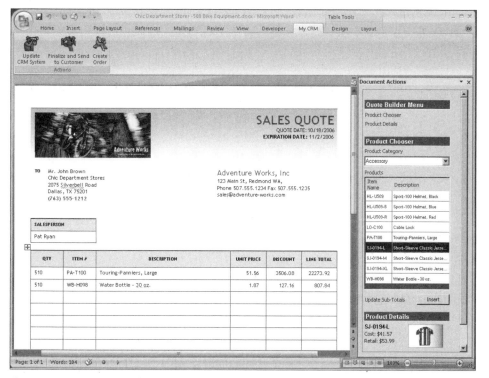

Figure 6-5   Creating a sales quote in Office Word 2007 based on information about an opportunity that is displayed in Office Outlook 2007.

After a sales quote document is completed, a salesperson saves it to the SharePoint document library. The library includes a site content type called Sales Quote. Saving the document to the library initiates a custom quote-approval workflow on the document. (The workflow is described in more detail in the following section.) The status of the approval is displayed in the document library as one of the columns in the library's view, as you can see in Figure 6-6.

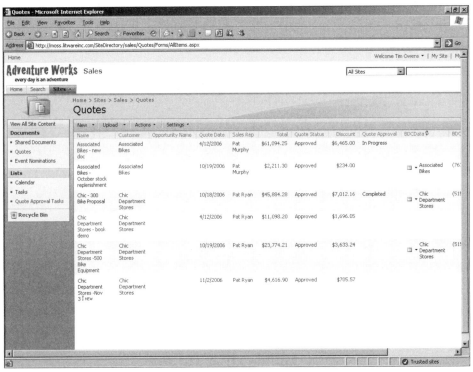

Figure 6-6   The status of the quote-approval workflow is shown in the SharePoint document library.

When a quote document is approved, a salesperson can use a custom Ribbon in Office Word 2007 to update the CRM system with data from the quote document. He can also submit the order based on this quote. Generally, order processing is a streamlined process defined in the CRM and ERP systems. An order is often originated in the CRM system and ends up being fulfilled through the ERP system. Most CRM and ERP systems offer workflow engines and integration technologies to automate this complex process. The OBA for SFA defers the order processing to the CRM or ERP system and simply submits relevant data from the Office Word 2007 document to these systems.

Sales Quote Approval Workflow

I defined a custom quote-approval workflow for the Sales Quote content type. As mentioned in the previous section, when a salesperson saves a quote document to the document library, the workflow is started on that document. The workflow I designed includes conditional logic based on the total amount and discount used in the quote. It routes the document to the appropriate person based on these conditions, and that person receives a notification in e-mail. The workflow then waits for the approver to record a decision. Using a link in the message, the approver navigates to the approval page, enters the necessary information, and submits the decision. The approval form is shown in Figure 6-7.

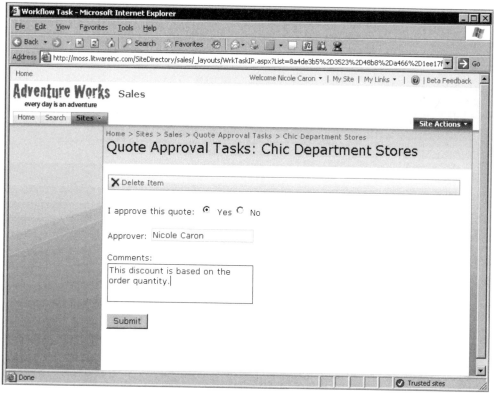

Figure 6-7   The approval form for the workflow.

The submission of the approval decision results in an e-mail notification being sent to the originator, and the workflow is complete. The quote approval is a simple workflow; however, it demonstrates the ability of SharePoint workflows to branch on the basis of data in a document. Obviously, you can develop more sophisticated workflows using Microsoft Visual Studio.

More Info   For more information, see the Windows Workflow Foundation Developer Center at *http://msdn2.microsoft.com/enus/netframework/aa663328.aspx.*

Architecture of the Sales Force Automation Solution

The architecture of the SFA solution consists of an Office Outlook 2007 add-in, an Office Word 2007 add-in, the SharePoint library and associated workflow, and the CRM system—including a process by which data is synchronized between the CRM system and the local database cache. Figure 6-8 outlines the architecture of the SFA solution.

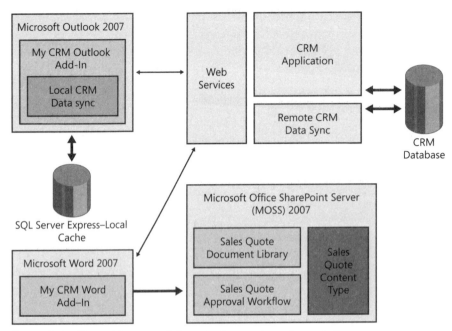

Figure 6-8   The architecture of the sales force automation solution.

A CRM application stores data in its own database. It provides access to the data it contains and to business processes via Web services. The CRM data is presented in Office Outlook 2007 through a Visual Studio Tools for Office (VSTO) 2005 SE Office Outlook 2007 add-in. The SFA solution also uses a SQL Server Express local database to cache CRM entities such as accounts, leads, and opportunities so that a user has access to them when the user is working offline.

I considered using a native Office Outlook 2007 store (an .ost or a .pst file) for caching data, but this approach would require using the Office Outlook 2007 object model for maintaining and synchronizing the cache. A mailbox's size becomes an issue with an .ost file as well, because it is synchronized with Microsoft Exchange Server. Also, in general, the performance of a native Outlook store suffers as the number of items and custom properties increases. Degraded performance is especially evident during Create and Update operations. With SQL Server Express, I have a lightweight database engine that provides excellent performance and can use SQL syntax. The local CRM data sync process is responsible for synchronizing the local cache with the CRM application's database.

In addition to cached data, the Office Outlook 2007 add-in presents CRM data in real time by calling CRM Web services. The real-time data is mainly contextual—for example, the order history for a customer—and is available only when Office Outlook 2007 can access CRM Web services. The decision to cache or display data in real time depends on a user's role and her pattern of using the application.

The functionality in Office Word 2007 that composes a sales quote document is provided by a VSTO 2005 SE Office Word 2007 add-in. Office Word 2007 content controls are used to separate data in the document from the document's presentation and formatting. The add-in gains access to CRM data using CRM Web services, including read access to the product catalog. It also provides product search and update functionality such as updating a sales quote and submitting a sales order.

Windows SharePoint Services provides collaboration functionality for the sales quote approval process. I defined a Sales Quote content type to capture sales quote semantics and a document library that is based on the Sales Quote content type. The quote-approval workflow, which I developed using Visual Studio 2005, is associated with the same content type.

Designing and Implementing the SFA Solution

Before I start explaining the design of this solution in more detail, I want to outline the guiding design principle behind this Office Business Application—the 80/20 rule. My goal for this particular OBA was to handle the most common scenarios and data elements required for an SFA solution. The SFA solution is not intended to entirely replace a CRM system's user interface, for example. If users need the capability to enter additional information about an opportunity or create a quote requiring complex product configuration, for example, they can perform this work through the CRM application's user interface. The approach I've taken results in a lightweight solution that is easy to develop and does not require a significant duplication of business logic and rules. Remember that OBAs are generally about extending line-of-business applications, not replacing them. After you adopt the 80/20 rule, you will find that you can develop relatively easily a number of task-centric OBAs that aim to solve specific business problems. Each OBA might be lightweight, but because each addresses a specific need, the combined results can lead to greater productivity for information workers.

With that principle in mind, let's walk through how I designed the OBA for SFA. I'll first describe the Office Outlook 2007 add-in and then move on to the CRM data synchronization process, the Office Word 2007 add-in, and the SharePoint workflow. I'll include implementation details such as code samples wherever appropriate. My goal in the following sections is to explain important design decisions and important areas of the solution's code to aid your understanding of how I built this OBA. Numerous resources are available about programming the 2007 Office system and VSTO that you can use to build a complete solution on your own.

 More Info   For more information about development resources for the 2007 Office system, see the section "Additional Resources" in the introduction to this book.

Developing the Office Outlook 2007 Add-in

The Office Outlook 2007 add-in, written in C# and developed with VSTO 2005 SE, uses the Office Outlook 2007 object model to manipulate Outlook items and its user interface. It also interacts with CRM data cached in the SQL Server Express database and with real-time CRM data exposed through Web services. In the following sections, I'll describe the steps I followed to create the customizations to the user interface shown earlier in Figure 6-3.

Creating CRM Folder Hierarchy

The CRM information is organized under the My CRM folder in the user's mailbox. Staying true to the 80/20 rule, the add-in targets three key CRM entities: accounts, leads, and opportunities. Items related to these entities are stored in subfolders of the My CRM folder. Salespeople on the road need access to these entities most of the time, and they tend to update information related to the entities while they are offline. The following code shows how to create this folder hierarchy.

```
using Outlook = Microsoft.Office.Interop.Outlook;

private void ThisAddIn_Startup(object sender, System.EventArgs e)
{
    . . .
    . . .
    CreateCRMFolders();
    . . .
    . . .
}

public void CreateCRMFolders()
{
    // Find the top level mailbox
    Outlook.Folder root =
        (Outlook.Folder)this.Session.GetDefaultFolder(
        Outlook.OlDefaultFolders.olFolderInbox).Parent;
    // Check if "My CRM" folder already exists and delete it
    int removeAt = -1;
    for (int i = 1; i <= root.Folders.Count; i++)
    {
        if (root.Folders[i].Name == "My CRM")
        {
            removeAt = i;
            break;
        }
    }
    if (removeAt >= 0)
        root.Folders.Remove(removeAt);

    // Create "My CRM" folder under Mailbox.
    Outlook.Folder crm = CreateFolder(root, "My CRM",
    Outlook.OlDefaultFolders.olFolderInbox, , "");

    // Create subfolders for accounts, leads, and opportunities
    Outlook.Folder acctRoot = null, leadsRoot  = null,
        opportunitiesRoot = null;
    if (crm != null)
    {
        acctRoot = CreateFolder(crm, "Accounts",
            Outlook.OlDefaultFolders.olFolderInbox);
        leadsRoot = CreateFolder(crm, "Leads",
            Outlook.OlDefaultFolders.olFolderInbox);
        opportunitiesRoot = CreateFolder(crm, "Opportunities",
```

```
                Outlook.OlDefaultFolders.olFolderInbox);
    }


    // Populate subfolders with data from SQL Server Express cache
    // See next section of the chapter for an explanation
    PopulateDataFromCache();
}
private static Outlook.Folder CreateFolder(Outlook.Folder root,
    string folderName, Outlook.OlDefaultFolders folderType)
{
    Outlook.Folder folder = GetFolder(root, folderName);
    if (folder == null)
        folder = (Outlook.Folder) root.Folders.Add(folderName, folderType);


    return folder;
}
```

Populating Outlook Folders with CRM data

After the add-in creates the folders for the CRM data, it needs to populate the folders with data
from the SQL Server Express cache. I used the ADO.NET *DataSet* object to interact with this
database. The dataset shown in Figure 6-9 includes two tables—Account and Opportunity—
with a one-to-many relationship. The columns in these tables are subsets of properties that
the CRM application maintains for underlying business entities. These subsets represent the
most commonly used properties of those entities; the CRM application includes many other
properties for these two entities in addition to those that I am caching in the local database.
The choice of which properties I cache is in accord with the 80/20 rule: If salespeople want to
look up or update properties that are not cached, they can do so in the CRM application
instead of in Office Outlook 2007.

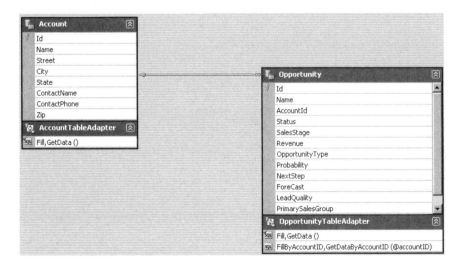

Figure 6-9   Tables from the SQL Server Express database represent a subset of properties from the
CRM application.

You can see that I define a *GetData* method for each table adapter to get all the rows. The code iterates through these rows and creates Outlook items in each subfolder. I used the Outlook *PostItem* object to model each entity and set the *MessageClass* property to a custom value to distinguish these entities from generic instances of the *PostItem* object. As you will see later in the chapter, I use the *MessageClass* property to display the appropriate form region for viewing and editing the item. Although the form region displays the data from the cache, I also created a few custom properties for each Outlook item. For the Opportunity item, for example, I created the custom properties *Opportunity Name*, *Revenue*, *Status*, and *Lead Quality*. The inclusion of these properties allows a user to create a custom view for the Opportunity sub-folder using the custom properties as columns for the view. Users can also define sort and filter criteria for the view based on these properties.

More Info   Replicating CRM data in custom properties and the item body creates a synchronization problem; in other words, we have to keep the properties in sync with the local cache. I'll discuss this issue in more detail later in the chapter in the section "CRM Data Synchronization."

Now let's look at the code. For the sake of brevity, I will show you the code only for the Opportunity item. The code for the Account and Lead items is similar.

```
// Get all opportunity rows from table
AccountOpportunity.OpportunityDataTable oppDT =

new OpportunityTableAdapter().GetData();

Outlook.UserProperty prop;

// Iterate through all rows creating Outlook items
foreach (OpportunityRow row in oppDT.Rows)
{
    // Create PostItem in Opportunities folder
    Outlook.PostItem post = (Outlook.PostItem)opportunitiesRoot.
        Items.Add("IPM.Post.CRMOpportunity");

    post.MessageClass = "IPM.Post.CRMOpportunity";
    post.Subject = "Opportunity: " + row.Name;

    prop = post.UserProperties.Add("OpportunityID",
        Outlook.OlUserPropertyType.olText,
        Type.Missing, Type.Missing);
    prop.Value = row.Id.ToString();

    prop = post.UserProperties.Add("AccountID",
        Outlook.OlUserPropertyType.olText,
        Type.Missing, Type.Missing);
    prop.Value = row.AccountId.ToString();

    prop = post.UserProperties.Add("Account Name",
        Outlook.OlUserPropertyType.olText,
        Type.Missing, Type.Missing);
    prop.Value = acctDT.FindById(row.AccountId).Name;
```

```
    prop = post.UserProperties.Add("Opportunity Name",
        Microsoft.Office.Interop.Outlook.OlUserPropertyType.olText,
        Type.Missing, Type.Missing);
    prop.Value = row.Name;

    prop = post.UserProperties.Add("Opportunity Status",
        Microsoft.Office.Interop.Outlook.OlUserPropertyType.olText,
        Type.Missing, Type.Missing);
    prop.Value = row.Status;

    prop = post.UserProperties.Add("Revenue", Microsoft.Office.
        Interop.Outlook.OlUserPropertyType.olCurrency,
        Type.Missing, Type.Missing);
    prop.Value = row.Revenue;

    prop = post.UserProperties.Add("Lead Quality",
        Microsoft.Office.Interop.Outlook.OlUserPropertyType.olText,
        Type.Missing, Type.Missing);
    prop.Value = row.LeadQuality;

    // Save Outlook PostItem
    post.Save();
}
```

Displaying CRM Data by Using an Office Outlook 2007 Form Region

Office Outlook 2007 comes with a new user interface extensibility feature called the *form region*. This feature provides an Office Outlook 2007 add-in with the capability to extend or replace built-in Office Outlook 2007 forms to render Outlook items. An add-in can render any Outlook item in the way you want and also implement the form's behavior by using managed code behind the form.

To implement a form region, follow these steps:

1. Design a form region using the Outlook Form Designer, and then save it as an .ofs file.

2. Compose a form region manifest file that conforms to the form region XML schema. This XML file specifies basic information about the form region and how to display it to the user.

3. Register the form region by adding a registry value to either HKEY_LOCAL_MACHINE or HKEY_CURRENT_USER.

4. Connect the form region to an add-in and write the code for the form region's behavior in the add-in.

Designing the CRM Opportunity Form Using the Outlook Form Designer   Various Microsoft Forms 2.0 controls are available in the toolbox and can be added to a form. I used the Label, Text Box, Combo Box, and List View controls. (The List View control is not available on the standard toolbox. It is a custom control that you can add to the toolbox by right-clicking the toolbox, selecting Custom Controls, and then selecting Microsoft

ListView Control version 6.0 from the list.) You should, of course, name each control appropriately. The name you assign is used to gain access to the control in managed code in the add-in. Figure 6-10 shows the Outlook Discussion item open in the Outlook Forms Designer.

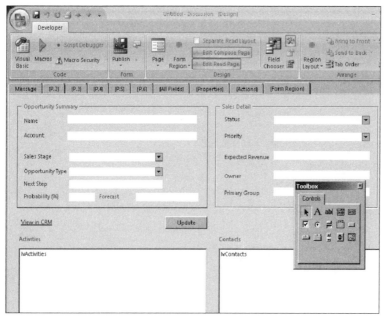

Figure 6-10   An example of designing an Office Outlook 2007 form region.

After I created the form region, I saved it as a file named CRMOpportunity.ofs in the C:\MyCRM\MyCRMOutlookAddin\FormRegion folder.

Composing a Form Region Manifest File   Here is the manifest file I created. I saved this file as RMOpportunity.xml in the folder C:\MyCRM\MyCRMOutlookAddin\FormRegion.

```xml
<?xml version="1.0" encoding="utf-8"?>
  <FormRegion xmlns="http://schemas.microsoft.com/office/outlook/12/formregion.xsd">
      <name>CRMOpportunity</name>
      <title>CRM Opportunity</title>
      <formRegionType>replaceAll</formRegionType>
      <showCompose>true</showCompose>
      <showRead>true</showRead>
      <showPreview>true</showPreview>
      <hidden>false</hidden>
      <addin>MyCRM</addin>
      <version>1.0</version>
  </FormRegion>
```

The *replaceAll* value specified for the *formRegionType* element replaces the built-in form for the Outlook Post item with our form region. The elements *showCompose, showRead,* and *showPreview,* all set to *true,* determine in which modes—compose, read, or preview—the form region is visible. We want it to be visible in all modes.

Registering a Form Region   This step associates the form region with a particular Outlook message class. Before displaying any item, Office Outlook 2007 checks whether any form region is associated with the message class for that item. If an association exists, Office Outlook 2007 displays that form region. I associated the SFA solution's form region with the *IPM.Post.CRMOpportunity* message class. (Remember that the add-in assigns the same message class to Post items it creates in the Opportunity subfolder.) The registry entry should look like the following:

```
[HKEY_CURRENT_USER\Software\Microsoft\Office\Outlook\FormRegions\IPM.Post.CRMOpportunity]
  "CRMOpportunity"="C:\\MyCRM\\ MyCRMOutlookAddin\\FormRegion\\CRMOpportunity.xml"
```

Connecting the Form Region to the Office Outlook 2007 Add-In   This step is carried out in two parts. First I'll describe the work required to connect the form region to the Office Outlook 2007 add-in, and then I'll describe how to implement the actual behavior of the form.

The add-in is required to return an object of type *Outlook.FormRegionStartup*, which is responsible for returning the appropriate form region file to Office Outlook 2007 and then managing multiple instances of the form region because multiple Outlook inspector windows showing the same form region can be open at the same time.

First you need to override the *RequestService* method in the *ThisAddIn* class of the add-in to return the instance of a class that implements the *Outlook.FormRegionStartup* interface.

```
public partial class ThisAddIn

{

    protected override object RequestService(Guid serviceGuid)

    {

        if (serviceGuid == Outlook.FormRegionStartup).GUID)

            return new FormRegionSupport ();

        else

            return base.RequestService(serviceGuid);

    }

}
```

The *FormRegionSupport* class implements the *Outlook.FormRegionStartup* interface and its *ComVisible* attribute is set to *true*. The *GetFormRegionStorage* method in the *Outlook.FormRegionStartup* interface returns the appropriate form region storage (.ofs) file. Office Outlook 2007 instantiates the form region stored in the .ofs file and calls the *BeforeFormRegionShow* method in the *Outlook.FormRegionStartup* interface. This method keeps track of multiple instances of the form region using a *List* collection. It uses the *OpportunityRegionWrapper* class to wrap the form region. The *OpportunityRegionWrapper* class implements the behavior of the form region, which I will describe next. First, the following code completes the operation of adding the form region to the Office Outlook 2007 add-in.

```
using Outlook = Microsoft.Office.Interop.Outlook;

[ComVisible(true)]
public class FormRegionSupport : Outlook.FormRegionStartup
{
    public FormRegionSupport()
    {
    }

    object Outlook._FormRegionStartup.GetFormRegionStorage(
        string FormRegionName, object Item, int LCID,
        Outlook.OlFormRegionMode FormRegionMode, Outlook.OlFormRegionSize
        FormRegionSize)
    {
        switch (FormRegionName)
        {
            case "CRMOpportunity":
                //Return path to the form region storage file
                return @"C:\MyCRM\MyCRMOutlookAddin\FormRegion\CRMOpportunity.ofs";
        }
    }

    // A list for keeping track of multiple instances of form regions
    private List<BaseFormRegionWrapper> m_KnownRegions =
        new List<BaseFormRegionWrapper>();

    void Outlook._FormRegionStartup.BeforeFormRegionShow(
        Outlook.FormRegion FormRegion)
    {
        try
        {
            BaseFormRegionWrapper wrapper = null;

            // Determine which form region wrapper class to use based
            // on the region name
            switch (FormRegion.InternalName)
            {
                case "CRMOpportunity":
                    wrapper = new OpportunityRegionWrapper(
                        Globals.ThisAddIn.Application, FormRegion);
                    break;

            }

            // Add the region to our list of known regions
            if (wrapper != null)
            {
                m_KnownRegions.Add(wrapper);
                // Handle the close event of the wrapper so we
```

```
                    // can clean up our resources
                    wrapper.Close += new EventHandler(FormRegion_Close);
                }
            }
            catch (Exception ex)
            {
                Debug.WriteLine(ex.Message);
            }
        }

        void FormRegion_Close(object sender, EventArgs e)
        {
            BaseFormRegionWrapper wrapper = sender as BaseFormRegionWrapper;
            if (wrapper != null)
            {
                m_KnownRegions.Remove(wrapper);

                // Clean up our unmanaged resources
                wrapper.Dispose();
            }
        }
    }
}
```

As I mentioned earlier, the *OpportunityRegionWrapper* class encapsulates the behavior of the Opportunity form region. This class has access to all the controls on the form region and can get and set the values of the controls. It also handles events for the controls on the form. This class derives from the *BaseFormRegionWrapper* class, which mainly provides cleanup functionality for underlying COM objects.

To demonstrate how I used the *OpportunityRegionWrapper* class, the following code is related to a few of the controls on the form region: *txtOpportunityName*, *ddStatus*, and *cmdUpdate*, which correspond to the Text Box, Combo Box, and Button controls, respectively. The code related to the List View control (*lvActivities*) is also very interesting. This list view shows e-mail messages, appointments, and meetings that are associated with the current opportunity. This association is established by attaching a custom property called *OpportunityID* to message, appointment, or meeting items and setting its value to the opportunity's unique identifier. The code also shows how the form's data is saved to the local cache when user clicks the Update button. The inline comments offer additional explanation.

```
using Outlook = Microsoft.Office.Interop.Outlook;
using Forms = Microsoft.Vbe.Interop.Forms;

class OpportunityRegionWrapper : BaseFormRegionWrapper
{
    private Outlook.OlkTextBox txtOpportunityName;
    private Outlook.OlkComboBox ddStatus;
    private Outlook.OlkCommandButton cmdUpdate;
    private mscomctl.ListView lvActivities;


    // Constructor
```

```csharp
        public OpportunityRegionWrapper(
            Microsoft.Office.Tools.Outlook.Application outlook,
            Outlook.FormRegion FormRegion)
            {
                // Save some important references. The variables are
                // defined in the BaseFormRegionWrapper base class
                this.Item = FormRegion.Item;
                this.FormRegion = FormRegion;
                this.UserForm = FormRegion.Form as Forms.UserForm;
                this.Application = outlook;

                // Hook up events
                FormRegion.Close +=
                    new Outlook.FormRegionEvents_CloseEventHandler(FormRegion_Close);

                // Initialize controls in the form region
                InitalizeControls();

                // Display opportunity data from local database in Read or Preview mode
                if (FormRegion.FormRegionMode ==
                    Outlook.OlFormRegionMode.olFormRegionRead
                    || FormRegion.FormRegionMode ==
                    Outlook.OlFormRegionMode.olFormRegionPreview)
                {
                    FillOpportunityRegion(txtOpportunityID.Text);
                }

            }

    // Member variables for controls in the form regions
    private Outlook.OlkTextBox txtOpportunityName, txtOpportunityID;
    private Outlook.OlkComboBox ddStatus;
    private mscomctl.ListView lvActivities;

    private void InitalizeControls()
    {
        // Unique identifier for the opportunity. This is a hidden field on the form
        txtOpportunityID =
            Outlook.OlkTextBox)this.UserForm.Controls.Item("txtOpportunityID");

        txtOpportunityName =
            (Outlook.OlkTextBox)this.UserForm.Controls.Item("txtOpportunityName");

        ddStatus = (Outlook.OlkComboBox)this.UserForm.Controls.Item("ddStatus");

        // Populate drop down values
        ddStatus.AddItem("Active", 0);
        ddStatus.AddItem("Waiting", 1);

        cmdUpdate =
            (Outlook.OlkCommandButton)this.UserForm.Controls.Item("cmdUpdate");
        // Add button click event handler
        cmdUpdate.Click += new
            Outlook.OlkCommandButtonEvents_ClickEventHandler(ButtonUpdate_Click);
```

```
lvActivities = (mscomctl.ListView)this.UserForm.Controls.Item("lvActivities");

lvActivities.View = mscomctl.ListViewConstants.lvwReport;

    // Set up list view columns
    object title, missing = Type.Missing;
    title = "Activity";
    lvActivities.ColumnHeaders.Add(ref missing, ref missing, ref title, ref
        missing , ref missing, ref missing);

    title = "Type";
    lvActivities.ColumnHeaders.Add(ref missing, ref missing, ref title, ref
        missing, ref missing, ref missing);

    // Add hidden column to store the EntryID of the Outlook item.
    // This will be used to open the Outlook item (email,
    // appointment, or meeting) when user double clicks on
    // the row in the list view.
    title = "EntryID";
    mscomctl.ColumnHeader h;

    h = this.lvActivities.ColumnHeaders.Add(ref missing, ref missing,
        ref title, ref missing, ref missing, ref missing);
    h.Width = 0;
    lvActivities.FullRowSelect = true;
    lvActivities.MultiSelect = false;
    // Add event handler
    lvActivities.DblClick +=new
            mscomctl.ListViewEvents_DblClickEventHandler(lvActivities_DblClick);

}

// Populate form region controls with data from local cache
private void FillOpportunityRegion(string oppID)
{

// Find the opportunity row based on unique opportunity ID
AccountOpportunity.OpportunityDataTable oppDT =
new OpportunityTableAdapter().GetData();
    System.Guid opportunityID = new Guid(oppID);
    AccountOpportunity.OpportunityRow r =
        oppDT.FindById(opportunityID);

// Show data from opportunity row in form region controls
txtOpportunityName.Text = r.Name;
ddStatus.Text = r.Status;

// Fill Activity list view with emails, appointments,
// and meetings associated with the opportunity
LoadActivityTable(oppID);
}

// Fill Activity list view with emails, appointments,
// and meetings associated with the opportunity. The association
// is done by attaching a custom property called "OpportunityID"
```

```
    // to these Outlook items. So we have to search for this custom
    // property to find the items and then load them in the list view
    private void LoadActivityTable(string opportunityID)
    {
        object missing = Type.Missing;

        Outlook.Folder mailFolder =
            (Outlook.Folder)this.Application.Session.GetDefaultFolder(
            Outlook.OlDefaultFolders.olFolderInbox);


    // Format query. Note that the string preceding "OpportunityID"
    // is very important. It signifies that the "OpportunityID" is
    // a custom property.
        string filter = String.Format("@SQL=\"{0}\" = '{1}'",
            "http://schemas.microsoft.com/mapi/string/{00020329-0000-0000-C000-
            000000000046}/OpportunityID",
            opportunityID);
    // Use new Table object to scroll through the filtered list
        Outlook.Table tbl = mailFolder.GetTable(filter,
        Outlook.OlTableContents.olUserItems);

        //Sort by ReceivedTime in descending order
        tbl.Sort("ReceivedTime", true);

        //Iterate the Table Rows
            while (!tbl.EndOfTable)
            {
                Outlook.Row nextRow = tbl.GetNextRow();
                //Set properties of ListViewItem
                object subject = nextRow["Subject"];
                mscomctl.ListItem li = this.lvActivities.ListItems.Add(
                    ref missing, ref missing, ref subject, ref missing,
                    ref missing);
                object index, itemType;
                itemType = "Email";
                index = 1;
                li.ListSubItems.Add(ref index, ref missing, ref itemType,
                    ref missing, ref missing);

                object entryID;
                entryID = nextRow["EntryID"];
                index = 2;
                li.ListSubItems.Add(ref index, ref missing, ref entryID,
                    ref missing, ref missing);
            }

        // Similarly find appointments and meetings in the calendar
            Outlook.Folder calendarFolder =
                (Outlook.Folder)this.Application.Session.GetDefaultFolder(
                Outlook.OlDefaultFolders.olFolderCalendar);

            tbl = calendarFolder.GetTable(filter,
                Outlook.OlTableContents.olUserItems);
```

```
            //Sort by Start time in descending order
            tbl.Sort("Start", true);

            //Iterate the Table Rows
            while (!tbl.EndOfTable)
            {
                Outlook.Row nextRow = tbl.GetNextRow();
                //Set properties of ListViewItem
                object subject = nextRow["Subject"];
                mscomctl.ListItem li = this.lvActivities.ListItems.Add(
                    ref missing, ref missing, ref subject, ref missing, ref
                    missing);
                object index, itemType;
                itemType = "Calendar";
                index = 1;
                li.ListSubItems.Add(ref index, ref missing, ref itemType,
                  ref missing, ref missing);

                object entryID;
                entryID = nextRow["EntryID"];
                index = 2;
                li.ListSubItems.Add(ref index, ref missing, ref entryID,
                    ref missing, ref missing);
            }

        }


// Handle double click event for Activities list view. When user
// double-clicks on a row in the list view, find the corresponding
// email, appointment, or meeting and open it.
void  lvActivities_DblClick()
{
    // EntryID is the hidden column in the list view. This uniquely
    // identifies an Outlook item
        string entryID = this.lvActivities.SelectedItem.get_SubItems(2);
        string itemType = this.lvActivities.SelectedItem.get_SubItems(1);
        if (itemType == "Email")
        {
    Outlook.MailItem mail =
        (Outlook.MailItem)this.Application.Session.GetItemFromID(
            entryID, Type.Missing);
        mail.Display(false);
        }
        else if (itemType == "Calendar")
        {
            Outlook.AppointmentItem appointment =
                (Outlook.AppointmentItem)this.Application.Session.GetItemFromID(
                entryID, Type.Missing);
            appointment.Display(false);
        }
    }

// Handle click on "Update" command button. This saves form region
// data to local database and Outlook item custom properties.
```

```
// If the form region is in Read mode, update
// existing row in the Opportunity table. If form region is in
// Compose mode,then new row is added to the table.
// Also remember that some of the values are also replicated
// as custom properties of the Outlook PostItem. So we need
// to update or create those custom properties.
// Following code shows updating only single property called
// "OpportunityName" for the sake of brevity. Other properties
// are handled in similar way. Also skipping handling of "Compose"
// mode for sake of brevity.
private void ButtonUpdate_Click()
{
    if (this.FormRegion.FormRegionMode ==
        Outlook.OlFormRegionMode.olFormRegionRead)
    {
    // Find Opportunity row in Opportunity table in local cache
    Guid opportunityID = new Guid(txtOpportunityID.Text);
        AccountOpportunity.OpportunityRow r = new AccountOpportunityTableAdapters.
            OpportunityTableAdapter().GetData().FindById(opportunityID);

        // Update Opportunity row in the local cache
        r.Name = txtOpportunityName.Text;

        AccountOpportunityTableAdapters.OpportunityTableAdapter ta =
            new AccountOpportunityTableAdapters.OpportunityTableAdapter();
        ta.Update(r);

        // Update custom properties associated with the Post Item
        Outlook.PostItem post = this.Item as Outlook.PostItem;
        if (post != null)
        {
            post.UserProperties["Opportunity Name"].Value = txtOpportunityName.Text;

            post.Save();
        }
    }


    // Handle form region close event. Need to clean up resources.
    void FormRegion_Close()
    {
        txtOpportunityID = null;
        txtOpportunityName = null;
        ddStatus = null;
        lvActivities = null;

    // Call close method on the base class to clean up resources.
        RaiseClose();


    }
}
```

Finally, here is my implementation of the base class *BaseFormRegionWrapper*, whose main purpose is to clean up underlying COM objects.

```csharp
abstract class BaseFormRegionWrapper : IDisposable
{
    private bool disposed = false;
    protected object Item;
    protected Outlook.FormRegion FormRegion;
    protected Forms.UserForm UserForm;

    // Event is raised when the wrapped form region raises its close event
    public event EventHandler Close;

    // Raises the close event on this class
    protected void RaiseClose()
    {
        if (Close != null)
            Close(this, EventArgs.Empty);
    }

    ~BaseFormRegionWrapper()
    {
        // call Dispose with false. Since we're in the
        // destructor call, the managed resources will be
        // disposed of anyway.
        Dispose(false);
    }

    public void Dispose()
    {
        // dispose of managed & unmanaged resources
        Dispose(true);

        // tell the GC that the Finalize process no longer needs
        // to be run for this object.
        GC.SuppressFinalize(this);
    }

    protected void Dispose(bool disposeManagedResources)
    {
        // process only if managed and unmanaged resources have
        // not been disposed of.
        if (!this.disposed)
        {
            if (disposeManagedResources)
            {
                // dispose managed resources
                Item = null;
            }

            if (FormRegion != null)
            {
                System.Runtime.InteropServices.Marshal.
                    ReleaseComObject(FormRegion);
                FormRegion = null;
            }
            if (UserForm != null)
            {
                System.Runtime.InteropServices.Marshal.
```

```
                          ReleaseComObject(UserForm);
                      UserForm = null;
                  }

                  disposed = true;
              }
          }

      }
```

Developing the Outlook Custom Task Pane

Now that you've seen how to create the form region to display Opportunity details, I'll describe how to create the custom task pane that shows contextual information about the selected opportunity. While details about the opportunity in the form region are cached in the local database, the contexual data is shown in real time. When a user selects the opportunity in Outlook Explorer, the custom task pane shows the related order history and service requests in the data grid by calling CRM Web services. You follow two steps to create this custom task pane:

1. Design a Windows Forms user control to display order history, service requests, and other information about the opportunity.

2. Add the user control to the custom task pane.

Designing the User Control   I added a Windows Forms user control named *Opportunity-InfoUserCtl* to the Visual Studio project. When developing a user control, be sure that you set the control's dimensions so that it is displayed appropriately within the boundaries of the custom task pane. I used *DataGridView* controls to display order history and service requests and wrote a *public* method named *ShowAccountInfo* that calls CRM Web services to get order history and service request information to fill the respective data grids. This code is a pretty straightforward, so I have omitted it for the sake of brevity.

Adding the User Control to the Custom Task Pane   I used the following code to add the user control to the custom task pane.

```
private Outlook.Explorer explorer;
private void ThisAddIn_Startup(object sender, System.EventArgs e)
{
    . . .
    explorer = this.Application.ActiveExplorer();
    explorer.SelectionChange +=
        new Outlook.ExplorerEvents_10_SelectionChangeEventHandler(
        Explorer_SelectionChange);

    this.ctp = this.CustomTaskPanes.Add(new OpportunityInfoUserCtl(),
        "My CRM");
    this.ctp.Visible = false;

    . . .
```

```
}
void Explorer_SelectionChange()
{
    Outlook.PostItem post = this.ActiveExplorer().Selection[1] as Outlook.PostItem;
    if (post != null && post.MessageClass == "IPM.Post.CRMOpportunity")
    {
        Outlook.UserProperty propAcct = post.UserProperties["AccountID"];
        Outlook.UserProperty propOpp = post.UserProperties["OpportunityID"];

        if (propAcct != null && propOpp != null)
        {
            string acctID = propAcct.Value.ToString();
            string oppID = propOpp.Value.ToString();
            ((OpportunityInfoUserCtl)this.ctp.Control).ShowAccountInfo(acctID,
                oppID);
            this.ctp.Visible = true;

        }
    }
    else
    {
        this.ctp.Visible = false;
    }
}
```

The user control also includes a link named Schedule Meeting that launches the Outlook Meeting Request form with the invitee list populated with the contacts associated with the opportunity. The meeting is also automatically associated with the opportunity in the CRM system. This association is made by attaching the *OpportunityID* and *AccountID* custom properties to the Outlook item.

```
private void linkLblScheduleMeeting_LinkClicked(object sender,
    LinkLabelLinkClickedEventArgs e)
{
    Outlook.AppointmentItem meeting =
    (Outlook.AppointmentItem)Globals.ThisAddIn.Application.CreateItem(
        Outlook.OlItemType.olAppointmentItem);
    // Get Contacts associated with the opportunity and call
    // meeting.Recipients.Add (email) for each contact.
    // I am omitting the code for brevity.

    meeting.UserProperties.Add("AccountID",
        Outlook.OlUserPropertyType.olText, Type.Missing,
        Type.Missing).Value = this.accountID;
    meeting.UserProperties.Add("OpportunityID",
        Outlook.OlUserPropertyType.olText, Type.Missing,
        Type.Missing).Value = this.opportunityID;

    object modal = false;
    meeting.Display(modal);

}
```

In addition, the user control has a New Opportunity link that launches an Outlook inspector window showing the Opportunity form region in compose mode. This operation is fairly direct. I just create an Outlook Post item in the My CRM/Opportunities folder and set the *MessageClass* property to *IPM.Post.CRMOpportunity*. Remember that Office Outlook 2007 will display the Opportunity form region based on this message class.

```
private void newOpportunity_LinkClicked(object sender,
    LinkLabelLinkClickedEventArgs e)
{
    Outlook.Folder root =
        (Outlook.Folder)Globals.ThisApplication.Session.GetDefaultFolder(
        Outlook.OlDefaultFolders.olFolderInbox).Parent;
    Outlook.Folder oppFolder =
        (Outlook.Folder)root.Folders["My CRM"].Folders["Opportunities"];

    Outlook.PostItem post =
      (Outlook.PostItem)oppFolder.Items.Add("IPM.Post.Opportunity");
    post.MessageClass = "IPM.Post.CRMOpportunity";
    post.Display(false);

}
```

Developing the Ribbon for the Office Outlook 2007 Inspector Window   The Ribbon that I developed for the Office Outlook 2007 inspector window is shown in Figure 6-11. As you can see, the custom Ribbon includes three buttons, one of which initiates a new sales quote document in Office Word 2007.

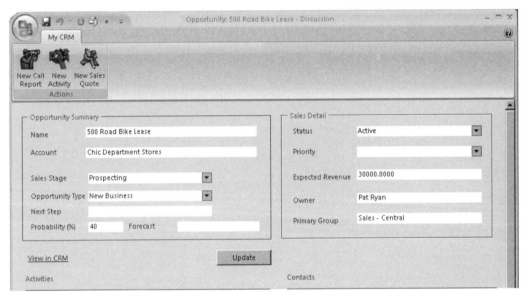

Figure 6-11   The custom Ribbon developed for the Office Outlook 2007 inspector window.

More Info   For more information about how to customize the Ribbon user interface in the 2007 Office system, go to *http://msdn2.microsoft.com/en-us/library/aa338202.aspx*.

The following XML defines the My CRM tab and the New Sales Quote button. The XML for the other two buttons is similar.

```xml
<customUI xmlns=http://schemas.microsoft.com/office/2006/01/customui"
    onLoad="OnLoad" loadImage="getImages">
  <ribbon startFromScratch="false">
    <tabs>
        <tab idMso="TabReadMessage" visible="0"></tab>
        <tab idMso="TabDeveloperTools" visible="0"></tab>
        <tab idMso="TabReportRendering" visible="0"></tab>
        <tab id="CRM.Opportunity" label="My CRM"
            getVisible="CRMOpportunityTab_GetVisible">
            <group id="CRM.Opportunity.Actions" label="Actions" visible="1">
                <button
                    id="crmSalesQuote"
                    size="large"
                    label="New Sales Quote"
                    onAction ="salesQuote_Action"
                    image="salesQuote_32"
                />

            </group>
        </tab>
    </tabs>
  </ribbon>
</customUI>
```

After defining the New Sales Quote button and the other buttons, I saved the XML file with the name OpportunityRibbon.xml and then added it to the Visual Studio project, setting the *Build Action* property for the file as Embedded Resource. I then used the following code to implement the custom Ribbon using the *IRibbonExtensibility* interface. The only method included in *IRibbonExtensibility* is *GetCustomUI*, which returns the XML that defines the custom Ribbon's elements as a string. I've also added the code required to show the Opportunity custom Ribbon only if Office Outlook 2007 displays an Opportunity item. Here again we use the item's *MessageClass* property to determine this. The *salesQuote_Action method* handles the click event for the New Sales Quote button in the Ribbon. It instantiates an Office Word 2007 document based on the template stored in the SharePoint document library and seeds the document with data related to the opportunity. When the document opens on the client, the content controls for customer name, address, and contact show the seeded data.

```csharp
using Office = Microsoft.Office.Core;
using Outlook = Microsoft.Office.Interop.Outlook;
using Word = Microsoft.Office.Interop.Word;

public partial class ThisAddIn
{
    protected override object RequestService(Guid serviceGuid)
    {
        if (serviceGuid == typeof(Office.IRibbonExtensibility).GUID)
            return new OpportunityRibbon();
        else
            return base.RequestService(serviceGuid);
```

```
        }

    }

    [ComVisible(true)]
    public class OpportunityRibbon: Office.IRibbonExtensibility
    {
        private Office.IRibbonUI ribbon;
        public OpportunityRibbon ()
        {
        }

        // Returns ribbon XML
        public string GetCustomUI(string ribbonID)
        {
            // Get XML from embedded resource
            if (ribbonID == "Microsoft.Outlook.Post.Read")
                return GetResourceText("OpportunityRibbon.xml");
            else
                return String.Empty;
        }

        public void OnLoad(Office.IRibbonUI ribbonUI)
        {
            this.ribbon = ribbonUI;
        }

        // Make this ribbon visible only if the inspector window is displaying
        // Opportunity. Remember that Opportunity is modeled as Outlook PostItem with
        // Message Class = IPM.Post.CRMOpportunity
        public bool CRMOpportunityTab_GetVisible (Office.IRibbonControl control)
        {
            Outlook.PostItem post = ((Outlook.Inspector)control.Context).CurrentItem as
                Outlook.PostItem;
            if (post != null && post.MessageClass == "IPM.Post.CRMOpportunity")
                return true;
            else
                return false;
        }

        public void salesQuote_Action (Office.IRibbonControl control)
        {
            Outlook.PostItem post = ((Outlook.Inspector)control.Context).CurrentItem as
                Outlook.PostItem;
            if (post != null && post.MessageClass == "IPM.Post.CRMOpportunity")
            {
                // Get OpportunityID from the custom properties
                string opportunityID =
                    post.UserProperties["OpportunityID"].Value.ToString();

                // Get parent account for the opportunity
                AccountOpportunity.OpportunityRow oppRow = new
                    AccountOpportunityTableAdapters.OpportunityTableAdapter()
                    .GetData().FindById(new Guid(opportunityID));
```

```
AccountOpportunity.AccountRow accRow = new
    AccountOpportunityTableAdapters.AccountTableAdapter().
    GetData().FindById(oppRow.AccountId);

// Create Word document based on template stored in the SharePoint
//document library
Word.Application wordapp = new Word.ApplicationClass();
object templateURL, missing = System.Type.Missing;
templateURL = @"http://moss.litwareinc.com/SiteDirectory/Sales/Quotes/
    Form/Quote/Quote.docx";
Word.Document doc = wordapp.Documents.Add(ref templateURL, ref missing,
    ref missing, ref missing);

// Find the document part that contains the XML data that is mapped to
// the content controls in the document
string NS_DocProperties =
    @"http://schemas.microsoft.com/office/2006/metadata/properties";
Office.CustomXMLPart part =
    doc.CustomXMLParts.SelectByNamespace (NS_DocProperties)[1];

string customerNameXpath =
    @"/ns0:properties[1]/documentManagement[1]/ns3:Customer[1]";

// Find the node in XML using the xpath and set the "Text" property of
// the node with Company Name. The implementation of the "UpdateNode"
// helper function is omitted for the sake of brevity
UpdateNode(part, customerNameXpath, accRow.Name);

// Similarly, set the XML nodes for Opportunity ID, Address (Street,
// City, Zip), Contact etc.
. . .

// Display the document
wordapp.Visible = true;

        }

    }

}
```

With the implementation of the custom UI elements in Office Outlook 2007, a salesperson is able to examine relevant information from the CRM system and initiate a sales quote when the opportunity requires it. I'll describe more about how the Office Word 2007 add-in works in the section "Developing the Office Word 2007 Add-In" later in the chapter. First, however, I'll describe the design and considerations for keeping the data in the CRM system in sync with the data in the local cache.

CRM Data Synchronization

A CRM application stores data in a database on the server. This data is accessed concurrently by multiple users. The OBA for SFA caches some of that data in the SQL Server Express database on the client to provide offline access to it through the Office Outlook 2007 user interface. This client-side cache is a single-user database. A subset of the cached data is also replicated in Office Outlook 2007 as Outlook *PostItem* objects that model the CRM entities and the custom properties attached to those items.

In the SFA solution, we have to keep three data stores in sync: the CRM database, the local cache, and the Outlook store. The architecture and implementation of the data synchronization process can vary significantly depending on factors such as the type of database used by the CRM, the database's ability to track changes, and how the database is accessed by an external process. In this section, I'll outline a general-purpose architecture and design for the synchronization process that assumes that the CRM database is relational and maintains a row-level modification time stamp. The architecture and process are outlined in Figures 6-12 and 6-13. Figure 6-12 shows the pattern of relationships between the different data fields that are synchronized. Figure 6-13 shows the synchronization steps themselves.

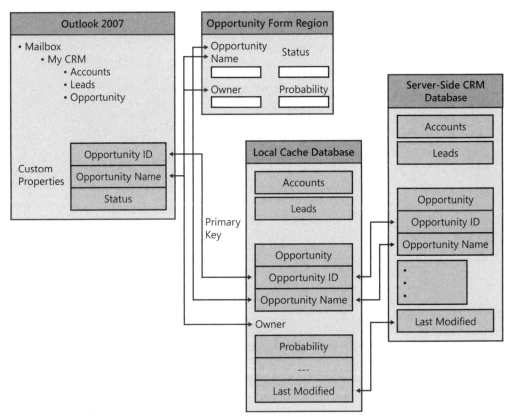

Figure 6-12   Custom properties defined for opportunities in Office Outlook 2007 relate to properties in the form region, local cache, and CRM database.

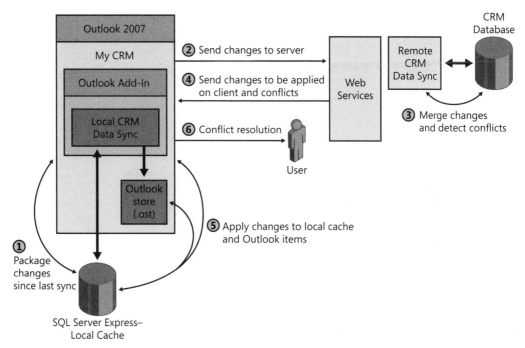

Figure 6-13   Changes made in the client are synchronized with the remote CRM database, and conflicts are shown to users for resolution.

The synchronization steps are as follows:

1. When a user makes changes to CRM data in Office Outlook 2007, you need to update the custom properties of the Outlook item as well as the corresponding row in the table in the local SQL Server Express cache. The relationship between the Outlook item and the table row is established through a custom property attached to the Outlook item that is the unique key for the table. For example, an Opportunity created from the *PostItem* object has a custom property called *OpportunityID*, which is the primary key for the Opportunity table in the local cache. When a row is updated in the local cache, it is marked as changed, a step that helps identify changes that have occurred since the previous synchronization.

2. When the synchronization process is initiated on the client, the Office Outlook 2007 add-in suspends write access to the CRM data. The user has read-only access to CRM data until the synchronization is complete. The CRM data sync process within the add-in packages the changes made by the user since the previous synchronization based on the row-level change flag mentioned in the previous step. The changes and the Last Sync Time Stamp are sent to the remote CRM data sync process on the server that has access to the CRM database.

3. The remote CRM data sync process merges the changes sent by the client with the server-side CRM database. It uses the Last Sync Time Stamp sent by the client to compare the client's changes with the server-side data that has been modified between the time

indicated by the Last Sync Time Stamp and the current time on the server. The current time is sent to the client as the new Last Sync Time Stamp. The merge results in changes that need to be applied to the client and in conflicts. The changes include any updates that other users had made to the CRM data. Conficts can arise in following cases:

❑ The row was updated on the client as well as the server.

❑ The row was updated on the client but was deleted on the server.

❑ The row that was deleted on the client was updated on the server.

After merging changes, the remote CRM data sync process sends the changes, conflicts, and Last Sync Time Stamp back to the client.

4. The local CRM data sync process receives the changes, conflicts, and Last Sync Time Stamp from the server. It stores the new Last Sync Time Stamp for the next scheduled synchronization and applies the changes to the local SQL Server Express cache and also to Outlook items and their custom properties. It displays conflicts sent by the server to the user for resolution. A conflict's resolution is sent to the server along with a Last Sync Time Stamp. Steps 3 and 4 are repeated until no more conflicts arise. At that point, the Office Outlook 2007 add-in restores write access to the CRM data.

As I mentioned earlier, a synchronization strategy can vary significantly based on the particular CRM application and its database capabilities. However, you need to keep a few things in mind regardless of the particular implementation.

■ Perform the local CRM data sync process on a separate worker thread in the Office Outlook 2007 add-in. Otherwise, this operation will block users from performing regular Outlook tasks such as sending e-mail, scheduling meetings, and so on for the duration of the synchronization. Little is more annoying in the midst of a workday than not being able to send an urgent e-mail message or look up the number of the conference room for an upcoming meeting.

■ Provide information about the synchronization progress or feedback to the user and allow the user to cancel the process at any point. Situations arise in which the user wants only to shut down his laptop and head out the door.

■ Allow users to configure the time and frequency for automatic synchronization. Also provide a capability to start and stop synchronization on demand (manually).

■ Anticipate conflicts between local and remote data and devise a scheme for presenting the conflicts to users and enabling them to resolve them.

Developing the Office Word 2007 Add-in

Additional functionality for the SFA solution is provided by a C# VSTO 2005 SE Office Word 2007 add-in. The add-in displays a CRM system's product catalog in a custom task pane and copies selected items to a product line items table in an Office Word 2007 document using the Office Word 2007 object model. These features of the add-in let a salesperson compile a sales quote directly in Office Word 2007. The add-in also implements Ribbon elements with which a user can submit a sales quote as an order to the CRM application. The add-in interacts with the CRM application using Web services. A sample of a sales quote and the custom task pane is shown in Figure 6-14.

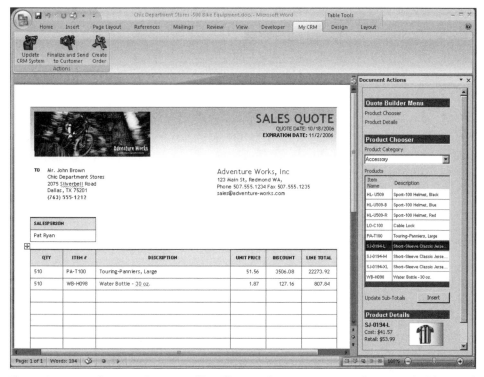

Figure 6-14   A sales quote is prepared in Office Word 2007. A custom task pane and Ribbon UI elements let a user search the the CRM system product catalog and create an order in the CRM system.

Creating the Office Word 2007 Template

The first aspect of developing the Office Word 2007 add-in was to create an Office Word 2007 template for sales quotes. The template can have any look and feel required by an organization (logo, titles, tables, and the like). The template uses Word content controls to display the customer name, contact, address, and similar information. The content controls should be bound to the custom XML part in the document. Documents based on the template are stored in a SharePoint document library, which will show some of the data bound to content control as columns. To create the template, follow these steps:

1.   Create an Office Word 2007 document and format it with the elements required for a sales quote. Save the document as Quote.docx on your local drive.

2.   Define a Sales Quote content type for a SharePoint site. The content type should have site columns for customer, street address, city, state, zip, and contact name.

3.   On the Advance Settings page for the Sales Quote content type, associate a document template by uploading the file Quote.docx from your local drive.

4. Create a Sales Quote document library on the SharePoint site. On the Customize page for the document library, associate the Sales Quote content type with the library.

5. On the document library's Settings page, click Change New Button Order And Default Content Type. On the next page, select the Visible check box for the Sales Quote content type. Selecting this option displays Sales Quote as a menu option when a user clicks the New button in the document library, allowing the user to instantiate a document based on the sales quote template.

6. Click the New, Sales Quote option on the document library menu. As mentioned earlier, this action will instantiate a document based on the sales quote template.

7. Now add content controls in the appropriate places in the document. For example, place the insertion point where you want to display the customer's name, click the Insert tab on the document's Ribbon, and then select Quick Parts, Document Property, Customer to add a Customer content control to the document and bind the content control to the Customer document property. Notice that as a result of you creating the Sales Quote content type and associating it with the document template, SharePoint creates document properties based on the site columns in the content type. Repeat this process to place all the content controls in the document. Save the document on a local drive, overwriting the files Quote.docx. This file now becomes the new template for the Sales Quote content type.

8. Go to the site content types page in Windows SharePoint Services, and associate Quote.docx from the previous step as the new template for the content type.

9. To test the content type, open the Sales Quote document library. Select the New, Sales Quote menu option to open a new Office Word 2007 document. This document should contain the content controls.

The combination of the Sales Quote content type, the Quote.docx template for the content type, and the Sales Quote document library based on the content type enables you to instantiate a sales quote from Office Outlook 2007 while viewing an Opportunity item and populating the content controls with opportunity-related data. I described the underlying mechanism in the section "Developing the Ribbon for the Office Outlook 2007 Inspector Window" earlier in the chapter.

Implementing the Custom Task Pane in Office Word 2007

The custom task pane in Office Word 2007 displays the product catalog and allows a user to copy items from the catalog to the product line item table in the Office Word 2007 document. This is a two-step process. You first need to develop a Windows Forms user control with the functionality you need, and then you need to add the user control to the custom task pane and manage the possibility of having multiple instances of task panes open—one for each open document.

Developing Product Catalog User Control   To create the user control, I added a new user control to the Visual Studio project and named it ProductChooser. The layout of the control appears in Figure 6-15.

Figure 6-15   The user control developed to show the CRM system's product catalog.

The user control calls CRM Web services to retrieve the product list by category and get detailed pricing and an image of the item. When a user clicks the Insert button, the item is added to the product line item table in the document. The following code shows a couple of the key methods for this user control.

```
using System.Data;
using System.Windows.Forms;

partial class ProductChooser : UserControl
{
    // Get products from CRM web services for given category and
    // fill the product data grid view on the user form
    private void FillProductList(string productCategory)
    {
        // Call CRM Web service to get products in given category
        // Web service returns a dataset
        CrmWS.Products products = new CrmWS.Products();
        DataSet productList = products.GetProducts(productCategory);

        // Populate dgProducts DataGridView
        Object[] item;
        dgProducts.Rows.Clear();
```

```
            DataRow[] rows = productList.Tables[0].Rows;
            foreach(DataRow row in rows)
            {
                item = new object[2];
                item[0] = row["ProductID"].ToString();
                item[1] = row["ProductName"].ToString();
            }
    }

    private void InsertItems()
    {

        string productID = dgProducts.SelectedRows[0].
            Cells[0].Value.ToString();

        // Get product details from CRM web service. The CRM uses
        // accountID to apply appropriate discount and price for
        // the customer
        CrmWS.Products products = new CrmWS.Products();
        CrmWS.ProductInfo productInfo = products.GetProductInfo(productID,
            accountID);

        // Get product line items table by name
        Word.Table itemTable =
            Globals.ThisAddIn.Application.ActiveDocument.Tables["ProductItems"];

            object missing = Type.Missing;
            Word.Row row = itemTable.Rows.Add (ref missing);

            // Set values in each cell of the row
            row.Cells[1] = "1";  // Quantity = 1
            row.Cells[2] = productInfo.ProductNumber;
            row.Cells[3] = productInfo.ProductDescription;
            . . .
    }
}
```

Adding the User Control to the Custom Task Pane   Now that we have the user control, we need to add it to the custom task pane and manage multiple instances of the task pane. For this purpose, I used the *DocumentWrapper* class. The following code is included in the *ThisAddIn* class.

```
//Create a new Wrappers collection
public Dictionary<Word.Document, DocumentWrapper> Wrappers =
    new Dictionary<Word.Document, DocumentWrapper>();

//Events objects to wire in document events
Word.ApplicationEvents2_Event appEvents;

private void ThisAddIn_Startup(object sender, System.EventArgs e)
{
    . . .
    appEvents = (Word.ApplicationEvents2_Event)this.Application;
```

```
    appEvents.NewDocument += new Word.ApplicationEvents2_NewDocumentEventHandler(
        appEvents_NewDocument);

}

void appEvents_NewDocument(Microsoft.Office.Interop.Word.Document Doc)
{
    this.Wrappers.Add(Doc, new DocumentWrapper(Doc));

}
```

The *DocumentWrapper* class creates a custom task pane and attaches it to the document being opened. It also handles removing the custom task pane when the document is closed. The following code is for the *DocumentWrapper* class.

```
public class DocumentWrapper
{
        Word.Document document;
        CustomTaskPane taskPane;

        public DocumentWrapper(Word.Document document)
        {
            this.document = document;

            //Wire up the close event for the document
            ((Word.DocumentEvents_Event)this.document).Close += new
                Word.DocumentEvents_CloseEventHandler(DocumentWrapper_Close);

            //Add a new ProductChooser user control as CTP for this document
            this.taskPane = Globals.ThisAddIn.CustomTaskPanes.Add(
                new ProductChooser(), "Document Actions",
                this.document.ActiveWindow);
            this.taskPane.Visible = true;

        }

        //Document Closing
        void DocumentWrapper_Close()
        {
            //Remove the Custom Task Pane from the collection when the document
            //closes
            if (this.taskPane != null)
                Globals.ThisAddIn.CustomTaskPanes.Remove(this.taskPane);
            this.taskPane = null;

            //Remove the document from the Wrappers collection
            Globals.ThisAddIn.Wrappers.Remove(this.document);
            ((Word.DocumentEvents_Event)this.document).Close -= new
                Word.DocumentEvents_CloseEventHandler(DocumentWrapper_Close);
            this.document = null;
        }
}
```

Developing the Office Word 2007 Custom Ribbon

The steps I followed to create the custom Ribbon in Office Word 2007 are essentially the same as those for developing the custom Ribbon for the Office Outlook 2007 inspector window. As a quick example of the work I did in Office Word 2007, I used the following XML to add a Create Order button as part of a custom Ribbon.

```
<customUI xmlns=http://schemas.microsoft.com/office/2006/01/customui
    onLoad="OnLoad" loadImage="getImages">
  <ribbon startFromScratch="false">
    <tabs>
        <tab id="MyCRM.Proposal" label="My CRM"
            getVisible="myCRMTab_GetVisible">
            <button
                id="createOrder"
                size="large"
                label="Create Order"
                onAction ="createOrder_Action"
                image="build_32"
            />

        </group>
        </tab>
    </tabs>
  </ribbon>
</customUI>
```

Handling the Ribbon in Office Word 2007 requires the same operations as handling the Ribbon in an Outlook inspector window, which I explained in the section "Developing the Ribbon for the Office Outlook 2007 Inspector Window" earlier in the chapter. Now I'll describe the event handler for the Create Order button. This method packages the order data from the Office Word 2007 document and calls the CRM Web service to create the order.

```
public void createOrder_Action(Office.IRibbonControl control)
{
    Word.Document doc = ((Word.Window)control.Context).Document;

    // Document properties are stored in XML part in document.
    // GetDocumentPropertyValue helper function retrieves the property value
    // using appropriate XPath search. The implementation of this function
    // is omitted for the sake of brevity
    string accountID = GetDocumentPropertyValue(doc, "Account ID");
    string total = GetDocumentPropertyValue(doc, "Total");


    crmWS.CRMOrderServices s = new crmWS.CRMOrderServices();
    crmWS.SalesOrder ord = new crmWS.SalesOrder();
    ord.customerID = accountID;
    ord.Total = total;

    // Get product line items table by name
    Word.Table itemTable =
        Globals.ThisAddIn.Application.ActiveDocument.Tables["ProductItems"];
```

```
// Construct ProductLineItems for SalesOrder
int numLineItems = itemTable.Rows.Count;
ord.productLineItems = new crmWS.ProductLineItem[numLineItems];
int i = 0;
foreach (Word.Row row in itemTable.Rows)
{
    ord.productLineItems[i] = new crmWS.ProductLineItem();
    ord.productLineItems[i].Quantity = row.Cells[1];
    ord.productLineItems[i].ProductDescription = row.Cells[2];
    // Set remaining product line item properties
    . . .

    i++;

}

// Call CreateOrder web method
string orderNum = s.CreateOrder(ord);

MessageBox.Show("Order created successfully in CRM system. " +
    "Order Number: " + orderNum, "Order Confirmation", MessageBoxButtons.OK,
    MessageBoxIcon.Information);

}
```

Through the Office Outlook 2007 and Office Word 2007 add-ins, the salesperson has been able to view information from the CRM system, capture important customer interactions, and initiate and build a sales quote—all within familiar 2007 Office system applications. Now we need to handle situations in which a sales quote needs to be approved before being distributed to a customer, which we do by implementing a SharePoint workflow that starts when a sales quote is saved to the document library.

The Quote Approval SharePoint Workflow

The workflow I developed for the SFA solution is a custom SharePoint workflow created using the Windows Workflow Foundation (WF) Designer in Visual Studio 2005. The workflow assigns an approval task to the sales manager if the discount given in the sales quote exceeds 10 percent. In these cases, the sales manager receives notification of the approval task in an e-mail message that contains an embedded URL to the quote approval form. The quote approval form is a custom form developed in Microsoft Office InfoPath 2007. The sales manager fills out the approval form in the Web browser. If the manager approves the sales quote, the workflow updates the Quote Status document property of the sales quote to Approved and sends notification to the originator of the quote.

The following steps are required to build this kind of workflow:

1. Design and code the workflow using the Visual Studio 2005 designer for the Windows Workflow Foundation.

2. Design an Office InfoPath 2007 task form that is used by the sales manager to approve the document.

3. Create a workflow definition file that binds the various workflow components together.

4. Create a feature definition file so that the workflow can be deployed as a Windows Share-Point Services feature.

5. Install and activate the feature using stsadm.exe.

In this section, I'll focus on the design aspect of the workflow—the first two steps in the list. I'll skip the deployment steps because they are not unique to the OBA for SFA.

> **More Info**   You can find information about workflow deployment on Microsoft Developer Network (MSDN) at *http://msdn2.microsoft.com/en-us/library/aa830816.aspx.*

Designing the Workflow

To start, I created a SharePoint sequential workflow project in Visual Studio 2005. I then used Windows workflow activities in the toolbox to design the workflow shown in Figure 6-16.

The next step is to add logic to the workflow by adding code behind the design. The following code shows a few of the key methods in the workflow code.

```
//This is the first activity in the workflow. Set some class level variable
//for later use.

public Guid workflowId = default(System.Guid);
private string documentURL = default(string);
private string customerName = default(string);

private void onWorkflowActivated1_Invoked(object sender, ExternalDataEventArgs e)
{
    this.workflowId = this.workflowProperties.WorkflowId;

    // Get to the list item in the Quote document library corresponding
    // to the document under review. From the list item, you can get
    // document properties
    SPSite site = new SPSite(this.workflowProperties.SiteId);
    SPWeb web = site.AllWebs[this.workflowProperties.WebId];
    SPList list = web.Lists[this.workflowProperties.ListId];
    SPListItem item = list.Items.GetItemById(this.workflowProperties.ItemId);

    this.documentURL = item.Web.Url + @"/" + item.File.Url;
    this.customerName = item["Customer"].ToString();

}
```

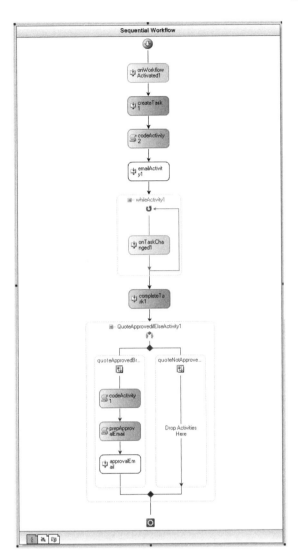

Figure 6-16   The quote-approval workflow in Visual Studio 2005.

The *createTask* method creates the quote approval task and assigns it to the sales manager (nicolec). The method also sets the properties of the created task object, which has built-in properties such as *AssignedTo* and *Title*. In addition, I created a custom property named Quote Document that points to the document properties page for the document in workflow.

```
private void createTask(object sender, EventArgs e)

{
    // Assign unique id to the task
```

```
    taskID = Guid.NewGuid();


    createTask1.TaskProperties.AssignedTo = @"litwareinc\NicoleC";
    createTask1.TaskProperties.Title = "Quote for: " +
        this.customerName;


    // Show document properties URL for the document under review
    string sURL = buildSummaryURL(
        this.workflowProperties.SiteUrl +
        this.workflowProperties.ListUrl);
    taskProps.ExtendedProperties["Quote Document"] = sURL;
}
```

I then added a code activity and an Email Activity to the workflow. The code activity executes the *PrepareEmail* method, which formats the e-mail message's text and associates it with the *Body* property of the e-mail activity (*emailActivity1*). It also sets up the *recipients* class member, which is assigned to the *To* property of the Email Activity in the workflow designer. The Email Activity then sends the message.

```
private void PrepareEmail(object sender, EventArgs e)
{
    string taskApprovalUrl = String.Format(
        "{0}/_layouts/WrkStat.aspx?List={1}&WorkflowInstanceID={2}",
            this.workflowProperties.WebUrl,
            this.workflowProperties.ListId.ToString("B"),
            this.workflowProperties.WorkflowId.ToString("B"));

    // Set the body of the email activity
    emailActivity1.Body =
    "Due to the discount amount of the associated quote, " + "your approval is
    required on the following quote: " + this.documentURL.Replace(" ", "%20") + ".
    Please review the quote task and then approve/deny " + "the quote by completing
    the task " + "that has been created for you at: " + taskApprovalUrl.Replace(" ",
    "%20");

    // The "recipients" is a private class member of type ArrayList and has been
    // initialized (new ArrayList()) in the constructor. The subsequent email
    // activity has its "To" property set to this variable.
    recipients.Add("NicoleC@litwareinc.com");

}
```

Later in the workflow I included a conditional branch. The condition for this branch is evaluated by the *IsQuoteApproved* method. This method checks whether the sales manager approved or rejected the quote in the Office InfoPath 2007 task form. The code is straightforward, but it highlights one important point: Data from an Office InfoPath 2007 workflow task form is not passed directly into the workflow the way it is for workflow association or initiation forms.

Rather, the task form changes the fields corresponding to the form's schema in the task item directly. This being the case, I retrieve the *Approved* property from the underlying task.

```
private void IsQuoteApproved(object sender, ConditionalEventArgs e)
{
    // Get the approval task item
    SPSite site = new SPSite(this.workflowProperties.SiteId);
    SPWeb web = site.AllWebs[this.workflowProperties.WebId];
    SPList list = web.Lists[this.workflowProperties.TaskListId];
    SPListItem item = list.GetItemById(this.afterProps.TaskItemId);

    if (item["Approved"] != null)
        e.Result = bool.Parse(item["Approved"].ToString());
}
```

Later in this conditional branch, the workflow updates the Quote Status document property of the document in workflow.

```
private void updateQuoteListItemStatus(object sender, EventArgs e)
{
    SPSite site = new SPSite(this.workflowProperties.SiteId);
    SPWeb web = site.AllWebs[this.workflowProperties.WebId];
    SPList list = web.Lists[this.workflowProperties.ListId];
    SPListItem item = list.GetItemById(this.workflowProperties.ItemId);
    item["Quote Status"] = "Approved";
    item.Update();
}
```

And finally, the workflow sends an e-mail message to the originator, informing the salesperson that the document has been approved, and then the workflow finishes.

Designing an Office InfoPath 2007 Task Form

When Office SharePoint Server 2007 displays a custom Office InfoPath 2007 form for a workflow task, Office SharePoint Server 2007 passes the task data to the form as XML. For my Office InfoPath 2007 task form to understand and parse the XML for the task data, I need to add the task schema to the form as a secondary data source. To do this, I created a file called ItemMetadata.xml that represents the task schema, and then I added that file to my form as a secondary data source. Finally, I bound form controls to specific elements of the task schema XML. The ItemMetadata.xml file contains the following XML.

```
<z:row xmlns:z="#RowsetSchema"
    ows_Approver=""
    ows_Approved=""
    ows_Comments=""
/>
```

The InfoPath form is shown in Figure 6-17.

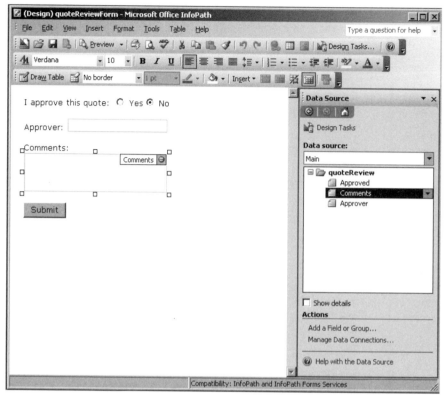

Figure 6-17   An InfoPath 2007 task form is used to approve the sales quote.

With the addition of the SharePoint workflow, the OBA for SFA handles each of the major steps in the opportunity-to-order process but without duplicating the functionality of the CRM system itself. In addition, the solution provides significant advantages: access to CRM data in the familiar Office Outlook 2007 user interface, preparation of the sales quote, and business process management through the SharePoint workflow.

Taking Advantage of Visual Studio 2008 and VSTO 2008

I developed this OBA using VSTO 2005 SE. Microsoft is introducing many new features in Visual Studio 2008 and VSTO 2008, and beta 2 versions of these products are available on Microsoft Developer Network (MSDN) at the time of this writing. In this section, I'll share some thoughts about how I could improve my OBA by incorporating some of these new features. Keep in mind that the points I am highlighting here relate to the scope of the OBA for SFA. Visual Studio 2008 and VSTO 2008 have many new features in addition to those described here.

Microsoft Synchronization Services for ADO.NET

The OBA for SFA caches CRM data locally in SQL Server Express to be used in the Office Outlook 2007 add-in. It also uses a proprietary scheme to synchronize the local cache with the remote CRM database. With Visual Studio 2008, I can base my caching and replication strategy on Microsoft Synchronization Services for ADO.NET, which provides the ability to synchronize data from disparate sources over two-tier, N-tier, and service-based architectures. Rather than simply replicating a database and its schema, the Synchronization Services application programming interface (API) provides a set of components you can use to synchronize data between data services and a local store. The Synchronization Services API, which is modeled after the ADO.NET data access APIs, provides an intuitive way to synchronize data. It uses SQL Server Compact Edition (CE) 3.5 to manage the local cache. SQL Server CE 3.5 is a free, lightweight, embeddable database that offers essential relational database functionality.

VSTO 2008 Document-Level Customization for Office Word 2007

The OBA for SFA uses an application-level Office Word 2007 add-in because that is the only type of add-in supported by VSTO 2005 SE for Office Word 2007. An application-level add-in is loaded as soon as any Office Word 2007 document is opened. As a result, the functionality provided in a custom task pane and Ribbon is available to any document, not just to a sales quote document, for example. This is not desirable behavior. I can employ some clever tricks such as examining a document property to check whether the document is of type Sales Quote and then control the visibility of the CTP and the Ribbon, but VSTO 2008 offers a cleaner way to implement such a solution by supporting document-level customization for Office Word 2007. A document-level customization allows me to associate my customization code with the Sales Quote template. My code executes only when a document based on the Sales Quote template is opened. It should be fairly straightforward to port my current application-level add-in code to VSTO 2008 Office Word 2007 document-level customization.

WPF and Windows Forms Controls in Outlook Form Regions

In my OBA, I developed Office Outlook 2007 form regions using built-in form controls (Office Outlook 2007 provides 15 of them) and a List View ActiveX control. This delivers a very plain user interface. VSTO 2008 allows you to design an Office Outlook 2007 form region by adding Windows Presentation Foundation (WPF) and Windows Forms controls, which will provide a better user experience.

ClickOnce Deployment

VSTO 2008 supports ClickOnce deployment of 2007 Office system add-ins and document-level customization. The deployment supports offline, automatic updating, and rollback. This ClickOnce behavior is similar to the ClickOnce deployment feature for Windows Forms applications. In addition, VSTO 2008 has simplified the security model by eliminating a dependency on code access security policy (caspol) without weakening the security of the solution. For me, the ClickOnce deployment and simplified security model are motivation enough to migrate my VSTO 2005 Office Outlook 2007 and Office Word 2007 add-ins to VSTO 2008.

Summary

The OBA for SFA manages a complex business process from start to finish, without requiring its users to work in applications other than Office Outlook 2007, Office Word 2007, and Office SharePoint Server 2007. As a result, salespeople have a more consistent user experience, gather important data more easily and more often, and can collaborate with customers and coworkers. I would stress again that OBAs are intended to complement and not replace line-of-business systems. They help organizations realize a return on the investment that the organization makes in a CRM and ERP system by helping increase user adoption and satisfaction and making line-of-business systems accessible to a broader user base.

Chapter 7

Business Intelligence: A Manufacturing Plant Floor Analytics OBA

–Karthik Ravindran, Microsoft Corporation

Business intelligence (often referred to simply as BI) is a business management term that refers to applications and technologies that are used to gather and analyze data and information about an organization's operations. Business intelligence systems can help companies gain more comprehensive knowledge of factors affecting their business in areas such as sales, production, and internal operations. Business intelligence solutions provide value at all levels of an organization when the flow of information across the operational, tactical, and strategic levels facilitates collaboration, business insight, and decision making. Data gathered at the operational level, for example, enables operational monitoring and real-time mitigations. Operational data is synthesized and consolidated to support tactical analysis, as well as strategic adjustments and directives provided by the managerial and executive levels.

The central aims of a well-designed business intelligence solution are to extract information from raw data and enable sound, fact-based decision making by presenting the information in context, tailored to each organizational role. A business intelligence solution should support and enable capabilities related to the following:

- **Planning**   Using information derived from data to analyze past trends, project future directions, and plan a course for successful business execution.

- **Monitoring**   Analyzing data and information synthesized from day-to-day transactional operations to mitigate real-time operational anomalies and risks.

- **Analysis**   Analyzing information synthesized over time from operational data to plan and implement tactical and strategic initiatives for the middle and long terms.

From a technology perspective, a variety of services and tools are needed to develop business intelligence solutions that can address these requirements. Required components include reporting tools, data marts and data warehouses, OLAP modeling and data analysis tools, data mining tools, and data visualization tools.

In this chapter, I'll describe the architecture for an Office Business Application designed for an oil and gas manufacturing plant, although the technologies and concepts I discuss are applicable to a broad segment of industries and solutions. The application is not fully implemented—it serves largely as a reference—but the architecture you'll read about illustrates how business intelligence solution capabilities are enabled by the OBA platform, Microsoft SQL Server, and the broader Microsoft platform. Relevant scenarios and sample code from the reference application accompany the key concepts I describe. The capabilities are discussed in a context that integrates a number of Microsoft technologies and services that span the 2007 Microsoft Office system (server and client) and the Microsoft SQL Server business intelligence product offerings.

This chapter assumes that you are familiar with general business intelligence concepts and the current Microsoft SQL Server business intelligence offerings (SQL Server Analysis Services, SQL Server Reporting Services, and SQL Server Integration Services). I'll describe more recent Microsoft business intelligence products and features included in the sample solution—those enabled by Microsoft Office SharePoint Server 2007 and Microsoft Office PerformancePoint Monitoring Server 2007, for example—at the level applicable to their role in the manufacturing plant floor analytics OBA solution architecture. Near the end of this chapter you'll see an example of how to implement Microsoft Silverlight, a technology designed for presenting media experiences and Rich Internet Applications (RIAs).

You can download a Virtual PC (VPC) image through the book's Web site at *http://msdn2.microsoft.com/en-us/architecture/bb643797.aspx* as a tool for exploring the OBA presented in this chapter. The system requirements for setting up and running the VPC are provided in the next section of the chapter.

> **Note**   The reference implementation of the OBA described in this chapter focuses solely on functional perspectives about a spectrum of products and tools that comprise Microsoft's business intelligence offerings. Architectural issues such as security, scalability, and availability are discussed briefly, but they are not the focal points of the reference solution implementation.

Walk-Through of the Manufacturing Plant Floor Analytics OBA

In the following sections, I'll walk you through the manufacturing plant floor analytics solution. You can follow along with the VPC available on the book's Web site. You will explore application scenarios and the user experience of an OBA, and you'll see details of the solution's implementation that will guide your understanding of the solution's architecture. I'll describe how users interact and experience the manufacturing plant floor analytics solution from three different perspectives. The walk-through begins by illustrating the use of business intelligence in operational execution for real-time monitoring and risk mitigations. It then proceeds to demonstrate how data collected at operational levels can be rolled up for tactical analysis and short-term and mid-term mitigations. In the third segment, you'll see how the solution can help provide insights for strategic planning and decision making.

Background Reading about the Plant Floor Analytics OBA

You can find additional background reading and demonstrations related to the manufacturing plant floor OBA on MSDN, at *http://msdn2.microsoft.com/en-us/ architecture/bb643797.aspx*. These materials include the following:

- A presentation aimed at business decision makers (Microsoft Office PowerPoint 2007 slides and video)

- A presentation about the solution architecture (Office PowerPoint 2007 and video)

- A click-through demonstration of the solution

The screen shots in the Office PowerPoint 2007 click-through demo will differ slightly from the portal pages on the VPC.

Software and Hardware Requirements for the Plant Floor VPC

To work with the VPC image of the manufacturing plant floor analytics OBA, your system must meet the following minimum requirements:

- A supported Windows operating system (Windows XP, Windows Vista, or Windows Server 2003)

- Microsoft Virtual PC 2007

- Minimum memory requirement for the VPC image: 1 gigabyte (GB)

- Hard disk space for the VPC image: 16 GB

- Processor (recommended): 1 gigahertz (GHz) or greater

Setting Up and Logging On to the VPC

In Microsoft Virtual PC 2007, create a virtual machine named PF Analytics OBA from the virtual hard disk (VHD) you can download from the book's Web site. To log on to the VPC image, follow these steps:

1. Use the VPC 2007 console to start the PF Analytics OBA virtual machine.

2. Log on to the virtual machine using the following user credentials:

   User name: **administrator**

   Password: **pass@word1**

3. Wait for the warm-up scripts to fully complete prior to proceeding to the next task.

Operational Monitoring: Exploring the Shift Foreman's Portal

To begin the walk-through, double-click the desktop shortcut to launch the WA plant/shift foreman's portal, which is shown in Figure 7-1. After the portal page is fully loaded in Internet Explorer, browse the page to view the Web Parts it contains. You will see the following Web Parts:

- A Silverlight rendering of an interactive plant floor map. (Animations are implemented in this version to only reflect activities at the input feed pumps.) You can see the code that creates this component in "Presentation Tier Architecture" later in the chapter.

- An Office PerformancePoint Monitoring 2007 scorecard that lists real-time key performance indicators (KPIs) of relevance to the plant operations.

- A list of active safety incidents reported in the plant.

- A list of quick links to frequently accessed resources.

- An Excel Services chart that is refreshed periodically to reflect the production performance over time for the product (Iso-Butane) manufactured by the plant.

- A list of the current shift workers and their clocked-in status.

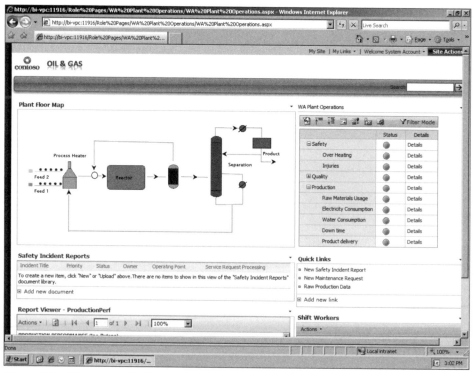

Figure 7-1 The plant shift foreman's portal.

Note   KPIs are the principal metrics used to measure the overall health of a business. Each KPI has four main attributes: a current value, the goal or target value, the current status, and the trend observed in relation to time. KPI scorecards are used in role-tailored business intelligence dashboards to display the current values, status information in relation to attaining the goal values, and trend over time for KPIs of relevance to users across an organization.

Now double-click the shortcut on the desktop to launch the Plant Simulator console application. You can use this application to simulate a plant operation exception condition and walk through a scenario that highlights the use of the important Web Parts on the page. (It will help you see the page if you position the Plant Simulator console window at the bottom right corner of the desktop.)

You will first simulate an overheating condition at the input feed pump. Type **1** in the Plant Simulator console and then press Enter. You will see a notification indicating that the overheating simulation is in effect. In 3 to 5 seconds you will notice that the input feed pump 2 turns red in the plant floor map Web Part to reflect an exception condition. A red traffic signal is also displayed over the feed line to reflect a danger condition. By moving the cursor over the traffic signal, you can see that the heat being generated at this input line is at a dangerous level.

Refresh the browser window, and you'll notice that the safety and overheating KPIs in the real-time scorecard have turned red to reflect the overheating condition. To mitigate the danger condition, you will now shut down the feed pump. To do this, select option 2 in the Plant Simulator console. After you do this, you will notice within 3 to 5 seconds that the feed line turns gray to reflect an inactive state. The danger signal is also removed as the overheating has been mitigated by turning off the pump. Refresh the browser window again and you will see that the safety and overheating KPIs are no longer red. However, you should notice that the downtime and the delivery KPIs have turned yellow to reflect a drop in production performance caused by one of the input feeds becoming inactive.

The next step is to file a safety incident report to get the affected feed pump examined and fixed. Click the New Safety Incident link in the Quick Links Web Part to open a Microsoft Office InfoPath 2007 browser form to report a new safety incident. Enter values into the fields to report an overheating condition at feed pump 2, set the priority to 0, and do not change the default Active (Not Assigned) status. Click Submit to create the new safety incident report. The form will be submitted, and you will be returned to the shift foreman's portal.

In the portal you will now see that the Active Safety Incident Reports Web Part lists the safety incident that you just reported. In a real implementation, a workflow would be connected to the Safety Incident Report content type to route the incident to an available service technician, who would service the request and close the incident. You can see the code that defines a workflow for service requests in "Application Services Tier Architecture" later in this chapter.

> **More Info** You can also see examples of workflows in several other chapters in this book. For example, Chapter 4, "Provisioning and Securing a Virtual Learning Workspace," demonstrates custom workflows built to help set up a SharePoint site.

Select option 3 in the Plant Simulator console to reset feed pump 2 and restore normal operations. In about 3 to 5 seconds you will notice that the feed line turns green again to reflect the active state of the pump. Refresh the browser window, and you will notice that the downtime KPI is no longer yellow. The delivery KPI, however, remains yellow because the overall feed downtime has affected production for the day.

If a minute or so has passed between shutting down the pump and the latest refresh of your browser, you will also notice a drop in a production performance chart to reflect the impact on production caused by the feed pump being inactive for a period of time. Select option 4 in the Plant Simulator console to reset the delivery KPI and restore the plant operation back to the state it was in at the start of this portion of the walk-through.

Tactical Analytics: Exploring the Plant Manager's Portal

As I mentioned previously, data gathered at the operation level can be synthesized and consolidated to enable tactical analysis and mitigations. In exploring the plant manager's portal, you'll see an example of how this capability is implemented.

Double-click the shortcut on the desktop to launch the plant manager's portal, and wait for the page to load in Internet Explorer. The portal is shown in Figure 7-2. Browse the page to view the Web Parts it contains. You will notice the following Web Parts:

- An Office PerformancePoint Monitoring Server 2007 scorecard that lists tactical KPIs of relevance to the plant operations. The values for these KPIs are consolidated and synthesized from a SQL Server Analysis Services (SSAS) cube that is refreshed on a daily basis.

- A contacts listing of functional managers at the Washington plant.

- Excel Services Web Parts that render charts that let the plant manager analyze the trends for tactical KPIs over time (across months of the current year). The plant manager can choose to open any of these charts in an instance of Office Excel 2007 to perform more detailed data analysis. Opening any of the charts will launch an instance of Office Excel 2007 that is connected to the source cube so that detailed analysis can be performed.

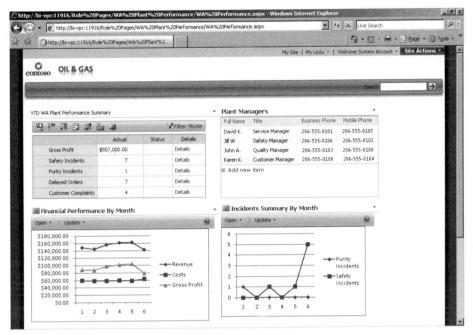

Figure 7-2   The plant manager's portal.

Looking at the scorecard, notice that the states of a few KPIs are not very favorable. Of specific interest is the safety KPI, which is in a nonoptimal state and is most likely causing the drop in customer service and the delayed orders KPIs. If you explore the charts on this page further, you can see that the safety incidents, delayed orders, and customer complaints KPIs have all experienced a spike in the month of June. As plant manager, you need to perform some detailed, ad-hoc analysis in Office Excel 2007 to try and determine the cause of the spike in safety incidents.

Click the Details link for the safety KPI in the PPS Monitoring KPI Scorecard Web Part. This launches an instance of Office Excel 2007 that is connected to a view of the SSAS cube that is the source of the KPI's values. The specific cube view (known as a *perspective* in SSAS) to which the Office Excel 2007 instance is wired enables exploratory analysis of safety-related metrics and related dimensions.

The plant manager can now build ad-hoc reports and charts in Office Excel 2007 that will enable her to identify the cause of the spike in safety incidents and take the corrective tactical action to mitigate the spike. A report that illustrates the results of the analysis performed by the plant manager is provided with the solution and can be found in the Microsoft Office SharePoint Server Reports Library.

Open the OBA PF RAP Quick Links, Reports Library link by selecting it from the Favorites list in Internet Explorer. You will be taken to the Microsoft Office SharePoint Server Reports Library, shown in Figure 7-3, which lists a collection of Excel Services reports. Select the Safety

Analysis Results reports and choose the option to edit in Office Excel 2007. This will open the report in a live client instance of Office Excel 2007 connected to the source SSAS cube. Explore the reports to view the field selections used to build them and understand the plant manager's analysis.

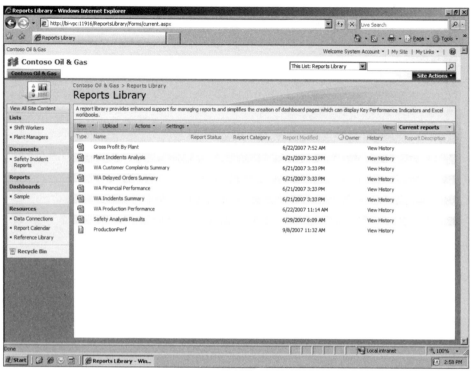

Figure 7-3   The Reports Library.

The safety incidents trend chart for the operating points over time shows that the spike in safety incidents occurred recently, in the month of June. The chart also shows that the incidents in June were all caused by overheating noticed at the number 2 input feed pumps. The plant manager, on seeing the safety incidents trend chart, recollects that she recently approved a request to experiment with a new model feed pump that was guaranteed to lower electricity consumption. The Maintenance Requests report indicates that this change has been implemented at the feed pumps. Relating this recollection to the recent spike in safety incidents and the trend analysis that indicates that this pattern was not seen earlier, the plant manager concludes that the new feed pumps are the cause of recent overheating incidents. The chart that displays electricity consumption across the feed pumps over time indicates that electricity consumption was indeed optimized after installing the new feed pumps. However, the optimization is by a few hundred units, and the overall cost benefit does not stack up to the downtime caused by the overheating incidents and the resulting impact on servicing customer orders.

Having detected the cause of the problem, the plant manager decides to immediately reinstate the older model feed pumps to address the spike in safety incidents. She also requests the vendor of the newer model pumps to examine the pumps for a potential resolution because the long-term benefits of conserving electricity consumption are beneficial from an overall costs perspective.

The manager returns to the portal and enters annotations for the actual values of the safety incidents and the delayed orders KPIs in the scorecard to explain the results of her analysis and detail the mitigation plans. To do this yourself, add the following annotations to the actual values of the safety and delayed orders in the PPS Monitoring scorecard. (Move your cursor over the actual values, click the drop-down arrow, and then select the Annotation option to add the annotations.)

- For the safety KPI, the annotation should read: Excessive heat generation by new FPX09 model feed pumps. Submitted Pri 0 service request to replace pumps. ETA for resolution is 1 day.

- For the delayed orders KPIs, the annotation should read: Cause: Downtime due to FPX09 safety incidents. ETA for resolution is 1 day.

Strategic Insight: Exploring the Vice President's Portal

You have now seen how data gathered at the operation level is consolidated for tactical analysis and decision-making. Now we'll take a look at how the data and decisions made at the tactical level roll up to inform strategic insights.

Double-click the shortcut on the desktop to launch the vice president's (VP's) portal (shown in Figure 7-4), and wait for the page to fully load in Internet Explorer. Notice the following Web Parts:

- A PPS Monitoring Server KPI scorecard that lists strategic KPIs that reflect the overall region's performance. The values for these KPIs are sourced from an SSAS cube that is refreshed on a weekly basis. The cube data in turn is consolidated and synthesized from the operational data stores and the tactical data marts.

- A Silverlight rendering of an interactive regional map that shows the various plant locations and visualizations to intuitively project the overall status of the region and the status of the strategic KPIs.

- An Excel Services chart that enables the vice president to monitor and analyze gross profit generation across the various plants.

- A contacts listing of the managers of the U.S. plants.

Figure 7-4 The vice president's portal.

In the scorecard, notice that safety and customer service for the region are starting to take a dip. In the adjacent regional map, you can see immediately that the Washington plant is the potential cause of this dip. You can also see that the drop in the safety and the customer service KPIs is reflected by the KPI dials in the regional map. The KPI dials currently reflect overall consolidated status across the various plants.

You now want to dig into conditions at the Washington plant to understand why it is shown as a "red" state. Clicking the WA state image updates the panel on the right to display a thumbnail photo of the WA plant manager and also updates the KPI dials to reflect the status of strategic KPIs related to the Washington plant. You immediately notice that the safety and customer service KPIs are severely down in Washington.

Note   You will be prompted for credentials when you click the WA state image for the first time. Specify **bi-vpc\Administrator** and **pass@word1** as the user ID and password to refresh the map display to show data for the state of WA.

By moving the cursor over the safety and the customer service KPIs, you can see the annotations recorded by the Washington plant manager explaining the observed dips. You review the explanations and are content with knowing that your plant manager is on top of the issue and is taking the required steps to mitigate the condition. You decide to wait until the mentioned ETA for resolution passes prior to reexamining the status and following up with the plant manager.

Solution Architecture Overview

This section provides an overview of the solution architecture of the manufacturing plant floor analytics OBA. You'll also find steps you can follow to explore the implementation of the layers in the architecture using the VPC image you used in the previous section when exploring the solution's scenarios. The steps in this section are designed to present a broad view of the Microsoft business intelligence offerings that are used in the implementation of this OBA.

The four principal logical layers of the OBA solution architecture are data, application services, productivity, and presentation. Figure 7-5 shows the logical architecture of the solution framework, and Figure 7-6 maps specific products and technologies used in the implementation of the manufacturing plant floor analytics OBA to the logical layers.

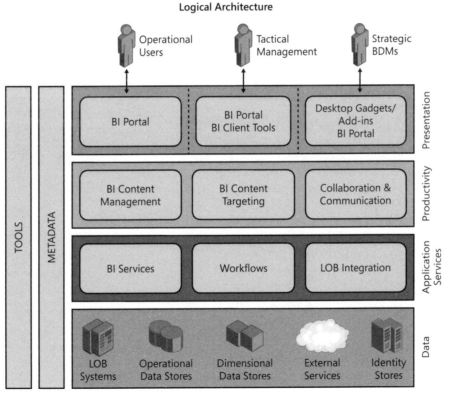

Figure 7-5   The logical architecture of the plant floor analytics solution.

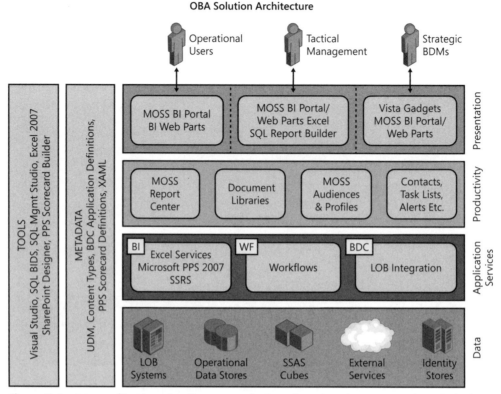

Figure 7-6   A map of business intelligence products and services that support the solution's logical architecture.

In the following sections, I'll describe the details of each layer and discuss the role of specific products and services in implementing the layers.

Data Tier Architecture

The architecture of the data tier, shown in Figure 7-7, is made up of the physical data stores from which data is consolidated and synthesized, and the data flows between them.

Each day, daily production schedules for the plant are transferred from a plant floor control (PFC) online transaction processing (OLTP) database to a plant execution and monitoring (PEM) operational database. Data pertaining to plant operations during the day is captured in the PEM database, and production statistics are transferred from the PEM database to the PFC OLTP database at the end of the day to update actual production figures. Periodic ETL (extract, transform, and load) processes modeled as SQL Server Integration Services (SSIS) packages are executed to transform transactional data to a dimensional plant floor data mart schema and eventually populate multidimensional cubes that provide data for tactical and strategic analysis.

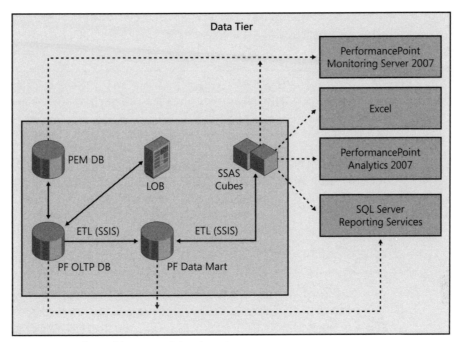

Figure 7-7   The architecture of the data tier.

The PEM database serves as the source of real-time KPIs and operational data visualizations used to monitor the plant's operations. SSAS cubes serve as high-performance data stores that are the source of medium-to-high-latency KPIs and enable exploratory data analysis using business intelligence clients such as Excel, ProClarity (included in the PerformancePoint Server Analytics module), and SQL Server Reporting Services. Data from the PFC OLTP database is used to update the plant floor (PF) data mart from which the SSAS cube gets its data.

You can also use the PFC OLTP database and the PF data mart for reporting and analysis. The PFC OLTP database can be accessed for zero-latency transactional reporting, and the PF data mart can serve as the source of data for detailed reporting and analysis, triggered to provide lower levels of details for the aggregated data in the SSAS cube.

Exploring the Data Tier

Using the VPC image for the plant floor analytics OBA, you can follow the steps outlined in this section to explore implementation details related to the data layer.

1. Use SQL Server Management Studio to explore the definitions of the following databases:

   ❑ PEM database. The plant monitoring and execution database for the Washington plant. This database consists of the tables shown in Table 7-1. By examining the table definitions, you can map the usage of the tables and their fields to the scenarios that you explored when walking through the shift foreman's portal earlier in the chapter.

Table 7-1   Tables in the PEM Database

Table	Description
OperatingPoint	Stores information about the operating points on a plant floor
OperatingPoint-SafetyMetrics	Records bit flags that are updated periodically to reflect the status of a variety of safety metrics of relevance to the operating points
PlantMetrics	Records bit flags that are updated periodically to reflect the status of a variety of metrics of relevance to monitoring the overall health of a plant
ProductionMetrics	Records the number of units of each product produced on an hourly basis
ShiftWorkers	Stores the list of workers scheduled for the current active production shift

❑   PF data mart. The relational data mart database. Data from this database is used to refresh the SSAS cube. The SSAS cube is the source of data for the KPI scorecards and Excel Services reports rendered on the SharePoint portals created for the plant manager and vice president. The definitions of the tables in this database are self-explanatory.

2.   Use Microsoft Visual Studio 2005 to open and explore the definition of the PFCubes Analysis Services database. Explore the definitions of the cube, the dimensions, and the measures to see how related data is sourced from the PF data mart. Take some time to map the dimensions and measures to the KPI scorecards and Excel Services charts that you explored when walking through the plant manager and the vice president portals earlier in the chapter.

Note   The sample implementation of the manufacturing plant floor analytics OBA utilizes only a PEM database, a PF data mart, and a PF SSAS cube. The interplays between the PEM database and the PFC OLTP database and the PFC OLTP database and the PF data mart are not implemented in the sample. You could extend the solution to add a PFC OLTP database and implement the scenarios described in this section to establish the data flows between the OLTP database and the related data sources.

Application Services Tier Architecture

The application services layer consists of business intelligence services that enable information analysis, workflows that trigger line-of-business processes in response to alerts and exception conditions, and line-of-business data integration services that enable integrated views of operational data that is relevant for business insight. The following sections describe the application layer services illustrated in the manufacturing plant floor analytics solution.

Excel Services

Excel Services, which is built into Microsoft Office SharePoint Server 2007, enables thin-client browser rendering of Office Excel 2007 workbooks published to Office SharePoint Server 2007 and exposes Web service interfaces that make Excel formulas and calculation services available from custom client applications. The architecture of Excel Services is shown in Figure 7-8.

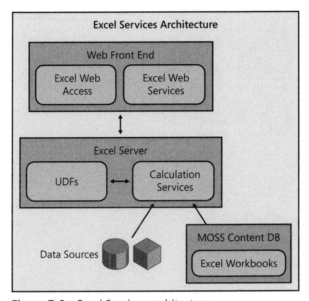

Figure 7-8   Excel Services architecture.

Excel Services, as you've read about earlier in this book, consists of three central components:

- **Excel Calculation Service**   This is the component that loads the spreadsheets published to Office SharePoint Server 2007, calculates them, refreshes external data, and maintains session state for interactivity. This component is the heart of Excel Services.

- **Excel Web Services**   This component provides programmatic access to the Excel Calculation Services. It is a Web service hosted in Office SharePoint Server 2007. You can use methods in this Web service to develop custom applications that incorporate calculations performed by Excel Services and to automate the refresh of Excel spreadsheets.

- **Excel Web Access**   This is a Web Part in Office SharePoint Server 2007 that performs the "rendering" (creating the HTML) of Excel workbooks on a Web page. This is perhaps the most visible component for the end user. As with SharePoint sites, you can use Excel Web Access like any other Web Part in SharePoint to create a wide range of Web pages.

In the manufacturing plant floor analytics OBA solution, Excel Services is used to publish Excel data views to SharePoint sites and to render the data views (using the Excel Web Access Web Part) in the plant manager and vice president portals.

PerformancePoint Monitoring Server 2007

The ability to define, monitor, and measure KPIs is a key ingredient for running a successful business operation. A business intelligence platform requires capabilities that support the definition of many types of KPIs, as well as the configuration of preferred latency levels for each KPI. The manufacturing plant floor analytics OBA includes KPIs for the following areas:

- Financial performance such as revenue, costs, and gross profit

- Customer service, including delayed orders and customer complaints

- Measures of quality such as impurities, off specification, and returns

- Production measures such as consumables usage, raw materials usage, and production performance

- Safety measures such as safety incidents and physical injuries

Some of these KPIs—those in the safety and production categories, for example—provide information that is required to monitor the real-time performance of a plant. These KPIs have near-real-time or even absolute real-time requirements with respect to data latency. A latency period of a longer duration can be tolerated for KPIs such as those in the financial performance and customer service KPI categories. These durations might be daily, weekly, monthly, or sometimes quarterly. It is therefore essential for a solution that enables the definition of KPIs to support the configuration of KPI latency intervals.

KPI definitions can range from simple aggregated measures to complex analytical expressions. Total revenue, for instance, is a simple KPI that retrieves its value from an aggregated measure field. A 52-week moving average of revenue is an example of a KPI whose definition is based on a more complex formula. The definitions of a single KPI's attributes such as its target or goal value and trend evaluation expression can also vary from simple scalar values or expressions to complex formulas. For instance, the target value for a gross profit KPI could be a scalar numeric value such as $1,000,000 or an expression that resolves to a certain percentage increase over the previous year's gross profit.

The plant floor analytics OBA uses Microsoft Office PerformancePoint Monitoring Server 2007 (PPS)—the next-generation release of Office Business Scorecard Manager—to define, deploy, and manage KPIs, scorecards, and business intelligence dashboards. Figure 7-9 shows an overview of PPS.

PPS is made up of a scorecard builder and a monitoring server. The scorecard builder is a client application used in defining KPIs, scorecards, and dashboards. KPIs can be defined to source values from Analysis Services cubes, SQL Server databases, ODBC data sources, SAP business warehouses, Excel workbooks, and SharePoint lists. Data source cache intervals are fully configurable to cater to the full range of data-latency requirements. Supporting report views (SQL Server Reporting Services reports, PivotCharts, PivotTables, and Office Excel 2007 reports) can be connected to KPI definitions to provide deeper analysis of the data they present.

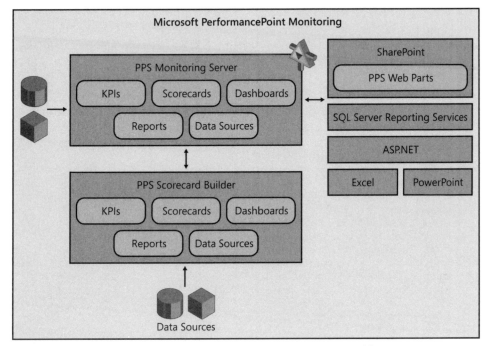

Figure 7-9   Microsoft PerformancePoint Monitoring Server 2007 architecture.

You can consolidate KPIs into scorecards, and you can consolidate scorecards and related report views into dashboards. In turn, you can deploy and publish dashboards to SharePoint document libraries, SQL Report Services, ASP.NET pages, Office Excel 2007, and Office PowerPoint 2007 to capture visualizations for business users.

Objects defined with the scorecard builder are published to the PerformancePoint Monitoring Server 2007 and can be accessed by business intelligence clients by using the Performance-Point Monitoring Web Service APIs. These APIs are used internally by the client components of the product to render the scorecards and dashboards, and they can also be used in custom solutions to access PerformancePoint Monitoring objects.

> **More Info**   You can find more information about Office PerformancePoint Server 2007 development at *http://msdn2.microsoft.com/en-us/office/bb660518.aspx*.

Windows SharePoint Services Workflows

The Windows SharePoint Services platform is tightly integrated with the Windows Workflow Foundation (WWF). This integration provides robust document processing and collaboration capabilities. Workflows can be implemented and associated with SharePoint document libraries and lists to activate content processing business logic and initiate and track human-centric document management and collaboration processes. Windows SharePoint Services extensions to WWF include specific workflow activities to manage collaboration tasks and respond to related events. Both Windows SharePoint Server 2007 and Office SharePoint Server 2007 are full-fledged WWF hosts that include services to initiate, persist, and track workflow instances to their completion.

The manufacturing plant floor solution includes a workflow project in which a workflow related to issuing service requests is defined. Listing 7-1 shows the C# code that defines the workflow.

Listing 7-1 The service request workflow.

```csharp
using System;
using System.ComponentModel;
using System.ComponentModel.Design;
using System.Collections;
using System.Drawing;
using System.Workflow.ComponentModel.Compiler;
using System.Workflow.ComponentModel.Serialization;
using System.Workflow.ComponentModel;
using System.Workflow.ComponentModel.Design;
using System.Workflow.Runtime;
using System.Workflow.Activities;
using System.Workflow.Activities.Rules;
using System.Xml.Serialization;
using System.Xml;
using Microsoft.SharePoint;
using Microsoft.SharePoint.WorkflowActions;
using Microsoft.Office.Workflow.Utility;
using System.Data;
using System.Data.SqlClient;

namespace ServiceRequests
{
    public sealed partial class AssignToTech: SequentialWorkflowActivity
    {
        public AssignToTech()
        {
            InitializeComponent();
        }

        public Guid workflowId = default(System.Guid);
        public Microsoft.SharePoint.Workflow.SPWorkflowActivationProperties
          workflowProperties = new
          Microsoft.SharePoint.Workflow.SPWorkflowActivationProperties();

        private void Execute(object sender, EventArgs e)
        {
            try
            {
                SPListItem item = workflowProperties.Item;
                if (item.Properties["Status"].ToString().Trim() == "Active (Not
                  Assigned)")
```

```csharp
            {
                item.Properties["Owner"] = AssignTechnician();
                item.Properties["Status"] = "Active (WIP)";
                item.Update();
            }
        }
        catch (Exception ex)
        {
            System.Diagnostics.EventLog log = new System.Diagnostics.EventLog();
            log.WriteEntry(ex.ToString(),
              System.Diagnostics.EventLogEntryType.Error);
        }

    }

    private string AssignTechnician()
    {
        SqlConnection cn = new
        SqlConnection("server=localhost;database=PEMDatabase;Integrated
          Security=SSPI");
        SqlCommand cmd = new SqlCommand();
        string technicianAlias;

        cn.Open();
        cmd.Connection = cn;
        cmd.CommandType = CommandType.Text;
        cmd.CommandText = "Select count(alias) from shiftworkers where
          clockedin='Yes' and available='Yes' and Role='Technician'";
        if (((int)cmd.ExecuteScalar() >= 1))
        {
            cmd.CommandText = "Select top(1) alias from shiftworkers where
              clockedin='Yes' and available='Yes' and Role='Technician'";
            technicianAlias = (string)cmd.ExecuteScalar();
            cmd.CommandText = "Update shiftworkers set available='No' where
              alias='" + technicianAlias + "'";
            cmd.ExecuteNonQuery();
        }
        else
        {
            cmd.CommandText = "Select top(1) alias from shiftworkers where
              Role='Service Manager'";
            technicianAlias = (string)cmd.ExecuteScalar();
        }
        cn.Close();

        return technicianAlias;
    }
}

}
```

Line-of-Business Data Integration Services

You can achieve line-of-business data integration by using services exposed by LOB systems and the Office SharePoint Server BDC service. (The BDC is a component of Office SharePoint Server Enterprise Edition and is not available in Windows SharePoint Services or earlier versions of Office SharePoint Server.) The BDC service enables the integration of LOB system data with a SharePoint site. The use of a service exposed by an LOB system is illustrated in the implementation of the plant floor map Web Part on the shift foreman's portal page in the manufacturing plant floor analytics OBA. More details about this service and its implementation are provided in the section "Presentation Layer," where its use in the context of the Silverlight plant floor visualization is discussed.

The BDC consists of LOB application definitions, which are based on the BDC application definition XML schema. An application definition is an instance of the BDC XML schema that defines the entities, the entity relationships, and entity actions of an LOB application that must be exposed in the SharePoint layer for consumption by users and Windows SharePoint Services. BDC application definitions can be consumed by the BDC Web Parts, SharePoint lists, and the Office SharePoint Server Enterprise Search service. You can also use them in a program by using the BDC APIs in .NET programming languages. The primary scenarios for the BDC in Microsoft Office SharePoint Server 2007 are to enable business users to configure Web Parts (the BDC Web Parts) that display LOB data in SharePoint portals, to integrate LOB data in SharePoint lists and document libraries, and to integrate LOB data with the Enterprise Search service. You can integrate LOB system definitions and data with the BDC using an ADO.NET provider or Web services.

 More Info   You can learn more about the BDC in Chapters 2 and 3 of this book. Chapter 3, "Managing Sales Forecasting with an Office Business Application," includes an example of an application definition file (ADF).

Exploring the Application Services Tier

You can use a number of resources and steps to explore and learn more about the application services layer, including the following:

- View the MSDN Channel 9 video at the following URL to get a broad overview of Share-Point workflow capabilities: *http://channel9.msdn.com/Showpost.aspx?postid=224539*.

- Explore the sequential SharePoint workflow implemented in the manufacturing plant floor analytics OBA solution that routes newly submitted safety incident reports to an available service technician. The workflow project can be found in the C:\PF OBA Bits\ServiceRequests folder on the VPC image.

- View the MSDN Channel 9 video at the following URL for a deeper look at the BDC: *http://channel9.msdn.com/ShowPost.aspx?PostID=221016*.

- Explore how the BDC is used in the shift foreman's portal page to display a list of shift workers. Examine the BDC application definition (using the SharePoint 3.0 Central Administration Portal) in the SharePoint farm used to enable this integration. To extend this solution, you could implement other use cases for the BDC in the context of the manufacturing plant floor analytics OBA.

- Open the plant manager's portal page and edit it to add an Excel Web Access Web Part. Configure the Web Part to display the report that you created and publish to the Reports Library.

- Execute the following steps to explore the use of Excel Services in the context of the manufacturing plant floor analytics OBA:

    1. Open Internet Explorer.

    2. Click OBA PF RAP Quick Links and then click the Reports Library favorite link to navigate to the Reports Library site.

    3. Open a few of the Office Excel 2007 reports listed in the Reports Library to see how they are rendered within the browser by Excel Services.

    4. Explore the content management options available for each Office Excel 2007 report item in the Reports Library.

    5. Explore the option available to open and explore an Office Excel 2007 report in a client instance of Office Excel 2007.

    6. Click OBA PF RAP Quick Links and then click the Data Connections favorite link in the Internet Explorer window to navigate to the Data Connections Library. The Data Connections Library is a list of Office data connections used by the manufacturing plant floor analytics OBA.

    7. Click the Plant Floor Safety Analysis Office Data Connection to launch an instance of Office Excel 2007 bound to a view of the solution's SQL Server Analysis Services cube referenced by the data connection.

    8. Explore the data model displayed in the PivotTable field pick list pane in Office Excel 2007.

    9. Build an Excel PivotTable or chart report by selecting measures and dimension attributes from the data source to construct a view of the count of the safety incidents reported at each of the plant operating points. You could also choose to build an alternative report.

    10. Publish the report to the SharePoint Reports Library for the manufacturing plant floor analytics OBA solution.

Productivity Tier Architecture

The productivity layer includes services that span content management, role-based business intelligence content targeting, and human-centric collaboration and communication services.

The Microsoft Office SharePoint Server Report Center is a productivity-layer offering for content management. Figure 7-10 shows the architecture of the Report Center, which is an enterprise site template that facilitates the storage and management of business intelligence content artifacts such as Office data connection files, KPI definitions, reports (both Excel and SSRS reports), dashboards created using Excel Services, and report schedules. The Report Center can be integrated with other products and services in the Microsoft business intelligence platform, including Office Excel 2007, SSAS, and SSRS.

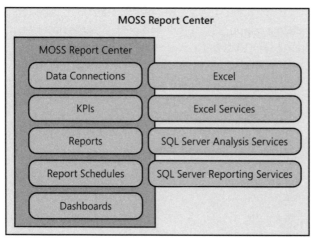

Figure 7-10 Microsoft Office SharePoint Server Report Center.

You can use SharePoint user profiles and audiences to target content for users of specific SharePoint portals. For example, you can configure Web Parts on a portal page to be visible only for a set of users who match a specified user profile or belong to an audience group. Content targeting enables the delivery of user experiences tailored for a particular role. This capability can improve user productivity and lessen the risks of unwarranted data disclosure. Collaboration and communication services include content management processes and integration capabilities with Microsoft Office Communications Server to provide presence information.

Note Integration with Office Communication Server is not illustrated in the manufacturing plant floor analytics OBA and is beyond the scope of this chapter.

Exploring the Productivity Tier

Following are some resources and steps you can take to further explore the productivity tier:

- View the MSDN Channel 9 video on creating Office SharePoint Server Report Center sites at the following URL: *http://channel9.msdn.com/Showpost.aspx?postid=214755.*

■ Define a SharePoint audience group for shift foremen. Configure the shift foreman's portal page to target the rendering of all its Web Parts to the shift foremen audience. You can test this by browsing the portal as a user who is a member of the shift foremen audience group and as a user who is not a member of this group.

Presentation Tier Architecture

The presentation tier, shown in Figure 7-11, provides the user interface elements through which a business intelligence solution presents information in context, tailored to a user's role. Presentation capabilities must support both pull and push business intelligence scenarios. *Pull* scenarios entail bringing information to the surface in response to requests from users. Users running predefined reports or performing exploratory analysis using a tool such as Office Excel 2007 are examples of these scenarios. *Push* business intelligence scenarios entail system-generated notifications whose purpose is to inform users of anomalies and important changes in trends in business performance.

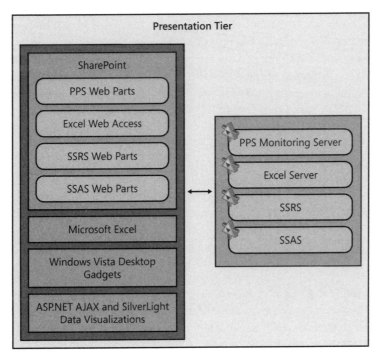

Figure 7-11   Presentation tier architecture.

The presentation capabilities illustrated in the plant floor analytics solution include SharePoint business intelligence Web Parts (Excel Services and Reporting Services), Microsoft Silverlight data visualizations, and the use of Excel for explorative data analysis. The presentation tier can also include third-party products and custom data visualization controls such as those provided by ProClarity and Dundas. The following sections briefly describe the presentation tier components illustrated in the manufacturing plant floor analytics solution.

SQL Server Reporting Service: The Report Viewer Web Part

The SSRS Report Viewer Web Part can be added and used on SharePoint portal pages to render SSRS reports. SSRS and SSRS reports are a good choice for operational reporting scenarios in which real-time and near-real-time data access is a requirement. SSRS is also the recommended platform for designing, deploying, and managing predefined reports in a solution.

An instance of the SSRS Report Viewer Web Part is used on the shift foreman's role portal in the manufacturing plant floor analytics OBA solution to render a near-real-time production performance line chart that displays the number of units of Iso-Butane produced over time (hourly production). The SQL Report Project that contains the definition of the production performance report can be found in the C:\PF OBA Bits\SSRS Report Project folder on the VPC image. Open the Visual Studio solution in this folder to explore the design of this report.

Excel Web Access

Excel Services was described in the "Application Services Architecture" section earlier in this chapter. Excel Web Access, a component of Excel Services, is a SharePoint Web Part that implements the functionality to render Excel workbooks on a Web page. It is the most visible component of Excel Services from the perspective of an end user. Users can add instances of the Excel Web Access Web Part to portal pages and configure them to bind to views of data published to SharePoint using Excel Services. Users can also open data views presented in Excel Web Access Web Parts in a client instance of Excel to customize the views and republish them. You can also enable user interactivity with the published Excel Services data views to facilitate capabilities such as a what-if analysis within the context of the browser. The plant manager and vice president role portals include Excel Web Access Web Parts that render charts created in Office Excel 2007 and published to SharePoint using Excel Services.

Using Office Excel 2007 as an Explorative Business Intelligence Client

You can walk through the Plant Manager scenario in the Manufacturing Plant Floor Analytics solution to explore the use of Office Excel 2007 as a BI client for explorative data analysis and reporting. Office Excel 2007 provides extensive capabilities for explorative data analysis. Business users can connect to data sources and create tools such as PivotTables, charts, data visualizations, and reports to access and view data. Advanced features include support for what-if analysis and off-line local cubes that you can use for data analysis when a user is not connected to an organizational network.

Office Excel 2007 works particularly well with SQL Server Analysis Services 2005. It provides a built-in data source explorer that is fully aware of the SSAS Unified Dimensional Model schema semantics. This integration provides a means for navigating general or role-tailored views of data models implemented using SSAS.

More Info   You can find more information about the Unified Dimensional Model at *http://msdn2.microsoft.com/en-us/library/ms345143.aspx*.

Microsoft Silverlight

In the walk-through of the shift foreman's portal earlier in the chapter, you saw an example of a Microsoft Silverlight visualization in the implementation of the plant floor map. Microsoft Silverlight is a cross-browser, cross-platform plug-in that is designed for developing Microsoft .NET Framework–based media experiences and Rich Interactive Applications (RIAs) for the Internet. Silverlight's programming model supports JavaScript, .NET, and other languages. In addition to its use for developing media experiences for consumers, Silverlight can be used to provide interactive user experiences within a business solution. The plant floor map that appears on the shift foreman's portal is a basic example of this use of Silverlight. The regional plant performance map on the vice president's portal is another example.

Listing 7-2 shows the code for this implementation. You can find the Visual Studio project in the folder C:\PF OBA Bits\Silverlight Projects\WAPlantFloor.

> **Note**   You can also copy over, open, and explore the project in Microsoft Expression Blend, which is not installed on the VPC. This IDE is a great tool for visually exploring and editing the XAML file, as opposed to reading raw XAML in Visual Studio.

Listing 7-2   The plant floor map Silverlight implementation.

```
using System;
using System.Windows;
using System.Windows.Controls;
using System.Windows.Input;
using System.Windows.Media;
using System.Windows.Shapes;
using System.Windows.Browser;
using System.Windows.Browser.Net;
using System.Net;
using System.IO;
using System.Xml;


namespace WAPlantFloor
{
    public class Page: Canvas
    {
        //Variables to store references to XAML objects
        //that represent plant floor operation points
        Canvas can;
        Image F2Danger;
        Rectangle FPump2;
        System.Windows.Shapes.Path Feed2;

        //The HtmlTimer type is an obsolete type and generally not suitable
        //for very short interval animations. A new updated Timer type will be
        //made available in a future release of Silverlight.
        HtmlTimer timer = new HtmlTimer();
```

```
public void Page_Loaded(object o, EventArgs e)
{

    can = o as Canvas;

    //Initialize references to operating point XAML objects
    InitializeOperatingPoints();
    //Check operating points and update functional status
    //in plant floor XAML
    CheckOperatingPoints();

    //Set up time to fire operating points status check
    //once every 5 seconds
    timer.Interval = 5000;
    timer.Tick += new EventHandler(timer_Tick);
    timer.Enabled = true;
}

void timer_Tick(object sender, EventArgs e)
{
    //Check operating points and update functional status
    //in plant floor XAML
    CheckOperatingPoints();

}

private void CheckOperatingPoints()
{
    //Check and update the operational status of Feed Pump 2
    //in the plan floor XAML. Only 1 operating point (Feed Pump2)
    //status is checked and updated in this sample application. Similar
    //checks could be executed for the other operating points.
    CheckFeed2();

}

private void CheckFeed2()
{
    //Check Temperature of Feed Pump 2 to monitor heat generation safety.
    //Temperature is the only metric checked in this sample application.
    //Similar checks could be executed for other metrics like pressure and
    // water consumption
    CheckFeed2Temperature();

    //Check the operational status of Feed Pump 2
    CheckFeed2Status();

}

private void CheckFeed2Temperature()
{
    try
    {
        int feedTemp = 0;
```

```
//Execute an HTTP POST to Invoke the Plant Monitoring Web Service
// method to check the temperature of Feed Pump 2
Uri serviceUrl = new Uri("http://bi-
   vpc:11916/PMService/Service.asmx/GetFeed2Temperature");
BrowserHttpWebRequest request = new
   BrowserHttpWebRequest(serviceUrl);
request.Method = "POST";
HttpWebResponse response = (HttpWebResponse)request.GetResponse();

//Parse the response XML to evaluate the temperature status
StreamReader responseReader = new
   StreamReader(response.GetResponseStream());
string RawResponse = responseReader.ReadToEnd();

XmlReader rdr = XmlReader.Create(new StringReader(RawResponse));
rdr.ReadToFollowing("int");
rdr.Read();
feedTemp = int.Parse(rdr.Value);

if (feedTemp == -1)
{
    //A -1 return code indicates a heat generation safety warning
    //Update the Feed Pump 2 XAML objects to reflect a danger
    //condition
    F2Danger.Visibility = Visibility.Visible;
    FPump2.Fill = new SolidColorBrush(Color.FromRgb(200, 0, 0));
    FPump2.Stroke = new SolidColorBrush(Color.FromRgb(200, 0, 0));
    Feed2.Stroke = new SolidColorBrush(Color.FromRgb(200, 0, 0));
}
else
{
    //Update the Feed Pump 2 XAML objects to reflect normal
    //functioning when a danger condition is not detected
    F2Danger.Visibility = Visibility.Collapsed;
    FPump2.Fill = new SolidColorBrush(Color.FromRgb(0, 255, 0));
    FPump2.Stroke = new SolidColorBrush(Color.FromRgb(0, 255, 0));
    Feed2.Stroke = new SolidColorBrush(Color.FromRgb(0, 255, 0));

    //Restore the visibility of the XAML Ellipse objects used to
    //represent raw material particles flowing into Feed Pump 2
    ((Ellipse)can.FindName("f2a")).Visibility = Visibility.Visible;
    ((Ellipse)can.FindName("f2b")).Visibility = Visibility.Visible;
    ((Ellipse)can.FindName("f2c")).Visibility = Visibility.Visible;
    ((Ellipse)can.FindName("f2d")).Visibility = Visibility.Visible;
    ((Ellipse)can.FindName("f2e")).Visibility = Visibility.Visible;
}
}
catch (Exception e)
{
    //Implement Exception handler

}
}
```

```
private void CheckFeed2Status()
{
    try
    {
        int feedStatus = 0;

        //Execute an HTTP POST to Invoke the Plant Monitoring Web Service
        //method to check the operational status of Feed Pump 2
        Uri serviceUrl = new Uri("http://bi-
            vpc:11916/PMService/Service.asmx/CheckFeed2Status");
        BrowserHttpWebRequest request = new
            BrowserHttpWebRequest(serviceUrl);
        request.Method = "POST";
        HttpWebResponse response = (HttpWebResponse)request.GetResponse();

        //Parse the response XML to evaluate the temperature status
        StreamReader responseReader = new
            StreamReader(response.GetResponseStream());
        string RawResponse = responseReader.ReadToEnd();

        XmlReader rdr = XmlReader.Create(new StringReader(RawResponse));
        rdr.ReadToFollowing("int");
        rdr.Read();
        feedStatus = int.Parse(rdr.Value);

        //Update the Feed Pump 2 XAML objects to reflect an inactive state
        //when the returned feed status = 0
        if (feedStatus == 0)
        {
            F2Danger.Visibility = Visibility.Collapsed;
            FPump2.Fill = new SolidColorBrush(Color.FromRgb(109, 106, 106));
            FPump2.Stroke = new SolidColorBrush(Color.FromRgb(109, 106,
                106));
            Feed2.Stroke = new SolidColorBrush(Color.FromRgb(109, 106,
                106));
            ((Ellipse)can.FindName("f2a")).Visibility =
                Visibility.Collapsed;
            ((Ellipse)can.FindName("f2b")).Visibility =
                Visibility.Collapsed;
            ((Ellipse)can.FindName("f2c")).Visibility =
                Visibility.Collapsed;
            ((Ellipse)can.FindName("f2d")).Visibility =
                Visibility.Collapsed;
            ((Ellipse)can.FindName("f2e")).Visibility =
                Visibility.Collapsed;
        }
    }
    catch (Exception e)
    {
        //Implement Exception Handler
    }
}

private void InitializeOperatingPoints()
{
```

```
        //Initialize references to XAML objects that
        //represent plant floor operation points manipulated in this
        //sample application

        //F2DangerFlag is the traffic signal XAML image object
        //displayed near Feed Pump 2 when an overheating condition is detected
        F2Danger = (Image)can.FindName("F2DangerFlag");

        //Register event handlers for the danger signal image object
        //to handle Mouse Enter and Leave events
        F2Danger.MouseEnter += new MouseEventHandler(F2Danger_MouseEnter);
        F2Danger.MouseLeave += new EventHandler(F2Danger_MouseLeave);

        //Obtain references to the Feed Pump 2 object and its related Path
        //object
        FPump2 = (Rectangle)can.FindName("FPump2");
        Feed2 = (System.Windows.Shapes.Path)can.FindName("Feed2");
}

void F2Danger_MouseEnter(object sender, MouseEventArgs e)
{
        //Display runtime stats for Feed Pump 2 when the user
        //hovers the mouse over the danger signal. The status indicators
        //for Heat, Pressure, and Electricity are hard-coded in this sample
        //since the only entry path to this segment is the detection of an
        //overheating condition at Feed Pump 2. The corresponding XAML objects
        //properties are set to reflect a danger status for Heat and a normal
        //status for Pressure and Electricity. In a realistic implementation
        //these status indicators would be dynamically configured based on
        //specific status checks executed by calling into the Plant Monitoring
        //Service.

        ((Rectangle)can.FindName("F2RuntimeStats")).Visibility =
          Visibility.Visible;
        ((TextBlock)can.FindName("F2Heatlbl")).Visibility = Visibility.Visible;
        ((TextBlock)can.FindName("F2Pressurelbl")).Visibility =
          Visibility.Visible;
        ((TextBlock)can.FindName("F2Eleclbl")).Visibility = Visibility.Visible;
        ((TextBlock)can.FindName("F2Heat")).Visibility = Visibility.Visible;
        ((TextBlock)can.FindName("F2Pressure")).Visibility = Visibility.Visible;
        ((TextBlock)can.FindName("F2Electricity")).Visibility =
          Visibility.Visible;
}

void F2Danger_MouseLeave(object sender, EventArgs e)
{
        //Hide the runtime stats for Feed Pump 2 when the user navigates the
        //mouse out of the danger signal image
        ((Rectangle)can.FindName("F2RuntimeStats")).Visibility =
          Visibility.Collapsed;
        ((TextBlock)can.FindName("F2Heatlbl")).Visibility =
          Visibility.Collapsed;
        ((TextBlock)can.FindName("F2Pressurelbl")).Visibility =
          Visibility.Collapsed;
```

```
    ((TextBlock)can.FindName("F2Eleclbl")).Visibility =
        Visibility.Collapsed;
    ((TextBlock)can.FindName("F2Heat")).Visibility = Visibility.Collapsed;
    ((TextBlock)can.FindName("F2Pressure")).Visibility =
        Visibility.Collapsed;
    ((TextBlock)can.FindName("F2Electricity")).Visibility =
        Visibility.Collapsed;

    }


    }
}
```

Listing 7-3 shows the code for the plant floor monitoring Web service invoked by the Silverlight plant floor map. Currently the service exposes only two methods to return status indicators that reflect the heat generation and operational status of feed pump 2. You could implement similar status monitoring methods for other operation points. An alternative approach for this feature would be to define granular, operating-point level, real-time PPS Monitoring KPIs and use the PPS Monitoring Web Service APIs to retrieve the KPI values.

Listing 7-3 The Web service invoked by the Silverlight plant floor map.

```
using System;
using System.Web;
using System.Web.Services;
using System.Web.Services.Protocols;
using System.Data;
using System.Data.SqlClient;
using System.Web.Script;
using System.Web.Script.Services;

[WebService(Namespace = "http://tempuri.org/")]
[WebServiceBinding(ConformsTo = WsiProfiles.BasicProfile1_1)]
[ScriptService]
public class Service : System.Web.Services.WebService
{
    SqlConnection pemDBConnection;
    SqlCommand pemDBCommand;
    string sql;

    public Service()
    {
        pemDBConnection = new
          SqlConnection("Server=localhost;Database=PEMDatabase;User
          Id=sa;Password=Pwd->123");
        pemDBCommand = new SqlCommand();
    }

    [WebMethod]
    [ScriptMethod(UseHttpGet = true)]
    public int GetFeed2Temperature()
```

```
    {
        pemDBConnection.Open();
        sql = "Select Heat from OperatingPointSafetyMetrics where OperatingPointKey
            = 1";
        pemDBCommand.CommandText = sql;
        pemDBCommand.Connection = pemDBConnection;
        return (int)pemDBCommand.ExecuteScalar();
        pemDBConnection.Close();

    }

    [WebMethod]
    [ScriptMethod(UseHttpGet = true)]
    public int CheckFeed2Status()
    {
        pemDBConnection.Open();
        sql = "Select OperationalStatus from OperatingPoint where OperatingPointKey
            = 1";
        pemDBCommand.CommandText = sql;
        pemDBCommand.Connection = pemDBConnection;
        return (int)pemDBCommand.ExecuteScalar();
        pemDBConnection.Close();
    }

}
```

Other Architectural Concerns

In this section, I'll describe considerations for architectural issues such as systems and data integration, security, and scalability.

Systems and Data Integration

Systems and data integration capabilities have increased in significance given the global marketplace that many businesses operate in today. Solution architectures should support the consolidation of data from a variety of collection points, including external systems, internal back-end LOB systems, and a variety of devices (a common requirement in manufacturing environments). SQL Server Integration Services, SQL Server Analysis Services, the Microsoft Office System, Microsoft BizTalk Server, and Microsoft Office PerformancePoint Server 2007 are among the products and technologies that enable systems and data integration. The OBA solution described in this chapter illustrated some data integration scenarios in the context of operations within a manufacturing plant. More advanced scenarios that integrate systems and data from across organization boundaries can also be implemented using these technologies. The OBA Reference Application Packs for Supply Chain Management and Loan Origination include complete solutions that illustrate such scenarios. You will find links to these solutions at *http://msdn2.microsoft.com/en-us/architecture/aa699381.aspx*.

Security

Security concerns are of paramount importance to business intelligence solutions. The functional requirements in these solutions to present information in context for different organizational roles by integrating data from multiple sources introduce additional challenges and more sophisticated needs. The Microsoft Office SharePoint Server 2007, Microsoft SQL Server, and Microsoft Office PerformancePoint Server 2007 security frameworks are tightly integrated with the security services in the Microsoft platform and add role-based security capabilities with flexible configuration options.

Microsoft Office SharePoint Server, for instance, is integrated with ASP.NET 2.0 and can use ASP.NET authentication options including Forms authentication and custom authentication providers. Single sign-on (SSO) authentication support in Microsoft Office SharePoint Server enables users to access multiple system resources without having to repeatedly provide authentication credentials. Office SharePoint Server user groups, permissions, user profiles, and audiences can be configured to address security requirements for each required role as well as content targeting. Microsoft Forefront can also be integrated into a SharePoint security architecture to help secure sites.

 More Info You can find out more information about Microsoft Forefront at *http://www.microsoft.com/forefront/default.mspx.*

Addressing security requirements also entails secure development practices in addition to the infrastructural aspects. Architects should thoroughly understand and document the security requirements for a solution prior to defining the architecture and implementation practices.

Scalability and Availability

All Microsoft server products discussed in this chapter (Microsoft Office SharePoint Server, SQL Server, and PerformancePoint Server) support scalable deployment architectures and disaster recovery options. As with security, addressing scalability and availability requirements also entails disciplined development practices in addition to careful plans for aspects of your IT infrastructure. Architects should thoroughly understand and document the scalability and availability requirements for a solution prior to defining architectures and implementation practices to address them.

Summary

This chapter explored an Office Business Application that incorporates a range of Microsoft business intelligence products and technologies, including Microsoft Office SharePoint Server 2007, Microsoft SQL Server (including SQL Server Analysis Services and SQL Server Reporting Services), Microsoft PerformancePoint Monitoring Server, and Office Excel 2007.

The solution demonstrates how the capabilities provided by an Office Business Application can facilitate information sharing and collaboration at all levels of an organization. Data collected from operational areas plays an important role in real-time monitoring, tactical planning, and strategic decision making. Through customizations of capabilities such as BDC Web Parts and Excel Services reports, information is presented in context for each organizational role.

Index

About the Authors

Rob Barker has worked for Microsoft Corporation for the past 7 years. He is a senior technical evangelist in Microsoft's Developer and Platform Evangelism group and focuses on Microsoft Office, SharePoint products and technologies, and Office Live development and architecture guidance. Check out Rob's blog at http://blogs.msdn.com/rbarker for information about his upcoming projects.

Joanna Bichsel lives in Redmond, Washington, and works at Microsoft as a program manager on the Office Platform Strategy team. She focuses on Microsoft Office development and helps provide architectural guidance and resources for building solutions. Originally from Ontario, Canada, she is often out enjoying the great outdoors.

Adam Buenz (MVP, CCSP, MCP) is an enterprise software architect for ARB Security Solutions, specializing in knowledge management, collaboration strategies, and business process automation with a focus on security. In 2006, Adam was awarded the Microsoft Most Valuable Professional (MVP) citation for Windows SharePoint Services for his contributions to the SharePoint community. Adam has contributed to two other books about Windows SharePoint Services: *Professional SharePoint 2007 Development* and *Real World SharePoint 2007: Indispensable Experiences from 16 MOSS and WSS MVPs* (both from WROX). Adam is currently completing his masters degree in mathematics. Adam blogs at *www.sharepointsecurity.com/blog* and can be contacted at adam@sharepointsecurity.com.

Steve Fox is a program manager for Microsoft, where he's worked for 8 years. His background is in the areas of social computing, search technology, natural language, and, more recently, Visual Studio Tools for Office (VSTO) and Office Business Applications (OBAs). He has presented information at many different conferences on VSTO and OBA and is co-author of the forthcoming *Programming Microsoft Office Business Applications* (Microsoft Press). He lives in Seattle, Washington, where he spends his time reading spy novels, watching movies, playing hockey, and, of course, working.

John Holliday is an independent consultant and Microsoft MVP for Office SharePoint Server 2007 with over 25 years of professional software development and consulting experience. John has been involved in a broad spectrum of commercial software development projects, ranging from retail products to enterprise information systems for Fortune 100 companies. After receiving a bachelor's degree in applied mathematics from Harvard College and a J.D. from the University of Michigan, John developed a specialized computing language for constructing legal expert systems. His expertise includes all aspects of distributed systems development, with a special emphasis on document automation, collaboration, and enterprise content management.

Bhushan Nene is a senior solutions architect in the Developer and Platform Evangelism group at Microsoft. He has worked at Microsoft for the past 5 years and has 15 years of software development experience. Prior to Microsoft, he worked for large and medium-size independent software vendors (ISVs), including IBM. In his current role he works closely with technical decision makers and architects at Microsoft's global ISV partners to help them envision and design Office Business Applications for their line-of-business applications. He lives in Southern California with his wife Aparna, son Gaurav, and daughter Trisha.

Karthik Ravindran has more than 10 years of industry experience, including 8 years at Microsoft, spanning services, product development, and architecture. Currently Karthik works as an architect on the Platform Architecture team in the Developer and Platform Evangelism group at Microsoft. His areas of focus include business and information worker solutions for the Microsoft platform. Prior to Microsoft, Karthik worked as a systems analyst and developer in the consulting industry and as a developer training specialist.

What do you think of this book?

We want to hear from you!

Do you have a few minutes to participate in a brief online survey?

Microsoft is interested in hearing your feedback so we can continually improve our books and learning resources for you.

To participate in our survey, please visit:

www.microsoft.com/learning/booksurvey/

...and enter this book's ISBN-10 or ISBN-13 number (located above barcode on back cover*). As a thank-you to survey participants in the United States and Canada, each month we'll randomly select five respondents to win one of five $100 gift certificates from a leading online merchant. At the conclusion of the survey, you can enter the drawing by providing your e-mail address, which will be used for prize notification only.

Thanks in advance for your input. Your opinion counts!

* Where to find the ISBN on back cover

ISBN-13: 000-0-0000-0000-0
ISBN-10: 0-0000-0000-0

0 000000 000000

Example only. Each book has unique ISBN.

Microsoft®
Press